The
Meaning
of Life

The
Meaning
of Life

Christian Truth and Social Change in Latin America

John A. Mackay

Edited and with an Introduction by
John M. Metzger

Foreword by
Dr. Samuel Escobar

WIPF & STOCK · Eugene, Oregon

THE MEANING OF LIFE
Christian Truth and Social Change in Latin America

Copyright © 2014 John M. Metzger. All rights reserved. Except for brief quotations in critical publications or reviews, no part of this book may be reproduced in any manner without prior written permission from the publisher. Write: Permissions, Wipf and Stock Publishers, 199 W. 8th Ave., Suite 3, Eugene, OR 97401.

Wipf & Stock
An Imprint of Wipf and Stock Publishers
199 W. 8th Ave., Suite 3
Eugene, OR 97401

www.wipfandstock.com

ISBN 13: 978-1-62032-872-9

Manufactured in the U.S.A.

To Isobel Mackay Metzger

Contents

Foreword by Samuel Escobar / ix

Preface / xv

Acknowledgments / xvii

Introduction: Christianity, Social Change, and Democracy / xix
 John M. Metzger

Abbreviations / xxxv

Part One: The Transforming Message

1. The Meaning of Life (1931) / 3
2. At the Feet of the Teacher (1930) / 40
3. The Christian Response to Secularism (1932) / 48
4. The Profession of Being a Man (1923) / 52

Part Two: The Message and Education

5. Young Students (1929) / 73
6. The Philosophy of the Red Triangle (1927) / 90
7. Is There a Relationship between the Young Men's Christian Association and Religion? (1927) / 103

Part Three: The Message and Intellectual and Literary Life

8. The Intellectuals and the New Times (1923) / 117
9. Don Miguel de Unamuno: His Personality, Work, and Influence (1919) / 133
10. The Christ of the Spanish Mystics (1929) / 157
11. The Cultural Value of Studying English Literature (1918) / 163

Part Four: The Message and Political Life
- **12** The Regeneration of Peru (1921) / 173
- **13** The Apra Movement (c. 1935) / 177
- **14** The Truth that Makes Men Free: The Relation of the Bible to Human Freedom (1939) / 187

Bibliography / 199

Foreword

ON JUNE 18, 1978, Peruvians elected their Constitutional Assembly after ten years of military government that had failed to accomplish its promise of radical social reform. A new Constitution would express the democratic convictions that had developed in a country tired of the inefficient authoritarianism of the military. The social democrat party APRA won the election and the persons that received more votes were Victor Raúl Haya de la Torre, Luis Alberto Sánchez, Ramiro Prialé, and Pedro Arana. Haya and Sánchez were good friends of John A. Mackay, had been influenced by him in their formative university years, and both had taught in the Anglo-Peruvian School that Mackay had founded in 1916. Arana represented a new generation: he had graduated from the same school in 1957, studied chemistry in San Marcos University, and had become a committed Christian through the influence of two books by Mackay that had been translated into Spanish: *The Other Spanish Christ* and *Preface to Christian Theology*.

It is also significant that three Latin Americans that have acknowledged the importance of Mackay's message in their lives would participate in politics, at crucial points in the history of their countries, and that their participation would be precisely in the writing of new constitutions: Pedro Arana in Perú in 1979, Jaime Ortiz Hurtado in Colombia in 1991, and José Míguez Bonino in Argentina in 1994.

Mackay and his wife Jane arrived in Lima in November 1916 for the beginning of their missionary career to Perú and Latin America. This was a period of transition in several countries: because the process of independence from the Spanish empire had taken place between 1810 and 1824, the first centennial was a time for a balance and inventory in politics and culture. Notably in Perú, which had declared its independence from Spain in 1821, Mackay got his doctoral degree from San Marcos University in Lima, and he came into contact with the so-called "Generation of the Centennial." He befriended men such as Haya de la Torre, José Carlos Mariátegui, and Víctor Andrés Belaúnde. Haya had become an intellectual disciple of Mackay and was the founder of APRA, a social democrat party with a moral and political renewal agenda. After a time of study in Europe, Mariátegui became the founder of the socialist party which eventually would become the Communist Party, and he educated his children in Mackay's school. Belaúnde was an active Roman Catholic diplomat and leader working for renewal in his church and eventually became the President of the General Assembly of the United Nations (1959–60).[1]

The genius of Mackay at his time of arrival was to grasp the decisive importance of this transitional period and develop a way of articulating the Christian message that especially attracted restless youth. Essays that have been collected for publication in the present volume were written originally by Mackay in Spanish during those first decades of his missionary assignment. As I read them again I find remarkable the quality and beauty of his use of this language. It brings back to my memory the surprise and admiration that I had in talking with him in Spanish, and his Castilian accent, when I first met him in Buenos Aires, in 1953.

The Christian message for Mackay was not just a conceptual reality, it was a way of life that included prayer and a daily life of obedience to God's law and commitment to truth. As he recalled his early years Mackay pointed out his experience of commitment of his life to God. The Reformed expression of the faith was passed on to him by his local church in Inverness and also by his teachers in Aberdeen. This perception was no doubt widened and enriched by his studies at Princeton in the years previous to the famous controversies of the 1920s. But his time in Spain added a new component that came from study of Spanish history and the mystics but also from his personal acquaintance with Miguel de Unamuno, rector of the University of Salamanca and a rebellious Catholic scholar. Through him Mackay became acquainted also with the work of Danish theologian Søren Kierkegaard.

As the essays collected in this volume show, his basic Reformed allegiance and culture allowed him to apply his thought to the intellectual task with a political dimension in mind. The majority were written during his time in Lima, Montevideo, and Mexico, and they allow us to grasp the ways in which his Latin American days had a formative role for him. In turn, several Latin American evangelical theologians, but also well-known intellectuals beyond the limits of the evangelical community, were reached by Mackay's way of articulating and communicating the Christian message. He found common ground as the basis for his long conversations with Latin Americans, and about Latin Americans, in the questions about the

---

1. Escobar, "La Huella," 5–15.

Christian view of humanity that were central in his public teaching. The component essays collected in his widely read and reissued book *El sentido de la vida* may be found in outline form in his speech in Tarma about the profession of man, chapter 4 in this book.

His time in Spain prepared him for his encounter with Latin American culture, and having grasped its Iberian sources, he was prepared to better understand the intellectual trends that he could detect in Latin America. Mackay became an interpreter of the Iberian sources of the religious dimension of Latin American culture, both for intellectuals and politicians that were looking for a renewal within Catholicism as well as for those that had rejected completely their Catholic background.

He also assumed a role of interpreter of Latin American reality for English speaking theological and missionary circles since the 1930s. Missionary literature in those days described the moral condition of Latin America, but it majored on the symptoms, the abuses and weaknesses of Catholic practice. Mackay was a careful observer but he also reflected theologically about what he found, and related it to the historical developments and cultural transformations that had taken place since the arrival of Christianity in the Americas in the sixteenth century. His book par excellence in that regard is *The Other Spanish Christ* (1932), a diagnosis of Latin American culture that continues to be valid.

Later on in 1935 Mackay published *That Other America*. He describes his intention and the conviction from which he departs, in a way that is valid for both books: "In writing this book I have not been interested in reproducing a miscellany of sounds from the incoherent din of a continent's life. My concern has been rather to interpret the undertones, the basic melody of its spiritual existence."[2] What is the perspective from which he writes? "My standard of judgment is an idea to which I am thralled, that Jesus Christ is the key to life's mystery and the solvent of its problem. This idea is the form, the *gestalt*, as some psychologists would say, that informs my outlook on life as a whole."[3]

In 1953 John Mackay presented the Carnahan Lectures in the Facultad de Teología, the Union Seminary of Buenos Aires, Argentina. These annual lectures had become a thermometer of the way Protestant thought was advancing in Latin America. Mackay's lectures were only published sixteen years later in English with the title *Christian Reality and Appearance* (1969). One year after that they were published in Spanish.[4] In these lectures it is

2. Mackay, *Other America*, ix.
3. Ibid.
4. Mackay, *Realidad e Idolatría en el Cristianismo Contemporáneo*, Buenos Aires:

possible to see how Mackay's theology had evolved and grown in depth, and how the basic convictions of his first essays in Latin America are kept within the new circumstances in both North America and Latin America.

When these lectures were published, Mackay's reading of the spiritual condition of Christianity around the world was realistic to the point of criticism: "The Christian religion has reached another crucial moment in its history. Across the boundaries of ecclesiastical tradition—Roman, Eastern Orthodox, and Protestant—a large proportion of those who bear the name 'Christian' are characterized by religious nominalism and theological illiteracy. Their conventional association with the name of Christ neither shapes their living nor controls their thinking. To a phenomenal degree, appearance has replace reality."[5]

In Mackay's writings we find a continuous reflection about Latin America which we can follow through decade after decade and find the development of a mature perspective that is put to the test when a dramatic situation arises, like that of the Cuban revolution in 1959. Mackay could help North American readers to see things with a well-informed missiological perspective but also in a politically relevant way. When a critical moment for the foreign policy of the United States came, such as the aftermath of the Cuban revolution, Mackay was able to propose a foreign policy that would not be conditioned by the extreme positions of the Cold War era. As in the case of China he proposed a mature political agenda in the face of the triumph of Communism.

As the end of the twentieth century was approaching in Latin America, there were Catholic, Protestant, and non-committed observers that agreed that since the decade of the 1960s the religious map of the region had changed significantly because of the rapid numerical growth of Protestantism, especially in its popular forms. Though a specialist wrote about the "lack of reliable quantification" of this process,[6] scholars and journalists insisted on the spectacular rate of growth. A Catholic observer went as far as predicting that, "If current growth rates continue Latin America will have an evangelical majority in the early 21st century."[7] Though this unexpected spiritual revolution had been taking place in Latin America all along the twentieth century, only in the final decade had it become the subject of continuous journalistic debate and scholarly research.

La Aurora, 1970.

    5. Mackay, *Reality and Appearance*, 13.

    6. Stoll, *Turning Protestant?* 6.

    7. McCoy, "Robbing Peter," 2.

Exactly forty years after Mackay's Carnahan lectures, José Míguez Bonino the well-known Methodist theologian from Argentina, offered in his own Carnahan Lectures of 1993 the best interpretation of the Protestant reality in Latin America, *Faces of Latin American Protestantism*, which was published two years later.[8] He shares a conviction that Mackay had expressed in different ways that the future of Protestantism has to be Evangelical or it will not be. Míguez's typology helps us to understand better the true impact of Protestantism. He presents four faces of Protestantism in Latin America: the Liberal face, the Evangelical face, the Pentecostal face, and the Ethnic face. His book is a mature observation of the way in which Protestantism has advanced in Latin America but also a realistic evaluation of its true impact and its failures: the promise of the Protestant message and the precariousness of its realizations.[9]

For those interested in the history of Protestantism in Latin America and its missiological significance the essays in this collection have a singular value. The present writer shares a conviction that John A. Mackay expressed eloquently in 1950. Recalling the fact that from the great Christian traditions, Catholicism, Eastern Orthodoxy, and Protestantism, the latter was the youngest in its institutional expression, Mackay went on to say:

> Protestantism, let it be emphasized, has not yet reached its religious majority, nor discharged its full historical mission. It is still in process of becoming; its heyday is not behind it but before it. The complete meaning of what happened at the Reformation four hundred years ago has still to be expressed in life and doctrine and ecclesiastical organization. Other things too must happen which did not enter into the thought of the Reformers.[10]

It is proposed here that in the growth of Latin American Protestantism there are enough signs to perceive it as a way through which "the complete meaning of what happened at the Reformation" will come to be expressed, together with "other things . . . which did not enter into the thought of the Reformers." This would mean that the significant numerical growth of Protestants in Latin America could contribute to the revitalization of church life, theology, and ecclesiastical organization in Protestantism at large, around the world. It would also mean that in the specific case of Latin America

---

8. Míguez Bonino, *Rostros del protestantismo latinoamericano*, Buenos Aires: Nueva Creación, 1995; English translation, *Faces of Latin American Protestantism*, Grand Rapids: Eerdmans, 1997.

9. This theme is developed in Escobar, "Promise and Precariousness," 3–35.

10. Mackay, *Christianity on the Frontier*, 123–4.

Protestantism could make a distinctive contribution to the social transformation that is now taking place.

Dr. Samuel Escobar
Professor Emeritus of Missiology, Palmer Theological Seminary
Professor, Facultad de Teología Protestante UEBE, Madrid, Spain

Preface

THE SELECTIONS FOLLOWING ARE taken from the early evangelistic writings of John A. Mackay, my grandfather. Twelve of fourteen were originally written or presented as lectures (*conferencias*) in Spanish or Portuguese. They are now made available to English speaking readers in one volume for the first time.

The original working title for this collection was Christianity, Social Change and Democracy. That title was intended to refocus attention on the specific, historical connection between Christianity and civic life in a pluralistic democracy. Since that title could imply an instrumental approach to Christianity, it was at variance with the meaning of Mackay's mission, and therefore the editor judged it potentially misleading. Accordingly, to emphasize the inherent value of faith and its propagation, the volume now bears the title of a major essay in the collection, and the subtitle directs attention to Christianity as a factor in social change.

To provide a conceptual view of Mackay's cross-cultural missionary strategy, the chapters are grouped thematically rather than in chronological order. Part One, The Transforming Message, focuses upon Mackay's theme of the importance of conversion and of acquiring a personal, interiorized experience of the founder of the Christian religion. Part Two, The Message and Education, illustrates how Mackay viewed the educational scene in Latin America and how he framed this message in dealing with the people, particularly the youth. Part Three, The Message and Intellectual and Literary Life, demonstrates how Mackay introduced and spoke on the importance of faith and ethics in connection with literature and culture. Part Four, The Message and Political Life, draws a connection between a well-functioning democracy and genuine, personal, biblical faith among a strong minority of a country's population.

American rather than British spellings are used throughout, and punctuation has been modernized and to some extent secularized in accordance with current conventions. In chapter 2, in particular, it was judged that using lower case would sometimes detract from the spiritual message that Mackay intended to convey by the original text, and therefore upper case has been retained for certain words. Introductory paragraphs for lectures are retained for their historical references and imagery, and to illustrate the speaker's personal manner that is manifested in them. Chapters differ in style and on occasion contain reiterations of particular facts, arguments, or illustrations. Since the essays in question have not been available previously in English, editing has been kept to a minimum in order to retain contextuality and the structure of the author's thought and message. Mackay did not always see a need to include citations to references for quotations he used. At times citations or notes have been added for convenience or to provide additional context. A bibliography is included for readers who wish to explore further the themes and ideas framed by the contents of the volume.

I am grateful for the friendship of Dr. Samuel Escobar and for his kindness in agreeing to write a foreword to this volume and for suggesting the subtitle. I am also grateful for the friendship and kind help of Dr. Raúl Alessandri whom I met while working on an earlier project. He made translations from Spanish of essays by and about Mackay and was the first person to suggest to me the possibility of publication of a collection of Mackay's Latin American writings. Dr. Alessandri made translations of chapters 1, 2, 4, 5, 6, 7, 8, and 9. Chapters 13 and 14 are English texts. Chapters 3, 10, and 11 are translations by the editor, and chapter 12 is Mackay's text. In addition, I had helpful conversations with Michael J. Gorman, Kenneth W. Henke, and James B. Metzger. Careful efforts have been made in the preparation of this volume, and any inaccuracies are my sole responsibility.

Above all, my deepest thanks are due to my wife, Sandra, for her love, cheerfulness, insights, and faithful encouragement.

John M. Metzger
Princeton, New Jersey

Acknowledgments

THE EDITOR ACKNOWLEDGES WITH gratitude permission granted by Isobel Mackay Metzger, Executrix of the Estate of John A. Mackay, to publish translations of works and material authored by John A. Mackay.

Chapter 1 is a translation of *El Sentido de la Vida, Pláticas a la Juventud.* Montevideo, 1931.

Chapter 2 is a translation of *A los Pies del Maestro.* Montevideo, 1930.

Chapter 3 is a translation of "A Riposta Cristã ao Secularismo." In *"O Cristo Vivo": Relatório Oficial da 11.a Convenção Mundial de Escolas Dominicais, Rio de Janeiro, 25 a 31 de Julho de 1932*, redator do volume em Português Rev. Galdino Moreira, 130–33. Rio de Janeiro: Conselho Evangélico de Educação Religiosa do Brasil, [1932].

Chapter 4 is a translation of *La Profesión de Hombre.* Lima, 1923.

Chapter 5 is a translation of *La Juventud Estudiantil: Primeras Indicaciones que se Ofrecen sobre este Tema a los Delegados al Congreso Hispano-Americano de la Habana para su Examen y Discusión.* Montevideo, 1929.

Chapter 6 is a translation of *La Filosofía del Triangulo Rojo.* Montevideo, 1927.

Chapter 7 is a translation of *¿Existe Relación Entre La Asociación Cristiana de Jóvenes y la Religión?* Montevideo, 1927.

Chapter 8 is a translation of *Los Intelectuales y los Nuevos Tiempos.* Lima, 1923.

Chapter 9 is a translation of *Don Miguel de Unamuno: Su Personalidad, Obra e Influencia.* Lima: Casa Editora De Ernesto R. Villaran, 1919.

Chapter 10 is a translation of "El Cristo de los Místicos Españoles." *La Nueva Democracia*, December, 1929.

Chapter 11 is a translation of "El Valor Cultural del Estudio de la Literatura Inglesa." Breve desarollo de la conferencia inaugural dada por el Dr. John A. Mackay en la Facultad de Letras, Sabado, 31 Agosto, 1918.

Chapter 12 is a translation from the Mackay Collection of "The Regeneration of Peru." *La Nueva Democracia*, July, 1921.

Chapter 13 is an unpublished article from the Mackay Collection, "The APRA Movement." C. 1935.

Chapter 14 is an article from the Mackay Collection, *The Truth that Makes Men Free: The Relation of the Bible to Human Freedom*. New York: American Bible Society, 1939. Portuguese ("A verdade que liberta os homens") and Spanish ("La verdad que hace libres a los hombres") versions were also published in 1939.

Introduction

Christianity, Social Change, and Democracy

THIRTY YEARS HAVE PASSED since the death of John Mackay. Many changes have occurred throughout the world since that time. With the advantage of hindsight readers can now consider Mackay's writings in the context of the social, cultural, and economic changes that followed. Like some other thinkers of his generation, he viewed history from a biblical viewpoint, judging events under the aspect of eternity, attempting to discern the "changing from the changeless." He believed that history had direction and purpose. Although its direction is not so easily judged contemporaneously, in retrospect the accuracy of his insights and the fruits of his work are apparent.

The propagation of Christian faith and social improvement based upon Christian principles stood at the core of Mackay's ministry, and the soundness of his approach stands the test of time. In retirement years he wrote about the qualitative wholeness of love that God requires. The love of God and the love of neighbor belong together in a proper observance of the two great commandments.[11] A committed love for God pours forth and overflows as love of neighbor as oneself, and the two commandments belong together.[12] A Christian performing social service makes known that the service is performed and motivated by loving commitment to his or her Lord and Savior. In this respect the essays presented here are important not only as a matter of Latin American history, but also for the example they bring forward of an effective balance of the spiritual and social message of Christianity.

11. Mackay, "American of the Sixties," 38.
12. Deut 6:4–5; Mark 12:29–31.

Religion is the basis of culture and civilization, and an accepted ethic is vital to hold a society together. For example, a level of honesty is essential to preserve the integrity of a free economic system; individual morality and responsibility are essential for a democratic political system to function effectively; the rule of law requires the enforcement of the rules and punishment of wrong doing. The power flowing from the Christian religion which teaches and practices individual conversion has been at the core of western civilization. John Mackay's theology and ministry provide a nexus for a comparison of the influence and direction of vibrant Protestantism in South and North America.

This foreword attempts to provide a perspective for understanding the essays that follow. First, a description of Mackay's early religious calling and training sets forth his background and preparation. Second, important cultural differences between North and South America are briefly outlined. Third, Mackay's South American mission and the advance of Protestantism in Latin America are sketched to contextualize his ministry there. Fourth, examination of North American religious and ideological trends after Mackay's retirement offers an historical and theological perspective on causes of later religious and cultural changes in North America. In conclusion, an introductory paragraph for each chapter in the collection ensues.

I

John Mackay's calling to foreign missions came to him gradually, and he prepared himself thoroughly for service through studies in Scotland, Princeton Theological Seminary, and the University of Madrid. As a student at Aberdeen University, Mackay attended a Baptist Church, where he joined a Bible circle focused upon missions in India. His interest in missions intensified the following winter when he attended an inspiring lecture on "Missions and the Native Churches," presented by Robert E. Speer. Mackay's pastor attended the Edinburgh Missionary Conference in June 1910, and Mackay supported the missionary effort through church meetings and prayer.

When he left Scotland to study at Princeton Seminary, Mackay had completed several theological courses under the guidance of ordained teachers of the Free Presbyterian Church and had developed connections with members of the Free Church of Scotland, who later arranged support for his missionary effort in Latin America. Mackay considered his time at Princeton as functional rather than merely theoretical and used his theological education to prepare himself spiritually and intellectually to be an effective missionary. As the result of his survey tour through Latin America after graduation from Princeton, Mackay's vocation crystalized, and he was drawn to work in Lima, Peru. In September 1915 in Buenos Aires at the conclusion of the survey tour, Mackay discussed his plans with experienced missionaries including representatives of the YMCA. Mackay judged that by beginning his work in Lima rather than a more progressive city like Buenos Aires or Montevideo, he would have more time to equip himself and to study further. At the suggestion of his professor at Princeton, B. B. Warfield, Mackay concluded his missionary preparation with one year of studies in Madrid, Spain. There he met Miguel de Unamuno whose thought became a key to understanding the Hispanic world and an important link with the Latin American people.

Intellectually well prepared, Mackay was deeply influenced by Reformation ideas and by the examples of nineteenth century leaders of his denomination, the Free Church of Scotland, particularly Thomas Chalmers (1780–1847) and Alexander Duff (1806–1878). Thomas Chalmers balanced evangelism and social action in his ministry, and emphasized the independence of a church's ministry. In his Glasgow parish he organized a method of caring for the poor, linking the better off citizens to aid those less well off in a personal fashion, actively involved the laity in home visitations, and developed educational programs. In later years Chalmers made great efforts to launch the Free Church and organize support for the ministers who joined in the Disruption in 1843, thus standing for the practice and principle of separation of church and state in Britain.

Alexander Duff was a Presbyterian missionary in India when the Disruption occurred, and he thereafter joined the Free Church. His influence on Mackay is apparent. As one small example, Mackay quoted a vivid passage that Duff wrote in Mackay's report for Free Church leaders that analyzed the possibilities for a church mission in Latin America. Christian education would set off new and positive forces in a non-Christian culture with power of a burned fuse that ignites an explosion. He wrote, "While you engage in directly separating as many precious atoms from the mass as the stubborn resistance to ordinary appliances can admit, *we shall, with the blessing of God, devote our time and strength to the preparing of a mine, and the setting of a train which shall one day explode and tear up the whole from its lowest depths.*"[13]

In September, 1916, just prior to Rev. and Mrs. Mackay's departure to begin mission work in Peru, the Free Church of Scotland held a gathering in Edinburgh to bid farewell to the couple. The convener of the Foreign Missions Committee presided, and Mackay and others accompanied him

---

13. Smith, *Alexander Duff*, 1:108–9 (italics original).

to the speakers' platform. Mackay's address to the assembly, reported in the *Monthly Record of the Free Church of Scotland*, illuminates his missionary calling and his understanding of the work he was about to undertake. He had considered a vocation in Scotland rather than a foreign mission; he had considered the timing and circumstances of undertaking work in Latin America rather than elsewhere; he understood that "the Church of Christ, above all else, [was] an essentially spiritual institution;" and he described the duty he felt to "teach God's truth in South America" and to "produce the principles of righteousness" in those lands.[14]

II

The religious and cultural contrast between North and South America has deep historical roots. They made the Free Church's new mission an ambitious project. Latin America was colonized in the sixteenth century by Spanish conquistadors, Pizarro, Cortes, Valdivia, and others motivated by dreams of wealth, glory, and power. Roman Catholic priests, who accompanied them, taught the indigenous people a centralized form of religion. North America, and especially the area that became United States, was colonized by people from Northern Europe, particularly England, who brought with them the religious principles of the Reformation. These colonists included the Pilgrims who settled in Massachusetts under the direction William Bradford's Mayflower Compact of 1620, a social contract based upon majoritarian principles and allegiance to the king. Based on these foundations the two continents continued to develop independently and separately for centuries.

Mackay crystalized differences between North and South America in religious heritage by focusing on two well-known representative literary characters: Robinson Crusoe and Don Quixote. He wrote, "Two different attitudes towards life, two kinds of spiritual achievement, two epochs of world history, two forms of world civilization lie hidden in the immortal heroes of Cervantes and Defoe."[15]

> The great library of Don Quixote, a historical symbol of the cultural universalism which has been one of the glories of the Iberian race, did not contain a Bible. The old sea chest which Robinson Crusoe, true prototype of the English Puritans, salvaged from the wreck contained a Bible, which became the means of his conversion. The Spanish knight and the shipwrecked sailor, the

---

14. "Farewell Meeting," MRFCS (November 1916) 158–59.

15. Mackay, *That Other America*, 12–13, and see discussion in 12–22; Mackay, *Heritage and Destiny*, 98–102; Mackay, "Two American Civilizations," 90–96.

manorial library and the storm-tossed chest, are the prototypes, respectively, of the two historic types which have influenced the Western world. They are also parables of the two civilizations which live together in the Americas.[16]

Other scholars helpfully illuminate additional aspects of the cultural dissimilarities. The first develops the economic consequences implied by cultural differences using the metaphor of the hedgehog and the fox: the hedgehog—who knows one big thing—and the fox—who knows many things. This image contrasts centralization and diversification in religion and society and suggests how these differences played out in economic development and entrepreneurial dynamics. This writer, Claudio Véliz, further notes the effects of liberation theology which broke through the "Baroque dome of the Counter-Reformation"[17] that had covered Latin America.

A second scholar, Mackay's colleague in Latin America, Julio Navarro Monzó, was a pioneer among learned Latin Americans in studying and writing about the religious problem in South America including from a political perspective. He wrote that copying institutions from one people to another is useless.

> Anglo-Saxon democracy without its historical setting, without the cultural antecedents of the Anglo-Saxon countries, is an impossible absurdity. The great tragedy of the Latin countries during the nineteenth century serves as an all-sufficient proof of this.[18]

Navarro Monzó articulated the links between authentic Christian practice and democracy as follows:

> The truth is that a political problem, like an economic problem, is one of culture, and above all else, of moral culture. The real problem has a religious character. Without Christianity, without a Christianity sincere and profound, which signifies a fundamental respect for moral laws, a deep appreciation of individual rights, a profound sentiment of human fraternity, it is impossible to have a democracy.[19]

Finally, José Enrique Rodó contrasted the regional identities and philosophical and intellectual differences of the two continents from the Latin American perspective. He wrote the essay, *Ariel*, in 1900, two years after the Spanish-American War. The work uses characters found in Shakespeare's

---

16. Mackay, "Theological Meditation," 158–59.
17. Véliz, *Gothic Fox*, 211.
18. Navarro Monzó, *Religious Problem*, 48.
19. Ibid., 49. On Navarro Monzó, see Mackay, *Spanish Christ*, 213–30, 260.

play the *Tempest*. It contrasts Prospero, who stands for South America, spiritual values, and classical beauty, with Caliban, who represents North America, utilitarianism, materialism, and other negative attributes. As a Scot Mackay had an advantage over his North American colleagues who also presented a Christian message in Latin America. Since his native country did not promulgate the Monroe Doctrine or fight the War of 1898, his presentations were free from those negative political associations.

III

Mackay's calling to Peru came at a spiritually auspicious moment for Latin America. He found there a sophisticated, secular, intellectual climate but a vacuum of authentic Christian understanding. Inspired by the educational precedent set by Alexander Duff in India, he knew and understood the culturally transformative effects of education saturated with the Bible which Duff's example demonstrated. The Colegio Anglo-Peruano, which Mackay founded in Lima on behalf of the Free Church of Scotland, became a seminal force in the education of the nation's youth. Its motto was the Biblical proverb, "the fear of God is the beginning of wisdom," underlining the Bible's role in education. Mackay also brought progressive ideas to Peruvian higher education as a lecturer and later as the holder of a chair in philosophy at the University of San Marcos. In due course he moved beyond the academic environment, lecturing to public audiences and providing essays to journals and newspapers. His seminal English language book, *The Other Spanish Christ: A Study in the Spiritual History of Spain and South America* (1932) synthesized his religious analysis. The book had great impact and legitimized the presence of Protestantism in the Iberian world.

Mackay's educational reforms and the group of younger teachers that he recruited to teach at the colegio had direct, progressive, generational influence in intellectual circles of Peru. Haya de la Torre, a teacher that Mackay recruited, led a social movement to train workers and artisans, and later founded the progressive APRA political party. Historian, Raúl Porras Barrenechea, a teacher at Anglo-Peruano in the Mackay era, and Luis Alberto Sánchez, the Peruvian politician and scholar, whose son was a student at the school, both influenced a young intellectual, Mario Vargas Llosa, who later won the Nobel Prize in literature. Vargas has recounted that he worked and studied with Raúl Porras for four and a half years, and that Sánchez's lectures inspired him to write a thesis on Rubén Darío's short stories.[20] Coincidentally, his half-brothers attended Colegio San Andrés.

20. Vargas Llosa, *Fish in the Water*, 270 (Porras); 394, 460 (Sánchez).

During a furlough to Britain Mackay recruited a young English Methodist as a teacher for the colegio, and this connection became the start of a lifelong friendship. Their correspondence and several books by Stanley Rycroft, Mackay's younger colleague, help document the evolution of Protestant mission work in Latin America. Mackay promoted the principle of interdenominational cooperation on the mission field to advance the Christian message. Its theological basis was "evangelical catholicity," a concept that he wrote about and articulated during the period from 1946 to 1964. Mackay maintained his missionary and educational contacts in Latin America and travelled there whenever possible, after he relocated to North America and took on the role of President of Princeton Theological Seminary in 1936.

Providence brought additional spiritual forces to impact the religious climate of Latin America. Pentecostalism, another wave of Protestant activity, grew from foreign missionary movements that preceded it. Liberation theology later challenged the political posture of the Roman Catholic Church in Latin America from within. Evangelical and Pentecostal Protestants advocated and practiced biblical virtues of honesty and reliability which in turn paved the way for economic advances. Although social change was more rapid in some countries of Latin America than in others, the new religious movements created conditions for social and economic improvement. In the last fifty years a vigorous religious pluralism has supplanted more than four centuries of religious and spiritual monopoly in Latin America. In Brazil, for example about twenty-five percent of the population now attends evangelical congregations.

A specific indication of the successful efforts to expand the Protestant Christian movement territorially in Latin America occurred when the World Alliance of Reformed Churches met in São Paulo, Brazil in 1959. It was the first time a world gathering of a Protestant religious tradition had met in Latin America. The Alliance was the first confessional group to recognize the Pentecostal movement as a robust, sound, and legitimate body.

Of course historical foundations run deep, and evangelism is an ongoing task for each generation. Contemporary Latin American leaders call for greater cultural reform as a fundamental factor promoting social, political, and economic development in the region. Oscar Arias, former president of Costa Rica, singled out four obstacles to overcome in making progress for development: "resistance to change, absence of confidence, fragile democratic norms, and a soft spot for militarism."[21] Osvaldo Hurtado, former president of Ecuador, referred directly to religious influences as factors that

---

21. Arias, "Culture Matters," 3.

affected Latin American culture before concluding that "Weak political institutions are not so much causes as effects of deeper cultural factors."[22]

Mackay understood clearly the national significance of Christianity in political, social, and cultural terms. In his essay, "The Meaning of Life," Mackay wrote that Toyohiko Kagawa, the Japanese evangelist, "makes efforts so that his Master will be reproduced in the life of his compatriots so that through the infusion of Christianity the national life may be revolutionized." The same may be written of the effect of Mackay's ministry in Latin America.

IV

A North American reader may say, "The essays are interesting for historians of Latin American Protestantism, but do they have anything helpful for me and other North Americans who are not specialists in that field?" In response, these writings are a counter example based on history to some current theological tendencies in the United States. Mackay's theology is characterized by *dynamic centrality*, a term that emphasized a leading status "given to the Evangel in theological thought and Christian life."[23] He successfully applied this principle on two continents and within two cultures. The presentation of the Evangel is the most basic and first work of the church. Therefore, the example of his ministry provides a touchstone to compare and contrast historical and theological trends on each continent. Studying Mackay's theology and methods facilitates understanding the expansion of Protestant Christianity in Latin America. Likewise, a generational change away from these Christian norms and methods in North America following his retirement helps explain the long lasting contraction in Protestantism on that continent, particularly in the historical Presbyterian and Episcopal denominations.

Mackay retired as President of Princeton Seminary in 1959 when he reached the mandatory retirement age of seventy. The generation that followed the leaders of his era in North America shifted their churches' vision and priorities. They turned away from the primacy of the traditional Christian message of redemption to agendas that stressed political and managerial goals and methods. This turn away from the approach of Oldham's responsible society and Mackay's dynamic centrality accommodated prevailing secular ideas that were time-bound and that failed to provide a counter-cultural Christian witness. The new direction had distinctive

22. Hurtado, "Know Thyself," 102, and see 93, 95.
23. Mackay, *Ecumenics*, 159.

characteristics including: an activist political role for Protestant churches in American society; an emphasis on institutional forms and managerial technique; the professionalization of church leadership following a secularized model; changes in the understanding of the nature of church leadership and in the credentialing of church leaders; relative neglect of an internalized Christian faith; ethical positions at variance with historical church teachings; and, in some cases, an absence of meaningful church discipline.

The label "new breed" is associated with some members of the generation of the 1960s. A journalist coined the term, and shortly thereafter an article described and advanced "new breed" ideas. The most distinctive feature of this tendency was its increased willingness "to lead the institutional church directly into the struggle for power."[24] The article linked the movement sympathetically with political activist and organizer, Saul Alinsky, who compared the church's role to that of a labor union. The article reflected an eagerness to take over church leadership from the preceding generation.

A second aspect of the new generation's approach was to advance a managerial, institutional, and organizational agenda in churches in the early 1960s. Leaders such as Eugene Carson Blake emphasized the structural dimension of church unity in contrast to a substantive understanding of the church as the community and fellowship of Christ. Mackay, whose theology had described the ecumenical movement as "a child of the Mission,"[25] and whose ecumenical focus had taught a balance of the worshipping, prophetic, redemptive, and unitive functions of the church, sharply criticized this institutional approach to church unity.[26] Mackay's experiences in Latin America with a politicized Roman Catholic Church, taught him the implications and consequences of clerical uses of political power. He foresaw the consequences for religion and belief when a secularized, organizational focus breached ecumenism from the church's missionary heritage.

Mackay pointed out the appearance of "ominous traits, psychological and sociological, political and religious," in North America that had had "fateful" results in Latin America. These suggested to him that the United States could be headed for a "tragic era."[27] The future was indeed tragic for some Protestant churches. The results of the new trends are apparent today.[28] Secularizing tendencies provoked schisms, fragmentation, and

24. Cox, "The 'New Breed,'" 148.
25. Beyerhaus, *Responsible Church*, 176.
26. Mackay, *Reality and Appearance*, 81–85; Mackay, *Ecumenics*, 202–7.
27. Mackay, "Discoveries," 5.
28. Membership in the Presbyterian Church (USA) decreased from 4,254,597 in 1965 to 1,849,496 in 2012. The Protestant Episcopal Church in the United States of America depleted its membership and financial resources by an aggressive and costly

diminished social significance for the Presbyterian and the Episcopalian denominations whose histories had been closely connected with the origins of the American republic. Early in the current century, the National Presbyterian Church of Mexico (INPM) separated itself from the Presbyterian Church (USA), and the Episcopal Church was fractured by division and dozens of law suits. In point of fact, these denominations departed from the ecumenical church movement.

While a number of internal and external causes are associated with the decline of mainline Protestant religion in North America, three educational and ideological factors are highlighted here: changes in theological education, changes within higher education more generally, and changes in ecumenical theology. Each had social consequences for American society and government, as well as for the churches. First, President Mackay had a well-developed vision of theological education that was set forth in his numerous writings on the subject. He attempted to embody that vision in the teaching, life, and practice of Princeton Seminary. His vision was consistent with the original conception of theological unity that was set forth in the Plan of Princeton Seminary by its founders.[29] His successor as President of Princeton Seminary in 1959, James McCord, who was supported for the office by Eugene Carson Blake, adopted a "dialectical" approach to theological education.[30] The sense of unity in the faculty that had been developed over the years was transformed by the expansion and changes to the composition of the faculty. Since the teaching function is crucial in transmitting the church's theology and culture[31] from one generation to another, the change in educational philosophy had real consequences. Over time the lack of unity in the faculty's teaching function was also manifested in a lack of uniformity of doctrine in the Presbyterian denomination itself.

Secondly, a closely related factor was the overarching secular influence found within higher education generally that also affected religious education. Some professors saw their academic role as separated from direct service to the church. They produced research and writings for other academics inspired by subjects created in non-theological disciplines, using those as sources for their own theological work. Many such efforts had less and less relevance to the spiritual needs of the laity. In some places Christianity was

---

litigation strategy, defending its "brand" despite the "product" having changed radically with the spirit of the age. Among other changes, both denominations departed from the *Didache*'s ancient teaching against abortion.

29. Mackay, "Rôle of Princeton," 1; *Charter and Plan*, "Introduction," 29–32.

30. Moorhead, *Princeton Seminary*, 464, 471.

31. For further discussion of the church's culture, see Jenson, "Christian Civilization," 157–58.

taught without reference to faith. Such a secularized academic environment is even exemplified by a character in a popular novel: dean Julia Carlyle, "a dedicated agnostic" "at a divinity school that only half believed in God."[32] When some academics produced a lectionary with secular goals in mind, a leading scholar referred to their effort as "a monstrous perversion of scripture."[33] For a long period a trend toward liberalism was the dominant point of view in writing the history of American religion.[34] Identity politics and identity Christianity followed the breakdown of a unified educational vision for theology. Theological pedagogy, like secular academic life, became fragmented.

Third, some members in the rising generation advocated a theological shift in ecumenical theory as well. For advocates of change, "the paradigm is not the old 'God–church–world' but rather 'God–world–church.'"[35] Under this theory, the world would set the agenda for the church. One of the weaknesses of the approach was that clerics did not bring subject matter expertise to debates in matters of public policy or secular subjects. As a result of a secularized orientation, the ecumenical significance of the World Council of Churches and the National Council of Churches was marginalized. A book review by a well-known former ecumenical church leader, Leslie Newbigin, decisively rejected the new paradigm.[36]

When students educated under secularized world views and fragmented theologies began to take their roles in churches and society in the next decades, American culture and politics were impacted by the relative absence of the presentation of orthodox dogma. Increasingly members in mainline churches accepted the premise that social change could and should be brought about through partisan political advocacy. However, when denominations and churches advocated specific legislative policy positions instead of offering general principals of ethical guidance to the laity and the public, divisive partisan lines occurred within denominations themselves. These in turn tore apart the churches' unity and culture. Corporate worship was also impaired since all congregants no longer accepted the same religious doctrines, including, in particular, the authority of scripture. Ironically, when churches tried to promote social change through political action, serious pathologies, including illegitimacy rates and divorce, increased within American society. The political aspirations of the radicals of

32. Carter, *New England White*, 116 (Julia); 201 (the school).
33. Metzger, "Implications."
34. Finke and Stark, *Churching of America*, 7.
35. Lindbeck, "Ecumenisms," 221.
36. Newbigin, "Review."

the 1960s proved counterproductive for both the North American churches and for the larger society. Protestant Christianity had been the historical basis for American civil society, but its theological influence now waned.

The essays in this volume were written to satisfy a need for evangelical literature in Latin America at a time when little of it existed. Nevertheless, although the essays were created for a particular audience the themes are universal and the core of the Gospel message is culturally transmissible. It is timely to recall Mackay's theological standard of dynamic centrality that is illustrated here. The essays embody his presentation of the Evangel to various segments of civil society, and the themes have continuing relevance. For example, Mackay addressed the true meaning of personality and the proper formation and education of youth in body, soul, and spirit. He dealt with vocation and meaning for living. He discussed moral and ethical issues in connection with the proper understanding of manhood. He presented the study of English literature by highlighting aesthetic and moral aspects. He challenged the intellectual class to be productive and to focus on the needs of its country. He squarely confronted the blindness of secularism with an image of a driver steering a car off the road. His explication of the Lord's Prayer taught reverence, humility, and the link between ethics and religion. He expounded the relationship between scripture and freedom. Finally, in terms of a comparative cultural contrast, contemporary readers can take note of the moral and ethical differences between the student revolution of Latin America of 1918 and the student revolution of North America of 1968.

Evangelical Christian teaching and preaching in Latin America helped bring about spiritual change and create preconditions for social, economic, and political transformation. The subjects of the essays include literature, politics, education, religion, and philosophy, but a persistent theme that runs through them is a focus on the nature and dignity of man in the light of God. The fruit of this teaching is self-confidence, courage, steadfastness, and other positive ethical attributes that in due time can bring progress and success to individuals and to peoples.

It is clear that Christian faith has intrinsic value. Persons of good will concerned for a nation's well-being and the common good will recognize the utilitarian social benefits of vibrant Christianity. The fabric of democracy wears thin when its Christian underpinnings are not vigorously upheld, and when opinion leaders are guided primarily by secularized visions and goals of social engineering. Similarly, with regard to foreign policy, it is not surprising that efforts to superimpose North American democratic institutions in foreign lands where Christian cultural foundations are missing are likely to miscarry.

Awareness of the connection between Christianity and democracy is not new or novel. Among many possible examples of the importance of religion (i.e. Christianity) for United States political history is George Washington's "Farewell Address," 1796, in which he stated, "Of all the dispositions and habits which lead to political prosperity, Religion and morality are indispensable supports."[37] Jasper Adams expounded the idea in his address, "The Relation of Christianity to Civil Government in the United States (1833)." During World War II, a writer located the Christian roots of democracy in the Christian ethic and understanding of human beings.

> There is . . . a definite correlation between the practice of the Christian ethic and the maintenance of democratic government . . . Organic correlation exists because of what the Christian ethic asserts about the nature of man and his role on this planet. The Christian view of man is that, earthbound as he is, he can here and now acknowledge and affirm his citizenship in the Kingdom of God.[38]

The church is not a labor union, a "snowplow," or a political faction. If the church becomes secularized and politicized, its ability to proclaim effectively its unique redemptive message as a leavening force within all of society is weakened and compromised. Ironically, the relation of South and North American Christianity has come full circle. Evangelical Latinos now have a growing presence in North America.[39] All Americans would do well to consider carefully the historic relationship of the sacred to the secular and the proper balance of church-state relations. A healthy Christian church is a crucial underpinning for democratic civic life. Mackay's mission to expand Christian influence in the global south is a profitable object lesson to consider. It is a fitting time to recall his thought provoking epigram, "Let the Church be the Church."

V

The essays are grouped thematically and not chronologically. The following introductory paragraphs are arranged in a sequence that corresponds to the order in which the essays appear below.

Chapter 1, "The Meaning of Life" (1931). This work has appeared in Latin America in Spanish and Portuguese and was a response to the recognized

---

37. Washington, "Farewell Address," 468.
38. Miller, "Faith to Democracy," 3–4.
39. Dias, "Evangélicos!"

need for first-rate evangelical literature in Spanish especially for youth. The six-part essay steadily builds to its conclusion, as it deals successively with the meaning of manhood, of vocation, of truth, of friendship, of the universe, and of Christianity. The latter is a creation from Christ's spirit, and the individual needs to take to heart his words, "Follow me."

Chapter 2, "At the Feet of the Teacher" (1930). This essay in seven sections is an exposition and reflection on the Lord's Prayer, in which Jesus responds to the disciples' request, "Lord, teach us to pray." There is no natural law of progress; the road of progress is the road of the cross. There is a tight bond between religion and ethics. Mackay prepared the essay for use at retreats of the YMCA in connection with a universal week of meditation and recollection organized in 1930.

Chapter 3, "The Christian Response to Secularism" (1932). This selection is the report in Portuguese of an address presented at the World's Sunday School Convention in Rio de Janeiro, Brazil. God is the response to secularism. The focus of the address was on reinterpreting the true meaning of personality and reinterpreting in the same terms the exact meaning of responsibility. The author states, "The function of the church is to create, inspire, and guide Christian personalities." Mackay, who travelled ten times in Brazil, lectured in Spanish, and he avoided use of a word in Spanish that had a different meaning in Portuguese.

Chapter 4, "The Profession of Being a Man" (1921). This lecture began Mackay's vocation as a public speaker in Latin America. The occasion was the inauguration of a lecture series in Tarma in the highlands of Peru, where José Galvez, Mackay's colleague in the Lima literary group, the Protervia, was mayor. It is a discussion of the philosophical idea of what it means to be a true human being. Mackay here uses the word "man" in context to convey the need for true masculinity and ethical conduct among the males of the society, yet the message of human dignity and a sober, confident approach to living applies, of course, to women as well.

Chapter 5, "Young Students" (1929). This report to the Evangelical Congress of Havana, Cuba, describes and evaluates the changes in Latin American education that Mackay both witnessed and influenced from 1917 to 1929. He evaluates the university revolution that began in Argentina with the Córdoba manifesto in 1918 and later swept over the continent. The report discusses the reform movement and the consequences of the university revolution in terms of academic reform, social reform, and political reform. The report concludes with a description of new ferments in university life such as spiritual awakening, and new philosophical, literary, and religious influences.

Chapter 6, "The Philosophy of the Red Triangle" (1926). This lecture was delivered in Montevideo, Uruguay, at the graduation of the class of 1926 of the Technical Institute of the YMCA where Mackay taught. The ideal of the organization was to build up the whole person in body, mind, and spirit. Using the phrase "The Christophilia of the Born Again," he distinguished religious nominalism from vital internalized religious experience. That experience permits one to move beyond mere virtue to kindness. The ideal for the organization is "realized only in so far as the members experience the transforming influence of Christ in their lives."

Chapter 7, "Is There a Relationship between the Young Men's Christian Association and Religion?" (1927). The author goes deeper into concepts developed in a companion essay. After defining relevant terms, he evaluates the religious problem in contemporary thought, describes religion as life and friendship, and focuses on the centrality of Christ in the religious thought of that time. The lecture concludes with discussion of links that bind the YMCA to religion: its goal to form Christian men and the treasure of a religious experience that it wishes to share with all people.

Chapter 8, "The Intellectuals and the New Times" (1923). Mackay delivered this address in historic Cajamarca, Peru, where the Free Church established a mission. After contrasting destructive and constructive forces of the times, he argues that new times challenge intellectuals to play a new role: not simply focus on esthetics, dry erudition, and historicism. The new intellectuals should study the world situation to learn the role of "their tongue and their pen in the definitive strife for justice and truth." The address sets forth the need to cultivate a new sense of humanity, a new sense of God in Christ, and a new sense of duty.

Chapter 9, "Don Miguel de Unamuno: His Personality, Work and Influence" (1918). The earliest work in the present collection, this essay, completed in 1917, opened the way for Mackay to enter intellectual circles of Lima and to present ideas to students, friends, and colleagues there. The essay, the first doctoral level essay on Unamuno, illustrates Mackay's early effort as a writer and linguist, and it illuminates particular ideas of Unamuno and his significance as a thinker for Latin America. Unamuno's thought influenced both John Mackay, personally and, in turn, Latin American culture.

Chapter 10, "The Christ of the Spanish Mystics" (1929). This essay in *La Nueva Democracia*, on whose board of advisors Mackay served, illustrates a method used in advocating Christian religious experience in Latin America. Mackay championed the need for a living, personal religion rather than a dead, institutionalized one. The essay exhorts readers to fight and struggle for the peace of Christ as the Spanish mystics did. Certain ideas are expanded in greater detail in his later book, *The Other Spanish Christ*.

Chapter 11, "The Cultural Value of Studying English Literature" (1918). This essay was Mackay's inaugural lecture at San Marcos University, Lima, Peru, the oldest university in the western hemisphere. After receiving his degree from San Marcos, but before being named to two teaching chairs at that institution, Mackay was asked to lead a course in English literature at the university. The lecture defines culture and offers reasons to study English literature in which life is described, life is sensed and perceived, life is idealized, and life is lived. This integration of ethics, theology, literature, and culture reflects the breadth of Mackay's academic capability.

Chapter 12, "The Regeneration of Peru" (1921). José de San Martín constituted Peru an independent nation on July 28, 1821. The article commemorates that occasion and stresses the need for an ideal that will serve the nation in the next century. Culture is not sufficient; rather a religious sentiment is needed as a great "dynamic and renovating force" in the nation. There is a religious basis for public morality.

Chapter 13, "The APRA Movement" (c. 1935). The APRA is a social and political movement founded by Víctor Raúl Haya de la Torre, in Mexico City, and today is the name of a political party in Peru. Before founding the party, Haya taught for several years at the Colegio Anglo-Peruano, where Mackay's friendship influenced him. This essay, written with a secular purpose, illustrates how ethical and moral ideals of social change were incorporated into a political party platform that had national and international influence.

Chapter 14, "The Truth That Makes Men Free" (1939). Mackay believed in God's revelation in the Bible. This essay, written for Universal Bible Sunday and a world plunging into war, was distributed in Latin America in Spanish and Portuguese versions. It notes that the last stand for freedom in many lands was inspired by the Bible. Touching on education, civil liberties, and the rights and privileges of citizens in a democratic order, the essay asserts that the pathway of the highest human freedom is reconciliation with God and loyalty to Jesus Christ.

John M. Metzger
Princeton, New Jersey

Abbreviations

AF	Association Forum
AHR	American Historical Review
AI	American Interest
AQ	American Quarterly
BR	Biblical Review
CC	Christian Century
C & C	Christianity and Crisis
CT	Christianity Today
CH	Church History
CQ	Congregational Quarterly
CuH	Current History
D	Daedalus
E de D	Espacio de Diálogo
FA	Foreign Affairs
IBMR	International Bulletin of Missionary Research
IRM	International Review of Missions
JPH	Journal of Presbyterian History
JPHS	Journal of the Presbyterian Historical Society
L	Leader: Organo Oficial del Colegio San Andrés, Lima, Peru
LAP	Latin America Press

MP	*Mercurio Peruano*
MRFCS	*Monthly Record of the Free Church of Scotland*
NI	*National Interest*
NYT	*New York Times*
PR	*Presbyterian Register*
PSB	*Princeton Seminary Bulletin*
SW	*Student World*
WD	*World Dominion*
WSJ	*Wall Street Journal*

Part One

The Transforming Message

1

The Meaning of Life

I. The Meaning of Hombridad

CHARLES WAGNER WAS RIGHT when he stated that, "There is something more unusual than a great man: a man." It is true that it is easier to be a physician, a lawyer, a writer, an artist, an engineer, than a man. And for the same reason that the profession of being a man is the only universal one, it is the most basic and important of human professions.

What does it mean to be a man, a full-fledged man? Where can we find a true human being, and how can we recognize him? Those farmers of Ibsen thought they had found one when they met the young clergyman, Brand, who had crossed the rough waters of the Norwegian fjord in a fragile little boat to do what he thought was his duty. "For a long time we have been told about the good way," they told Brand, "and they point it with their finger. More than one has pointed to it, but you are the first one who has followed it. A million words are not worth one deed. For that reason we come to seek you, because what we need is a true man." Pilate, too, that skeptic and feeble-spirited Roman governor of Judea, thought he was looking at a man in a certain prisoner brought to him on an unforgettable occasion. "Ecce Homo," he said to the contemptible accusers of the Nazarene. "Look at the Man."

Unamuno has called this quality of man, in the exact sense of the word, "hombridad." He tells us in one of his essays that, reading the great Portuguese historian and psychologist, Oliveira Martins, his imagination was struck by the word "hombridad," that he applied to the Castilian people.

He thought "hombridad" was a good discovery. The way Unamuno uses it, this word involves wider qualities than simple probity or honesty that are meant by "integrity." Its real sense is much more comprehensive and manly than "humanity" or "humanism," words that reek of pedantry, of a sect, of an abstract doctrine. Hombridad is the "quality of being a man, a whole and true man, of being a full man." "And there are so few men," adds Unamuno, "of whom we can say that they are fully men!"

Adopting this attractive linguistic coinage of the great Basque—who, by the way, is one of the most legitimate examples of hombridad on the contemporary scene—we will attempt to provide the portrait of a true human archetype.

1

The real man must be, first of all, the negation of some bastard archetypes that still enjoy wide prestige whether among the masses or among the intellectual or social elite.

One classic human archetype that enjoys great prestige in a certain sector of society, and in some countries more than others, is called Don Juan Tenorio. Don Juan, who received original literary personality in *The Seducer of Seville* by Tirso de Molina, shares with Faust the sad honor of being the most universal character of European literature from the Renaissance until now. Who is Don Juan? In fact, there are sharp differences in moral sensitivity between the Don Juans of Tirso, Zorrilla, Molière, Byron, and those of a South American city. But in the end they are identical. Don Juan does not change; he always proclaims the same motto, "Myself and my pleasures." But, in spite of all his bragging and his gallant airs, he is a perfect rake, turned foolish by his lust. He is rarely a man of great passion, instead, almost always cold and calculating. He boasts of his freedom. He lives, none the less, in complete slavery, being uncontrollably led by the impulses of his flesh, or the irresponsible commands of a ceaseless desire: "Because that is what I want." A short time ago the distinguished Spanish physician, Dr. Gregorio Marañón dropped a bomb in the camp of Tenorio, calling Don Juan "a biological monstrosity." Yet, he deserves this qualifying adjective, because there are no two ways about it: he is an abnormal person from a moral or a physical point of view.

But there are many youths, unfortunately, who, although they do not become Don Juans, believe that to be a man one has to take lessons in the school of Tenorio. I remember the sad case of a Peruvian young fellow who was looked at as a hero by a group of his companions, when it was found that he had acquired one of the diseases that follows the path of being a Tenorio. In the opinion of those naïve youths, he had now become a man. But a man is something different. A man recognizes that the sexual instinct is perfectly natural, as natural as any other, and then takes one or the other of the following attitudes towards it. Without repression, to avoid forming Freudian complexes, he sublimates it, looking for some higher activity that will absorb his passion. Or, alternatively, he honestly directs his instinct within the channel of marriage, accepting and even seeking the natural consequences brought about by the foundation of a new home.

I believe that if the young could reflect a little on the possible consequences for others of an irregular passion, they would reject forever any form of Tenorial behavior. I will never forget an experience I had in the city of Valparaíso. I had addressed some encouraging words to a group of youngsters, newspaper sellers, who each evening used to attend a class organized for them by the Young Men's Christian Association of that Chilean city. When I was leaving the place, I asked the secretary who was coming out with me, "How do you explain the extraordinary contrast between the intelligent and beautiful faces of many of those kids and their rags and their low social position?" My companion answered with these words so tragically suggestive, "Not a single one of them knows his father." What about those fathers? Tenorios of a higher social stratum.

2

Another human archetype, perhaps more cultured and correct, but no less a bastard and subhuman, is the snob. The snob belongs to the Old and Aristocratic Order of the Peacock. By virtue of the blood that courses through his veins, or the social position that he occupies, or the properties he owns, or the culture that he has acquired, the members of this order feel the greatest contempt for other people, and do not miss the opportunity to strut, taking care not to socialize with anybody who is not in their circle.

From the social point of view the snob is often a beautiful animal, who, not being able to find his genial society, shows preference for dogs and horses. Considering this branch of snobbism, Bernard Shaw said something about it, "It is allowed for ladies and gentlemen to have friends in the kennels, but not in the kitchen." The number of people that exhibit their sub-humanity, being closer to dogs or horses than to humans, certainly is astonishing and disconcerting.

Another kind of snob devotes himself to letters. What the literary snob seeks is to shine, more than to give off light. He has an obsession for the form, and is unconcerned about the substance. Trumpeting the words "art for art's sake," he spends his life looking for new cuts and colors, in this way becoming a tailor of the ephemeral when he ought to be a sculptor of the eternal. The only aspects of life that the snob is interested in are the showy and gaudy. As a spectator sitting in his ivory tower or his carved aristocratic balcony, keeping away from every contact with real and true life, he will never consider placing his talent at the service of a noble cause or idea. And if it were ever the case, as may happen, that a literary snob writes a book of substance, it will almost always be about a subject that is fashionable. When he deals with human problems, he takes good care not to touch those aspects of the problems that are burning in his own country. To deal with thorny issues could prove very inconvenient. I know a great work of sociology, written by a South American professor, in which not a word is said about the huge sociological problems from the author's country because he was only interested in the critical opinions of foreigners and not the national well-being.

Such people lack hombridad. All of them are little men, traitors against beauty, goodness, truth, or their own land. Every educational system is also traitorous and damned that tends to produce individuals who live contemptuously apart from eternal human reality and the actual reality of their country.

3

The third archetype of a man who lacks hombridad is the self-worshiper. He makes the ego and his own interests the reason for all activity. He pretends to create for himself a cosmos revolving on an axis of him, himself. Don Juan was an egotist, but not a self-worshiper, given that his actions were not inspired by the objective idea of the ego, but by a simple carnal passion. The same could be said about the snob. Unquestionably, he acts for egotistical motives, but while what drives him is a good image or the good opinion of some elite, what drives the self-worshiper is an immensurable desire to place himself in the center of every picture, making everything a means for the realization of his goals without him serving as a resource for any outside interest.

To follow will and self-interest at all times, without considering others at all, is nothing but an aristocratic form of madness. The perfect willful one, with all his airs of an independent gentleman, is possessed by the most tragic of all demons, the demon of the ego. No one can perform a lasting work if his only motive is selfish ambition. Sooner or later the one possessed of the ego will fall headlong in one of his reckless flights because he will meet in the heights the driving wind of a universal law. "The stars in their courses fought against Sisera," says the old Book of Judges.[1] And Victor Hugo, in *Les Miserables* asks, "Who won the battle of Waterloo?" . . . And he answers, "It was God!"

Perhaps the most accomplished egomaniac presented in literature is Ibsen's Peer Gynt. This young man adopts the motto, "To be myself," and flings himself on the world in search of fortune. After a series of adventures in foreign lands, during which he has earned and lost several huge fortunes, he returns to the land of his birth as a man with a white beard. On the way to his town, he enters an old vegetable garden that he knew. He takes an onion in his hand and starts removing the onion skins. To each skin he gives the name of some role that he has played in his life . . . the castaway, thrown by the sea on an American beach, the seal hunter in Hudson Bay, the gold prospector in California . . . until he gets, at the end, to what should be the heart of the onion. But . . . nothing! The onion is just skins. "My life," he says, "has been like an onion, all skins, appearances . . . On my tombstone the following should be carved, 'Here lies nobody.'"

Peer Gynt was Mr. Nobody because he did not consider in his long life anything but his ego and his own interests. He had not placed himself at the service of anything that could benefit others. Not a single surviving grateful heart would keep his name undying. In the long run the egomaniac must end up being either crazy or a nobody, but never a man.

4

Who is, then, the true human archetype? Whoever deserves to be called a true man possesses three basic qualities.

He is a free man who thirsts for what is real. His freedom stands out when compared to the prior types. Don Juan is a slave of a low passion; the snob is a slave of aristocratic prejudices; the egomaniac is a slave of the greatest devil, his ego. The true man, having assured his freedom with respect to his passions, his prejudices, and his wretched ambition, opens the doors and windows of his soul widely to the inspirations and voices that come from the real world. He thirsts for reality.

The human being lives in two worlds, a world of ephemeral appearances and a world of permanent values. The true man, once out of the platonic cave of appearances, contemplates everything under the light of reality. He can look straight to the sun.

---

1. Judg 5:20. —Ed.

A part of Keyserling's message to the contemporary world is his insistence on the need to adopt a passive attitude towards those things that we want to investigate or that should be investigated.[2] We have to let them speak first. Free of forethoughts and prejudices, we have to allow ourselves to be steeped in their atmosphere. Afterwards, whatever is not satisfying, after we have understood it, we reject. But our critical attitude should not come first but last. Then we will be able to be critical with full knowledge of the facts.

In this way we will avoid the complaint that those who criticize the most are generally the ones who know the least. The true man who is eager for reality proceeds in his search for spiritual things in the same way that a scientist does. Scientific discoveries are made on the basis of applying a hypothesis in a reverent and conscientious way to objective reality. Spiritual discoveries will take place only by a process of honest verification of the theory or the attitude presented for investigation.

Another feature of the true man is his passion for something higher. There are great regions of the real world that will not be discovered by theoreticians, priceless experiences that they will never be able to share. The only creative attitude towards life is that of the person who joins a higher cause that absorbs all the energies of his brain, his heart, and his arms. He has to be a worker in one way or another. He has to place his talents at the service of something of indisputable importance, that he may find, in other words, his calling in life. And with reference to the intellectual difficulties, they tend to solve themselves as soon as one starts working to fulfill a duty or to flesh out an ideal in life. There are problems that turn out to be insoluble in the solitude of a library that could be easily solved in the solitude of the road. "Action," said Amiel, "is the quintessence of life, as combustion is the quintessence of fire." How frequently it happens that the cause makes the man both intellectually and morally! Who has not known mediocre men who became giants, managing to engrave immortal feats in the pages of history because they risked their life for a superior cause!

Passion and not apathy is the normal condition of man. The only creative ones are the greatly impassioned ones. They are the only ones capable of great accomplishments, starting with the preliminary conquest of a proven personal character. "No heart is pure," it has been said, "that is not passionate; no virtue is safe if it is not enthusiastic." Live in a vertigo of passion, Unamuno cries out. Read and be inspired by the burning prose of

---

2. Hermann Graf Keyserling (1880–1946) was a German social philosopher from a wealthy aristocratic family. —Ed.

the crusader, it says in his prologue to the *Life of Don Quixote and Sancho*, whoever has seen the star and is prepared to proceed!

And if one is a true man, one will turn out to be of one piece, in thought and action. Steeped in reality, he will be a true man, or of the Truth, as the Galilean said to Pilate. His life will be of one piece, and he will have no mask of any kind. Whatever his soul believes, that is what he will say and do. He will prefer death to abandonment of his principles. Thinking about men of this kind, Romain Rolland states, "Those of you who have to die, should die. Suffer, those who have to suffer. One does not live to be happy, but to fulfill a law. Suffer or die, but make an effort to be what you should be: a man."

II. The Meaning of One's Calling

Upon Don Quixote's return home after the sad adventure that put an end to his first sortie, he directs a phrase to the farmer, Pedro Alonso, who is with him, that turns out to have a deeper meaning than the long speech to the goatherds. "I know who I am," says the nobleman of la Mancha to his unbelieving neighbor, "and I know what I can be," and he said this when he was all crushed and battered.

"I know who I am." These words could be taken, certainly, as symbolic of the so-called Spanish pride that Quixote embodies. But they have a more universal and human meaning. They are the words of a man who is strongly convinced of the role he has to play in life, that is, of someone who has a superlative sense of his calling. Quixote knew who he was. He knew he had been born to be an arm of God on earth, to right all wrongs. Consistent with the sense he had of his mission, he did not miss the opportunity to charge at the windmills and to liberate the chained galley slaves, not weakened in his faith and daring by the fact that they left him beaten, and that they, upon recovering their freedom, stoned their liberator. What he was looking for was not success and gratitude but the satisfaction of having answered an inner calling that imposed on him a duty and not happiness as his life's ideal.

The vocational sense of the immortal man of la Mancha was at the same time craziness and his glory. For that reason, he "lived crazy"; freed from it, in the twilight of his life, he "died sane." But it is not as Alonso Quijano the Good, but as Don Quixote, the Crazy, that he will be the eternal inspiration and emblem of those called to play a role in the world.

1

There is no question that the sense of one's calling is one of the highest senses of man. It is the sense that leads him to undertake the greatest ventures with altruism and bravery. In dark moments it provides light; in difficult junctures it infuses renewed dash. It makes a man ignore all the taunts and slanders, and, if at the end of the road he would not see his hopes fulfilled, it will provide consolation in the idea that others who have seen the star of their destiny in the sky, through his luminous example, will carry out the work. So that it will be possible to declare that the day a man can truthfully say, "I know who I am," knowing himself through the light of a new vision of a mission he had to accomplish in life, on that very day he will begin to live in all truth. From then on he will live in his work, and his work, in him. In that instant he will stop being nobody and become somebody. He will be a "nobleman," son of someone, that is, of his work, or rather, of the new and holy sense that pushes him to undertake work.

We have great need of this superior sense of calling. Its acquisition and development will bring a sure solution to a portion of the serious problems of our society. Unamuno has expressed some concepts of this kind in his book *The Tragic Sense of Life* that have to be considered attentively. He says, "This question of the proper vocation is possibly the gravest and most deep-seated of social problems, that which is at the root of all the others. That which is known par excellence as the social question is perhaps not so much a problem of the distribution of wealth, of the products of labour, as a problem of the distribution of vocations, of the modes of production. Pray that each one will find his true role; that he experience the religious value of his civil vocation; that he will work at it with so much love and effort that he will be irreplaceable to those that he serves." "Looking at each one as a servant of the others, as if we had to give our entire enthusiasm to do something of public usefulness; the religious attitude, undoubtedly," Unamuno concludes, "is to endeavor to make the occupation in which we find ourselves our vocation, and only in the last resort to change it for another."

Such would be the ideal, but in our current society what do we find? On the one hand, a great number of people who lack a profession or vocation, and, on the other, a much greater number who do not recognize their job as a vocation. Among the first ones there are millions, undoubtedly, who would like to work in some job, but they cannot. We find here the tragic problem of unemployment, part of the instant legacy of the Great War to the contemporary world. This is, notwithstanding, an incidental situation, a product of abnormal circumstances, and it is destined to disappear little by little.

Much more serious than the problem of those who do not have a vocation because they cannot find a job, is that of those who, able to get a job, refuse to work. They are well to do and prefer parasitic sloth to productive work.

What can we do with the parasites, with men who live from inherited monies, without contributing anything useful to the society that protects them? There may be different ideas about the measures that could be convenient to adopt towards such people, but none regarding the eternal ideals of the adages that say, "The one who does not work, should not eat" (always assuming that he can do so), and, "All will produce according to their capacity and receive according to their need." But only a deep sense of vocation among all the citizens of a country could bring about a social condition in which this ideal could be realized.

2

We have stated, on the other hand, that there are many people who do not recognize their job as a vocation. A few years ago I had the opportunity to pay a visit to a prison in Buenos Aires at a time when the institution was run by the illustrious expert, Eusebio Gómez. Towards the end of my visit, I asked the director to answer a few questions about the behavior of some of the prisoners. Among the reports that he gave me, I heard a phrase that has remained engraved in my memory. Dr. Gómez told me that frequently, when a prisoner spoke in confidence in his office, he would say, "Director, I know how to be a prisoner." He knew, that is to say, to accommodate himself perfectly to the regulations of the institution, adhering to such behavior that was most likely to render him attractive to the authorities. He did not feel any vocation to continue as a prisoner. What he felt was the yearning to be a free man; but to be able to recover his freedom more quickly, he had to know how to be a prisoner.

"I know how to be a prisoner." How many people learn to carry out a role that they do not like, not feeling any vocation for it! A number of them are poor, and society has denied them the opportunity to develop their higher capacities, sentencing them to work at the same jobs as their parents and grandparents. This is a great injustice. Each society is morally obliged to provide to all the children of their citizens, through proper cultural facilities, the opportunity to discover their aptitudes and select freely a vocation in life.

But there is another much more serious problem than the unconcern of the government to discover higher values among the members of the proletariat. It is that many men and women that have enjoyed all the advantages that society could provide, and who occupy important positions, have a total lack of a vocational sense in the jobs that they fulfill. They are doctors, lawyers, legislators, public employees, priests, professors, students, and who knows how many other professionals, of whom the only thing that can be said is this: they know how to be. Each one has the job of his job, but no one has a vocation. Just like the prisoners that I have mentioned, they know how to be what they are not, and they know it for the salary or the position, or the influence of their situation. They consider only the advantages that they receive, and not the good that they may do. Sad cases! They do not know who they are; they only know how to be what they are not and what they do not want to be.

3

What a tragedy when a large portion of the people of a country seeks jobs instead of vocations! Let's look at the teaching profession. How few of them are true skilled teachers, men who, for their love of teaching, do not dream of anything but to be real leaders of souls, making efforts at all times to be models of virtue and conscientious researchers!

It will escape the notice of no one who is informed about the real meaning of the university disputes during the last decade, that the basic cause, the origin of the reform movement of the students in Latin America, was the feeling of tragic forlornness of the students seeing themselves without professors. "We want teachers, we want teachers!" That is the crux of the historical document, put out by the students from Córdoba, "To the Freemen of America." When will it be possible to fulfill the dream of those and other young students for a cultural home in which "only those true builders of souls, the creators of truth, beauty, and greatness will be able to be teachers"?

It will happen when everyone who calls himself a teacher, be it from superior, middle, or primary education, will have a similar sense of vocation to the one reflected by Gabriela Mistral in that moving piece of prose, "The Prayer of the Teacher." The humble country teacher says to the Supreme Master,

> Give me the unique love of my school; so that not even the withering of beauty may be able to take away my lasting tenderness. Master, make my fervor lasting and my disillusionment fleeting. Take away from me this impure desire of justice that confuses me, the wretched suggestion of complaint that boils in me when they hurt me, that I will not feel pain for the lack

> of understanding nor will I be saddened by the forgetfulness of those I taught. Grant me to be more of a mother than the mothers; to be able to love and defend, like them, what is not flesh of my flesh. Give me the far reaching capacity to make a perfect verse of one of my girls, and leave fixed in her my most penetrating melodies, for that time when my lips will sing no longer. Show me your Gospel as possible in my time, so that I will not renounce the battle of each day, of each hour, for it.

Who could measure the influence of a teacher moved by such a sense of vocation? Among the true teachers of the modern world, a prominent place is occupied by Don Francisco Giner de los Ríos. He was the perfect teacher. Everything will be known later on, when his disciples and those of Don Miguel de Unamuno, will one day found the new Spain. At the end of *The Lawyer of Glass*, Azorín depicts Don Francisco among his students.[3] Here is the passage.

> The imagination takes flight, and we see a large, aristocratic house, and in it rich libraries and wide rooms, apart from the bustle in which lives, in pleasant harmony with the muses, a learned and good man, and some youngsters full of illusions and hopes. Don Francisco directs their readings, pointing out the beauty of the Latin and Greek classics, reading with them the great Spanish poets, bringing them up, in the end, not with the severe frown of a tutor, but with the sweet softness of a sincere and passionate friend . . . and later on they amble, take long outings, soak up the landscape and the smells of the fields.

There is something, though, that Azorín does not say, something told to me by one of the same disciples of Don Francisco. It seems that on those meetings and outings of friends, the professor, in intimate conversation with one or another of his disciples, used to ask each one of them, "And you, what are your plans in life?" He wanted to infuse the sense of vocation. He wished that each one would know who he was, seeking and finding his true vocation.

The kind questioning of Don Francisco elicited, no doubt, questions like this in the minds of his young friends. What should I do in life? Which should be my vocation? How could I know what profession I should embrace?

---

3. José Martínez Ruiz (1873–1967) used the pseudonym Azorín. A Spanish man of letters, he was the longest lived member of the Generation of 98, his artistic and literary group. —Ed.

4

In view of the huge vocational problem there is nothing like immersing oneself in the biographies of great men. No youth should cross the threshold of coming of age without having read all those classic collections of biographies such as Plutarch's *Parallel Lives*, Carlyle's *Heroes*, *Exemplary Lives* of Romain Rolland, and in a special way, *The Life of Jesus* in the Gospels. At the fire of these superior men is where the flames of the ideals are to be lit, and we can make out the horizons of destiny.

History tells us that many of the top men felt called as if by a supernatural voice to undertake the revolutionary works that have made them immortal. Such was the case of Moses, of Jesus, of St. Paul, and of not just a few figures of the religious history of the world.

There have been cases, also, in which great soldiers, explorers, and revolutionaries have possessed a mystical sense of the historical importance of the role that they played and of their own importance as men of destiny. Columbus, for example, looked at the discovery of the New World as the fulfillment of a prophecy of Isaiah[4] and saw himself as the tool of providence to bring it about. His mystical sense gave him the intuition of a continent to be discovered and an unbreakable will to search for it.

But, in general, one finds his own vocation in one of two ways: the discovery of a special capacity, or the vision of an urgent need.

Modern education is geared to discover in different ways the latent capacity of the students, as well as their innate tendencies. As soon as they are discovered, there is an effort to cultivate them by all means, encouraging the students to seek their vocation through their own aptitudes. It would seem that it was his reading of the feats of Achilles in the *Iliad* of Homer that led Alexander the Great, as a young man, to discover his own soul and his destiny. He had to be the Achilles of his times.

Romain Rolland unveils to us how Jean-Christophe discovered his vocation. He was just a child when his grandfather believed to have found in his grandchild the budding talent of a musical composer and told him that. Jean-Christophe took the enthusiastic opinion of his grandfather seriously, and from then on, as he was carrying out the unending and boring musical exercises imposed by his father, "he heard in his interior a proud voice that said repeatedly, I am a composer, a great composer. Given that he was a composer, from that day on he dedicated himself to compose."

---

4. Isaiah 60:9 is cited in Mackay, *Other America*, 17. By quoting 2 Esdras 6:42 to the Spanish sovereigns, Christopher Columbus helped to secure financing for his voyages of exploration. Metzger, *Apocrypha*, 232–34. —Ed.

Some others, and I would say the majority of humanity's benefactors, have discovered their vocation by finding themselves, in a given moment of their lives, confronting a serious situation that demanded immediate remedy. In this way Oliver Cromwell found his vocation as father of English freedoms; in this way José de San Martín and Simón Bolívar found theirs, as fathers of South American independence. Steeped in the anguish of his country, Benito Juárez discovered his vocation as builder of a new Mexico. Mahatma Gandhi was a simple lawyer at the time when, due to an offense against the rights of Indians in South Africa, he canceled his ticket for his return trip to India, on the eve of the day he had to leave, in order to defend the cause of his fellow countrymen. A temporary need led him to a lifelong vocation. All the great humanitarian institutions were founded by men and women who—like Florence Nightingale, founder of the Red Cross—discovered their vocation in the task of facing up to pressing needs. "Somebody has to do it," they told themselves, "Why not me?"

Why not? This is the creative question, the question of those who, in the middle of the present have been able to catch a glimpse of some ideal, something that does not exist, but that should. Each one of them, inspired by their particular dream, challenges with an eternal "why not?" all the difficulties that impede its realization. The superior tension that is engendered in the heart of all those who want to develop their vision of what is good into a reality will lead them, inevitably, to find a role in life, infusing them with the creative meaning of their vocation.

III. The Meaning of Truth

"What is truth?" said Pilate to Jesus of Nazareth, without granting the time to get an answer. The same question has been asked through the centuries since then, as had been done, prior to that, by the philosophical schools of Greece. It involves a problem of persistent interest, that has resulted in a number of solutions.

Without going into the history of the problem, and without subjecting the multiple theories proposed to a critical examination, we will look at it directly and in my own way.

The field of the truth is a field of relations. It has to do with the relation between what is and what is said to be, or what is made to appear, that is, between reality and its expression.

When there is correspondence between them, the truth is recognized immediately. So that it could be defined as the perfect correspondence between reality and its expression. When there is a lack of correspondence between them, error or lies result. If, when trying to describe reality, we make an involuntary mistake, an error crops up. On the other hand, if the description of reality turns out to be inaccurate because we wanted to make it that way, then a lie shows up.

But, since what we have called reality consists of several aspects, it will be necessary to develop a harmonious picture of the truth, to point to what it means in relation to each one of the aspects.

1

Reality presents itself, first of all, as an object for our knowledge, so that it presents an intellectual problem immediately: how to think about what is real? What is the essence of conceptual reality?

In the field of knowledge man has to be a "hunter of truth," as Plato called a true philosopher. He must make an effort to know things as they are. Free of all prejudices or bastard interests, he must not give rest to his brain in the loyal attempt to try to find correspondence between the objects or facts that he is studying and the ideas he forms of them.

The passion to seek the truth in this sense has been a feature of a great number of superior spirits. Some reached it by their search for a principal idea that would illuminate the whole of reality, bringing peace to their restless hearts. Such were, for example, Buddha and Spinoza. Some others found so much vital satisfaction in the search itself, that they grew attached to it. For these the strife was even better than victory. It was not the goal but the race that made them happy. They did not look for rest but for agitation. They would say with Malebranche,[5] that "if I had the truth captive in my hand, I would open the hand and let it fly, to be able to go after it and catch it again." But the ones or the others had the same meaning of truth. The thirst was the sole spring of their life, and they swore eternal loyalty to it. They would never accept an error knowingly, nor would they proclaim or live a lie. They were intellectually honest.

Intellectual honesty is one of the worthiest features and unfortunately one of the most difficult to find. It is characterized by the custom of keeping open the doors and windows of the mind to the lights and breezes of reality, and also by the unbreakable resolution to draw the logical consequences of

---

5. Nicolas Malebranche (1638–1715) was a French Oratorian and rationalist philosopher. —Ed.

every new glimpse of the truth without avoiding the consequences of loyalty to it. But there are few honest intellectuals.

An eminent Spanish author tells of a doctor, his friend, who was called on some occasion to a boarding school to see one of the boarders who was sick. In a reserved hallway he saw a painting representing St. Michael, the Archangel, fighting with Satan, the devil. The Archangel had at his feet the rebellious angel, who held in his hand . . . a microscope! The microscope was for the authorities of that school a symbol of over analysis. They considered an extremely thorough investigation as satanic work, and those who carried it out turned out to be demons.

How much has human progress suffered because of those who, due to their prejudices or vested interests or lack of moral courage, have resisted matching their ideas to reality! Intellectual honesty of a man of science is put to the test when he trips on some finding or findings that do not fit within his hypothesis. If he were to possess a real sense of truth, he would be willing to revise the laws and formulas involved. If not, he will try to sidestep the new problem found, or to kill the inconvenient facts that brought it up.

It is said of a biologist, a disciple of Louis Agassiz,[6] who once found some mollusk which seemed to be a transitional species among the many mollusks that he was studying, that after examining it for a long time, he threw it angrily to the ground, grinding it with the heel of his shoe. Having thus destroyed the finding that was challenging his biological theory, the pseudo-scientist exclaimed, "This is the way to deal with a damn transitional species."

On the other hand, true scientists, inspired by the meaning of scientific truth, have always had a special interest for all the data that appeared to be resistant to being pigeonholed in the current theories. Very often the honest study of the rest of the data has led to new discoveries. We have to face all the trustworthy data that we find without avoiding any. We have to concentrate our mind on them in silent and patient consideration. Afterwards, when we least expect it, and when the mind is already in a receptive mood, the longed for new truth will come to us, like a spark of light. In this way Henri Poincaré[7] has said his mathematical discoveries "came" to him. Because, if it is true that we have faculties of an acquisitive character that seek out the truth, we have others of a receptive nature that recognize and welcome it as soon as it arrives.

---

6. Jean Louis Rodolphe Agassiz (1807–1873) was a Swiss earth scientist who formulated theories of the ice age and later became a professor at Harvard University. —Ed.

7. Jules Henri Poincaré (1854–1912) was a mathematician and philosopher of science whose cousin, Raymond Poincaré, became President of France 1913–1920. —Ed.

2

A second aspect of reality claims our awe. In the same way that the correspondence between the idea, on the one hand, and some data on the other, gives rise to conceptual truth, correspondence between behavior and some eternal values give rise to ethical truth. A moral man is one in whom those values or norms have been made flesh. He will internalize them in such a way that his actions will turn out to be the transparent expression of a person completely identified with the good. He will do good for good's sake, and not from some external imposition or personal convenience.

Conceptual truth and ethical truth are intimately linked. In the last analysis, science rests upon virtue. If there is no absolute sincerity in the scientific investigator, his research will have scant value. There are, also, intellectual problems of such transcendence that they have no solution except through a determined attitude towards life. For example, one may pretend to define the ultimate reality. One wants to explore the "why?" of the universe and get to know the matrix principle that rules its destiny. For such a case, as someone has stated, "Ethics is the best source of spiritual clairvoyance." It offers a clue to interpret the frightful mystery. Reality is one, and human life is an integral part of it. In such a way the intuitions of the moral conscience have enormous value. Quite often loyalty to it has saved a man at the moment when he finds himself adrift, subjected to the gales of skepticism. "In the darkest night that a human soul can experience, even if everything else were in doubt, this at least is true: if there is no God or future life, even in that case it is better to be generous than selfish, better chaste than licentious, better loyal than false, better brave than a coward." Whoever said these words was saved by his sense of the ethical truth, grasping in his intellectual desperation to the immovable basis of morality. And it is nothing else that Unamuno advocates in his masterpiece *Tragic Sense of Life*. The prime moralist of Europe says, "to act in such a way as to make our annihilation an injustice, in such a way as to make our brothers, our sons, and our brothers sons, and their sons' sons, feel that we ought not to have died."[8]

There are, notwithstanding, those who only pretend to have this precious sense of ethics. The most out and out enemies of virtue, the most dangerous elements of society, are the hypocrites. According to the etymology of the word, the hypocrite is an "actor," one who plays a role that is not his, one who feigns to be what he is not. He is a masked person who adopts the disguise most convenient to his wretched interests. The most frightening

---

8. Unamuno, *Tragic Sense*, 269. —Ed.

disguise is that of the face of an angel that hides the heart of a devil. This is the most applicable for a traitor. The English novelist George Eliot has depicted the picture of the perfect traitor with unsurpassed mastery. He is one, she says, who has "a face in which vice leaves no track, lips which lie with a sweet smile, eyes of such brightness and depth that they do not get tarnished by any infamy, cheeks that get up from a murder without paling." But in the entrails of Tito, the traitor, hypocrisy had begotten a child, fear. Down through time, this terrible child became an inseparable and sole companion of his father.

And it always happens this way. The hypocrite cannot be happy. To be able to be happy, he will have to take off his mask. To be able to feel manly, a man who respects himself, a man not cowed by the most searching gaze, has only one resort: to take off the mask and confess frankly why he wore it. A sincere confession, which is nothing but the brave reaffirmation of the numbed sense of reality, destroys the covenant with lies, returning balance and simplicity to the whole person.

3

A third feature of reality produces our emotions. From the correspondence between the emotion produced and its expression in a poem, a song, a symphony, a picture, or a statue springs esthetic truth. When someone attempts to give artistic form to something that he does not feel deeply, a farce results. A good deal of poetry, for example, is plain farce, because it is written with the head and not with the heart. A number of would be poets would do well to remember the advice of Carlyle that one should not say in verse what can be said in prose. Most of the speeches made to commemorate the great leaders and historical anniversaries are also farces. There is no style of speech more false and pompous, more unbounded and strident, than the one used in the panegyrics with which such occasions are celebrated. The bucket of superlatives and hyperboles ends up by incapacitating the devotee from experiencing a soaring emotion or expressing it in a natural and proper way, even when he may experience it.

"To make songs one has to be like them," said Gottfried, the peddler to his little nephew, Jean-Christophe, the night they spent at the river edge, soaking in the music of nature. This lesson of musical esthetic was never forgotten by our small composer, who turned his whole life as an artist into a perfect symphony of matching his emotional state and the musical expression that he gave to it.

But in dealing with esthetic reality one also has to recognize another correspondence: the one that must exist between the emotions felt by the artist and whatever caused them. The true artist feels the universal significance of what he contemplates, hears, or meditates so that the expression that he then gives to his emotion will not be just a simple realistic reproduction of its cause, but an interpretation of its meaning.

We are fed up with realists who believe that esthetic truth consists in using art as a photographic camera to reproduce the most disgusting aspects of human life. There are realists whose works are mere open sewers, that plague the moral atmosphere of their readers, producing in them a sort of asphyxia, rendering them incapable of seeing and sensing life in its proper perspective. The urge of realism, suffered by so many so-called artists and others, is nothing more than a sick and amoral condition.

What is missing, in reality, in these American lands, are artists that will discover for us the universal out of the particular and the eternal out of the ephemeral; and who, sharing the feeling of the reality that surrounds them, will make us feel and see it in its true human meaning: rejecting crafty imitations, absorbing the core of the native soil in order to sing and paint after that the sorrows and hopes of the plains, the forest, and the mountains! Because art is for life and not life for art.

4

The last relational correspondence to which we are going to refer may be the most important of all. It is, in fact, the correspondence between the central current of our life and the central current of the cosmic process. That such current or trend may exist, is a postulate of the idea of progress itself. That it is pushed by forces of goodness and is directed towards the perfecting of the human person, is a postulate of our moral conscience. There is no more valid philosophical principle than this: "the *whole* has to be good." We do not live in a phantasmagoria, in spite of the high relief with which the chaos and the mystery of human things are brought to our attention. Neither can one believe for a moment without being at risk of overturning the same foundation of reason, that the universe may not be essentially good and that it moves across millennial history to a sublime purpose of good. If that is so, the most basic harmony that each man must attain is to adapt his life to the veritable trend of things. He must make use of all possible means to be connected to it. By allowing his life to flow in the same river bed with it, man will become a center that will create progress. This transcendental correspondence could be called the religious truth.

But a second question arises: how to interpret this cosmic flow of goodness? What is its quintessence? According to the old philosophical principle that one should interpret the reality of a thing according to its fruit, not according to its root, it is necessary to interpret the supreme reality as willing the good, the archetype of the highest reality that we know. The central current of things is, accordingly, the expression of a supreme will for good, that impels the world through the way of progress and leans towards the perfection of human life. But all progress, as well as all refinement, depends on the spontaneous and full abandonment, on the part of man, of his selfish will, in order to identify himself, as a loyal cooperator, with the will of God.

Thus religious truth is the correspondence that arises from the sublime adventure of delivering one's particular will to the universal will. Only by means of this surrender will we be able to know the higher truth. Only in this way will the human soul find the rest and the indispensable energy for a work of created good.

On the road to the supreme truth, a voice breaks the mysterious silence, a firm but tender voice, of the Wayfarer. It says, "I give you my hand. Follow me."

IV. The Meaning of Friendship

There is no more sacred word than friend. There is no more spiritual and sublime relation than friendship.

The relationship between friends is more elevated than the one between brothers, brides and grooms, or spouses, given that many brothers, brides and grooms, and spouses are not friends. With a high frequency brothers just tolerate each other, a petty interest may associate the bride and groom, and spouses may have nothing more in common than the house they live in. But when a sense of friendship is instilled to fraternal tolerance, to the exalted state of the engagement, to the routine life of marriage, these relationships become sublime, thus reaching their most perfect expression.

1

How can we define this superior reality? It consists in the reciprocal devotion of two or more human beings with the highest confidence and the purest of motives. To find a friend, a person that shares our same interests, whose disposition may be different but complementary with ours, and of whose affection and loyalty we do not have the smallest doubt, is the most precious discovery that we may encounter in life. The friendship of that person constitutes, for every one that has the happiness to have found it, a spur to fulfill our daily duties, a bastion in the dark hours of temptation and doubt, a consolation in suffering, and a luminous target for the constant effort to improve.

Among the many merits that could be pointed out in that marvelous novel *Jean-Christophe* of Romain Rolland, one takes precedence over all the others: it is the apotheosis of friendship. Christophe, a figure as epic in its greatness as Brand but infinitely more human and closer to us than Ibsen's hero, became what he became thanks to the male and female friends that he had along the path of his life. Even at the twilight hour they continued in his life. The volume titled *Morning*, that describes the youth of Jean-Christophe, contains a precious passage in which the emotions of the solitary child are depicted in warm colors when he finds for the first time a friend of his age. After a day spent walking in the countryside with his friend, Otto Diener, Christophe returned home alone; it was night already. His heart was singing: I have a friend! I have a friend! He did not see or hear anything; he was falling asleep and did fall asleep as soon as he got into bed. But twice or three times he woke up during the night with a fixed idea. He repeated: I have a friend! And he would fall asleep again.

2

Since the experience of friendship has an incalculable spiritual value, it causes deep sorrow and even holy indignation to find so many parodies that carry its sacred name.

The first parody of friendship is by a Chilean author who has denominated it "bar friendship." He was referring to those casual encounters, or the arrangement of some group of acquaintances to meet in bars, clubs, cafes, taprooms, or other places of public gatherings. There is no stronger link between these bar friends than the common desire to kill time, to drink something, to tell some off color jokes, to curse their neighbors, or to go on a binge. They do not know each other intimately; they are even scared to open up to one another. They barely know themselves. All of them have disguises so that their companions will not see their faces. "All the world is a mask, and the whole year is a carnival," was the title Mariano José de Larra[9] gave to a famous satire of his. This phrase depicts very well the way and the ideals of "bar friends." Whenever one of them finds himself in dire straits, he will never go to his carnivalesque companions to ask for advice or help

---

9. Mariano José de Larra (1809–1837) was a Spanish romantic writer whose life ended with suicide. —Ed.

because he knows well that it would be counterproductive. From that day on, when one of them will have nothing to contribute to the merrymaking, the others will shun him. He should go elsewhere to dance!

To another parody of friendship we could give the name "utilitarian friendship." It is that in which every "friend" is a convenience, an actual or potential means to foster one's interests. For them life, even the most sacred that they have, is reduced to a kind of fishing, to fish for favors, honors, positions, profits. And given that the fastest and surest way to reach all those ends is to have the support of "influential friends," they devote themselves to seeking friendship, employing for that all the resources within their reach. "One will have to be in trouble to seek a friend," a Greek adage stated. Utilitarian friends fulfill to a tee the spirit of the adage, given that they seek friends not for the spiritual necessity of having them, but for the material urge to exploit them. As soon as these friends, for any circumstance, cannot or do not want to serve the interests of those who have sworn so much friendship, they harass them and erase them from their memory.

This utilitarian friendship is becoming a threat to public morality. Positions are distributed not out of personal merit of the applicants, but by the number of "friends" that they have. It is necessary to have objective and impersonal norms to fill public jobs that should be assigned only to those who have true ability and vocation for them. In any case, the sacred name of friendship should never be invoked to grant positions or privileges to those who do not deserve them through their own virtues.

3

Friendship, that is true friendship, supposes the fulfillment of some postulates. The first of them is that whoever wants to get soul friends has to start removing every mask.

Life in the large cities is something like a masked ball. Those same ones who see each other every day rarely know each other. It is because everyone carries a mask of some kind. Some wear the mask of the scowling civil servant, others that of a man of business who does not stop working except to state how busy he is, and still others the gallant man of the world, specializing in conventionalisms and contemptuous of any superior concern. At the same time a large proportion of persons hide their true self behind the mask of morbid and hostile melancholy, a consequence of disappointments and of spiritual isolation. There is no possible friendship among those wearing a mask. If they crave friends, they will have to take off their masks and go in search of those kindred spirits who have done the same.

But where? And how to take off the false mask? The most suitable place is the bosom of nature. So that the masked men should go out of the city, bound for the sierras, or the fields, or the sea shore! May they go where the flattering voices or those who are backbiting cannot reach, where urban conventions have no say, where the nakedness of nature will invite the souls to bare themselves, where a multitude of sylvan creatures will offer them their friendship, and where this new thirst for reality will be quenched by a breeze filled with aromas and the vision of far horizons tinted by the changing face of the sky. The contact with nature reveals us to ourselves and prepares us for friendship.

Whoever may have attended those camps organized in different settings of the South American continent by the Young Men's Christian Association will never forget it. A throng of urban masked men arrives at the beach of Piriápolis, or to the sierra of the Ventana, or to Angol in southern Chile, or to Chosica, at the edge of the Peruvian River Rímac. On the first or second day after arrival, one is heard to say, "Well, I do not recognize myself here." His companions do not know him either. Together with the conventional city clothes, he has taken off many mental garments, the prejudices, the snobbish airs, the critical spirit, the tendency to repress his emotions, and most others that have incapacitated him for a friendly exchange. The beauty of the place and the expansive and fraternal environment of the camp have taken possession of him. He feels like a child again, and now he sings, shouts, and plays with all the naturalness of childhood. He will talk later, in the night called "the open heart," when all the campers, united under the stars around a great hearth, will tell, just prior to their farewell, their impressions of those days spent together. He will state that for the first time in his life he has known what friendship is. A few years later, he will come back to the same sacred place and will tell a new group of campers, united around a symbolic fire, how he found at a prior camp the best friends of his life.

A second postulate of friendship is the cultivation of common interests. It is understood that such interests are of a pure and elevated character. But within this category there are a great number of interests that tend to create a suitable atmosphere for the formation and cultivation of friendships. We could mention recreational sports, hikes and excursions to the country, a mutual enthusiasm for the arts or the letters.

Much more efficient, however, in order to establish an unbreakable friendship is the consecration by two or more persons to a common cause. Because, we have to recognize that friendship is like happiness: one finds it when one does not consider it as the supreme goal but cooperating in some objective completely alien to a selfish interest. There is no friendship comparable to that of those who live a self-sacrificing life completely devoted to the propagation of ideas that they believe are transcendental for human welfare, or that of those whose life merges with an altruistic endeavor destined to improve the life of their peers. If, by any chance, they would suffer for their ideals, their friendship will be purified even more. The gale will only be able to make the true friends develop deeper roots, intertwining their smaller roots in the ground of eternal love.

Reader, if you start to feel boredom instead of pleasure and disgust for disloyalty of friends that were not so, when the soul cries over its solitary condition and experiences hunger for love and friendship, seek then a noble cause with which to bind yourself. Finding it and devoting yourself to it, you will encounter the friendship that you so desire in the path of altruistic service.

The third postulate is absolute loyalty on the part of friends. How often we have seen a friendship of many years undone because one of the friends has paid attention to some malicious gossip! Gossip is the bane of a simple, unsuspecting friendship. No friend should ever believe a piece of gossip about the other. What is due as a friend is to get the proper clarification from the same mouth that has always deserved his affection and confidence. This is what loyalty demands, and this is what loyal friends will do.

And they will do something else also. If they were to observe in a friend some less than honorable feature or gesture, they will feel the duty to call his attention to it. True friendship can live only on the basis of truth and mutual respect in all the relations of friends. There are occasions when one has to be willing to sacrifice even the very friendship of the other for the sake of truth. The friend that will not stand for friendly criticism, and also the one who does not dare to make it when needed, are equally disloyal to the ideal of friendship. There are times in which the greatest test of friendship is to accept the risk of losing it in the name of that friendship.

4

While friendship has postulates, by the same token it imposes responsibilities. Whoever has experienced this inexpressible enjoyment is obligated to have a friendly attitude towards all others. A superior friendship is sublimated when the friends make an effort to suffuse with its spirit, all the environment where they move. Friendship should not make us selfish. Someone has said that "a friend is the first one to come in after everybody has abandoned the house." He crosses the threshold and looks inside. Somebody sitting in the middle of a scary solitude looks askance at the intruder. But this person, not with a protective air but with the candid smile of a friend, will disarm any mistrust and will give confidence to the heart, and he will shake hands with the deserted. Here we have someone who is coming, not to take anything away, but to offer everything: his friendship. The sun shines again, a sun of spring, over the frozen barren plain of his heart. The thaw is there, and afterwards, the greening of rekindled hope . . . "I have a friend! I have a friend!" A friendly world, the only one in which justice and peace will have deep roots, will come about only if friends transmit to others the spirit of their friendship.

And how can it be transmitted? One way to do it has been mentioned already. Here is another one. The friendliest act that can be done, the one that contributes more than any other to the advent of universal friendship, is to offer the example of such goodness that not even ingratitude is capable of shriveling it. There are so many souls that anxiously seek the live manifestation of an ideal that will set their heart on fire! How could they not be impressed by a friendly spirit that will sacrifice itself in the name of friendship . . . for those very ones who dislike him? From boundless friendship, the highest symbol is a cross, a cross that proclaims that we have to deal with our enemies as if they were friends, dressing friendship with sacrifice, so that hatred may disappear from the earth. Identifying oneself with the eternal symbol of the cross, we will attain the most sublime meaning of friendship.

V. The Meaning of the Universe

When Nietzsche was asked why he praised that formidable character of superman who did nothing but release energies, the only reply he could imagine to give was, "Because I like Zarathustra." The famous, extraordinary companion of the German thinker had not been generated in the depths of reason but in those of feelings.

It is a commonplace of thinkers that the main factors that determine our attitude toward life do not originate in reason or logic, but in the region of the subconscious or from an emotional state of consciousness. For the most part impulses, likes, prejudices, intuitions, or ideals lead us to act and determine what we are. They are the creative elements that bring out the motives which provide the force for our behavior. Reason is not a creative principle, but a regulator; it only criticizes, explains, and ordains the raw material supplied by the creative faculties, rationalizing it into a system that it then tries to justify.

"A philosophical theory," said Lotze, "is the attempt at justification of a fundamental concept of the world which has been adopted in youth."[10]

Count Keyserling has used the term "sense" to designate the creative principle that, operating in the depths of being, gives a determined direction to all the psychic life. "That which I call meaning or sense," he says in *The World in the Making*, "underlies life, in all circumstances, as creative principle, however the particular matter may best be described in terms of collective psychology, morphology, race biology, and astrology or any form you care to name." For Keyserling the "sense is a spiritual impulse communicated to life by philosophy, interpreting this, not just as an abstract system of knowledge but as concrete and creative wisdom, the capacity for magic, to influence and transform life directly through the spirit." Here we have a luminous concept, that we have already used in prior studies, but whose reach and importance will be more evident in the present study about the meaning of the universe.

1

Each person experiences the universe in his own way. It may be that he will not define, either for himself or for others, the whole impression that it produces in him. Notwithstanding, the sense he possesses of the world must determine both his conduct and his thinking. So that everything that we are, everything that we do, and everything that we think, in the last analysis, are reduced to how we perceive the world around us and in which we live.

Let us consider some of the main ways in which the universe is perceived.

There are those who consider it as a gigantic machine, therefore holding a mechanical sense of life. For them, life and things are nothing but cogs in the wheels of a cosmic machine. Their power and efficiency are admirable, awakening in them the desire to imitate it. It may happen that they have not consciously adopted a materialistic way of thinking; it is possible that many of them would strongly reject such idea. But, if they do not consider the universe as a machine, at least they *sense* it as such, and the thought of the machine leads them to the practical apotheosis of mechanical values.

The mechanical meaning of the world is the basic meaning of the current civilization. The driver, as stated by Keyserling, is the typical individual of our times. He is the symbolic man of the twentieth century, as the priest and the knight were in prior times. All the awards and applause are for the

---

10. Hermann Lotze (1817–1881) was a German philosopher and logician. —Ed.

one who manages to confer speed to existence, who knows how to organize and direct large enterprises that will guarantee order and increase efficiency.

In the current world the driver is very powerful. One can find him in all spheres of life. He is dominant not only in commerce and industry but also in politics and religion. In that capacity he squeezes out the last drop of sweat and blood of millions of human beings, who are turned into fuel for the operation of his machine. He has introduced into the sacred room of religion, that ought to be reserved for the renewal and restoration of souls, the entire bustle and the mechanical organization of an automobile factory.

But it is in the political sphere where one can nowadays study the meaning and tendencies of the sovereign driver. Fascism and bolshevism are two fully complete creations of the mechanical meaning of the world. The drivers, who rule the respective destinies of Italy and Russia, with all their ideological differences that set them apart, agree completely in the form that they understand the political ideal. Each one advocates a perfect political machine, and they try to suppress every spiritual ideal, every scientific or philosophic concept, and any expression of public opinion that may create a risk for the workings of the machine. In this way a new ethics has surged, the fascist one, reduced to a decalogue for the young Italian driver, according to which, the eternal principles of morality have been subordinated to the interests of the governing machine. In the same way, a Soviet science has appeared in which every fact not in favor of the clumsy materialistic ideology that supports the policies of the bolshevik bosses has been zealously suppressed. It could be said that they have a horror of the microscope, because it could reveal disquieting facts, while the fascists are terrified by the telescope, which, by placing the present regime in a historical perspective, may proclaim the inevitable failure of any system that despises the eternal laws of human freedom.

Anywhere the mechanical sense of the world is in command, either among individuals or social groups, the human spirit reveals itself as cruel; man is enslaved, treated as a means, not as an end. Values that do not contribute to immediate success are despised. The ideal of the hegemony of race, nation, or social class is substituted for the ideal of human brotherhood. Spiritual perfection is confused with material progress. The supreme need of contemporary civilization is the creation of men with equal energy and passion to the driver but with a world view that is more spiritual and constructive.

2

There are others who possess an orphanage sense. They feel themselves orphans in the universe. Without failing to recognize that the world is full of goodness and tenderness, everything seems to them to be an illusion. Everything is an attempt to make man forget that he is an orphan.

The orphanage is one of the human institutions that best embodies feelings of tenderness. There is a time in the life of the little exiles when they believe that the nice couple who takes care of them is their parents. They may call them "pop" and "mom." But the time comes when they become disappointed. They do not have parents; they are orphans.

Many people live as disappointed orphans. In the early years they used to send to a Heavenly Father their naïve, infantile prayer. Years went by. Perhaps as a reaction to the religious protection of home or school, perhaps due to studies that they made, or to a moral failure that they suffered, what happened is that they felt like orphans, or at least they thought they were, against a world that they had thought was ruled by a Father.

What a tragedy is that of spiritual orphans who have abandoned a faith that does not satisfy them in the shape that it was presented to them in their early life, or who reject every belief in a transcendent being merely because the official religion they see appears disgusting! They reject the Divinity as an anachronistic concept, and religious experience as an illusory creation of a feverish imagination. The one and the other turn out to be something like the ringing of bells of that legendary city mentioned by Renán, that the fishermen of Brittany used to hear on quiet days, sounding from the oceanic abyss.

Some others, not as brave, even when they are subconsciously convinced that they are orphans, are afraid to say it out loud, even to themselves. Unamuno described one of them in these terms, "Having been baptized, he will not abjure publicly the social fiction of his supposed belief, and he does not think of it, not a little nor a lot, neither to develop it nor to abandon it and claim another, or search for a lesser one." That person will never be able to be a creative spirit.

But we should not reject all belief in the transcendent because we do not wish to have to make a complete revision of our religious beliefs. The religious intuition is eternal and equally as valid as any other intuition or instinct. It puts us in touch with a spiritual world as objective and real as the visible and tangible world in which we move every day. It is necessary to fight to have a manly faith, an adventurer's faith that will not be intimidated before mystery, nor be resigned to the idea that the universe may have gestated and given birth to us only to abandon us.

Unamuno himself was forced to abandon his primitive faith but fought searching for another one until he found it. In one of his essays, "My Religion," he describes for us his fighting attitude towards the universe. "My religion," he says, "is to wrestle unceasingly and unwearyingly with mystery; my religion is to wrestle with God from nightfall until the breaking of the day, as Jacob is said to have wrestled with Him. I cannot accommodate myself to the doctrine of the Unknowable or to that of 'thus far and no farther.'"[11] In a beautiful paragraph of his book *Tragic Sense of Life*, he makes us feel the peace that his heart experiences by the conviction that the world is not an orphanage. "I believe in God as I believe in my friends, because I feel the breath of His affection, feel His invisible and intangible hand, drawing me, leading me, grasping me; because I possess an inner consciousness of a particular providence and of a universal mind that marks out for me the course of my own destiny."[12]

3

A third group has the sense of a cemetery. It is the sentiment of those that live by means of a conviction that everything human, the beautiful and good or the ugly and bad, ends up equally at the grave. As a result everything is transitory and relative; nothing is absolute and eternal. Why strive excessively, then, to reform the world? To reform is immoral. Let all be as it is. It will be more interesting that way. In the meantime, let us press from the grapes of life the sweetest juices that they have, and, when there is nothing more, then die.

Cemeteries are frequently very beautiful. All the resources of money and the arts have been employed to beautify them. They have corners that look like enchanted cities. Strolling there it turns out to be difficult to believe that they are the dwellings of the dead. One expects that some beautiful face will appear behind a little window, or some knight will open, with a majestic gesture, the gates of his castle. But these dwellings, marvelous imitations of the houses of the living, are nothing but death chambers. They are inhabited by the remains of beloved treasured loved ones, which, after each one had drained his goblet, slipped away in silence to repose.[13]

---

11. Unamuno, *Essays and Soliloquies*, 156. —Ed.
12. Unamuno, *Tragic Sense*, 194. —Ed.
13. For example, Recoleta Cemetery in Buenos Aires is a very grand cemetery in

Is the philosophy of Omar Khayyam the only reasonable one considering the transitory nature of the human and the absolute certainty of death? Is it worthwhile to continue striving for a disinterested ideal? What guarantee do we have that it will ever come about? Given that the only absolute certainty that we have is that everything will end, should not our ideal be to enjoy life as much as possible?

Looking at the problem with serenity, the least we are able to say is that the cemetery approach has never created idealist or lasting works; it has made nothing but a cemetery of the heart itself. If everybody were to have it, the world would come to an end, but not in a nirvana free from desires, but in a hell of frustrated desires.

It is a terrible thing not to be able to grasp anything eternal or absolute that will allow the overcoming of doubts, passions, and human ingratitude! What a tragic voice is that of Mariano José de Larra at the end of his famous satire "All Souls Day, 1836"! At the end of the depiction of all the graves of Madrid, he said, "Madrid is the cemetery, a vast cemetery, where each house is the niche of a family, each street the sepulcher of some happening, each heart the urn containing the ashes of some hope, some desire," Larra ended with this painful cry, "Holy heaven! Another cemetery, as well. My heart is nothing more than another sepulcher. What does it say? Let us read. Let us read. Who has died in it? Terrible sign! Here lies hope . . . Silence, silence!!!" Shortly thereafter the author shot himself, and silence became his.

4

There is still another way to sense the world, the most adequate and dynamic feeling of them all, the perception that digs deepest into the interior of things, the one that best intuits the heart of reality itself. It is the one that provides man with the clearest vision of his meaning in the world and gives him the greatest energies for the realization of his destiny. I will call it the home-loving meaning of the universe.

The human institution that represents, or, to be faithful to its character that should represent, the summit of spirituality is the home. This is the sphere of love, of trust, and of perfect friendship. Why should we not think that the true home is a microcosm of the universe? Instead of projecting onto the infinite the machine, the orphanage, or the cemetery as that which most resembles ultimate reality, why do we not project the home? Do not say that such a procedure is not licit from a philosophical point of view, because it is based on an anthropomorphic concept. Are not the machines,

---

this Spanish style with many rows of ornate burial vaults and sarcophagi. —Ed.

orphanages, or cemeteries anthropomorphic concepts? How could man think in terms other than what he is, what he feels, and what he knows? He has to think about the ultimate in accordance with the categories adequate to the proportions of experience. On the other hand, it would not be possible to have science or philosophy since they are, in the last analysis, anthropomorphic because they are man's creations.

If this is so, what is more just, to try to explain the universe with reference to the lowest or the highest of our experiences? We do not hesitate to state that we have to think of the cosmos in terms of the highest reality of human experience, that is to say, the friendly personality; not the abstract and cold personality, but the specific personality, warm and loving. And given that the home is the place where we have to search for the most perfect expression of this sublime reality, let us consider it as our interpretive category of the universe. Supreme reality has to be friendly, and the human sentiment that most faithfully interprets what is the most intimate in life is what we have called the home-loving sentiment.

Life can be compared to an old stately citadel. It has towers bathed with sunlight and vaults submerged in darkness. Now one can enjoy in the heights the morning splendor, the precious views, the invigorating breezes; then one can find himself sinking in the lower darkness, where one suffers and despairs. But whether one is ecstatic in a lookout or stifled in a dungeon, a loving heart is not far off. It takes only a sigh for peace and purity, a stammering but sincere confession of having sinned against virtue, an agonizing prayer requesting new strength, for the friendly and fraternal heart that beats continuously keeping time with human pain, to flood the dungeon of the heart with light, bringing into it the friendly atmosphere of the home, of the hearth.

The moral world is created in such a way that not a single sigh of a broken and longing heart is lost on deaf ears. It will always awaken an echo in the infinite Heart of a Friend that pulses behind the curtain of our unbelief, intent in pushing aside the dividing veil, to enrich our life. The sentiment of this Presence, so friendly and excellent, gives to us, as to Unamuno, peace in war and confidence in destiny. The struggle for personal and worldly perfection will not be in vain, nor the victory uncertain, because the final reality is holy and paternal.

VI. The Meaning of Christianity

"If you call me Christian," a Hindustani said recently to a Western man, "I will take offense, but if you call me a Christian man, that will be a great honor for me." The words could not be more suggestive. To be Christian meant for that oriental only to profess a given religion, but "Christian man" was for him a person who lived in consonance with the spirit and principles of Christ.

Much has been written on Christianity as a historic religion, as an ecclesiastical organization with a dogmatic system, but much less, and extremely little in Spanish, has been said about it as a vital and renewing experience. I do not intend to get busy here with the plan of this or that Christian confession being the legitimate heir of primitive Christianity.

I am not interested at this moment to state which of the dogmatic banners waved by the diverse Christian groupings best interprets the sacred texts. For I consider that many persons can support their right to call themselves Christian by their ecclesiastical links or by the purity of their ideology that may not be at all infused with Christianity, that is to say, by the new spirit or meaning introduced into the world by Jesus. They are Christian by birth or by profession, but they are not Christian men, persons in which the spirit of Christ, the very one mentioned so beautifully by Ricardo Rojas in his book, *The Invisible Christ*, has become flesh, transforming their whole life, making them full men, true men. They may be Christians by profession or office, but they are not Christophers, carriers of Christ.

That is the kind of Christianity that I am going to talk about now. What is Christianity? How do we have to experience it? What is its intimate meaning? In what form does it give its best expression?

To be able to acquire the proper meaning of Christianity it is necessary to consider it from two points of view: first, from the point of view of the influence that it has exerted and exerts, and second, from the point of view of its essence. Looking at the action of Christianity through the centuries, we will be convinced that it contains a reality that deserves our careful attention. Grasping the core of Christianity, our heart will acquire a new meaning, the most powerful and creative of all the known meanings.

1

Christianity is a creation of Christ's spirit. It is the expression of all the superior influences flowing from Jesus that have tended to transform life. "Everything that is vital in the Western world," Count Keyserling has said in one of his latest books, "is owed to Christianity." That is unquestionable. The emancipation of women, the abolition of slavery, the workers legislation, popular education, philanthropic societies, campaigns against diseases, even democracy itself, and the internationalist spirit, they are all clear products of

Christianity. All of it reveals the presence of Christianity, of the Christianity of Jesus. "Even bolshevism," says Keyserling, "the first movement that has radically denied Him, has descended in a direct line from Him. Without Jesus, without Him who proclaims the infinite value of the human soul and gives preference to the wretched and afflicted, it would not be possible to conceive bolshevism."

Let us cast a glance at the contemporary world, especially to Africa and to the Oriental countries, in order to see to what extent Jesus is having influence over them.

In the African continent the white man has written one of the most shameful pages of history. Such has been the imprint of the so-called Christianity on the continent of the blacks that one of them said not long ago that if Christ were to come back to the world as a white man the blacks would reject him. For many centuries the so-called Christian whites used to leave Christ in the ocean abyss upon arriving at the African shores. They dedicated themselves to the hunt of blacks and elephants, to take from these their tusks, and from those their freedom, carrying them to the lands of America. Even today blacks are forbidden in South African towns to walk on the sidewalks: they have to walk through the middle of the road, the same as oxen or horses. And even if a man of color has graduated from a foreign university, it does not matter; not even he can rub elbows with the whites on the sidewalk!

But among the shadows there are flashes of light. In the history of the nineteenth century there is no one figure more full of Christianity than David Livingstone, a man who devoted his life to the double task of discovering for civilization the heart of the African continent and extending to the heart of the indigenous peoples the meaning of the divine friendship, interpreted, and mediated by his own. He fought with Christian courage against the infamous slave traffic, which was still present in his time; he did not carry weapons except to get food and protect himself against the wild animals. Finally he got sick, when he found himself at Lake Tanganyika, which he was the first to explore. In a letter to an American newspaper written shortly before his illness, the scout for the sources of the Nile recorded these words, that today are engraved in his tombstone, "All I can say in my solitude is, may heaven's rich blessing come down on every one—American, English, Turk—who will help to heal this open sore of the world." He was talking about the commerce in human flesh.

One morning towards four o'clock the faithful Africans who accompanied Livingstone on all his trips found him dead in his tent, kneeling next to his bed. He had elevated his last prayer to the Most High, for the beloved African land. His inseparable black friends took out the heart from the body of their beloved hero, burying it at the foot of a large tree. Once the body was embalmed, the same hands carried him to the coast, arriving after nine months of painful voyage to the port of Zanzibar. He rests now in Westminster Abbey, and his heroic heart, near the heart of Africa; a beautiful epic of Christianity, when with the infinite friendship of one heart it can communicate itself to other people's hearts.

Some fifty years passed. The Hindustani immigrants in South Africa, in whose defense Gandhi had become famous in the prior decade, suffered great indignities once again. When at last the South African authorities became willing to settle the problems with the Indian colonists, who do you think was appointed as their representative in the negotiations? A man called Andrews, of English origin, but Hindustani in the heart, a close friend of Gandhi and Tagore. Identified with Christianity, Andrews had gone to India as a simple missionary of God's friendship, becoming totally identified with the aspirations and needs of the Hindustani people.

Let us now go to Asia. There is no more significant phenomenon than the fact that present day India seems willing, more and more each day, to accept Christianity and Christ, although it denies vigorously all the sectarianism and religious dogmatism of the West. The group of friends of Christ increases at a fast pace. Jesus is becoming the conscience of the new India. When Gandhi's fellow countrymen wanted to give their venerated leader the highest adjective that they could think of, they called him, "Man resembling Christ." There are Hindustanis and Muslims who avoid some attitudes because they are antichristian. Because of the influence of Christ, the indigenous religions are being modified.

The last Chinese revolution, that grand movement of resurgence of a millenarian race and purification of the sources of its life, is inspired in Christianity. A new generation had been educated in Christian institutions of China and also in other lands. Seven out of the ten members of the government in Nanking are disciples of Jesus.

One of the most extraordinary men in contemporary Japan is called Toyohiko Kagawa. He is the Dostoyevsky of the Orient. One of his novels, *Before the Dawn*, in which he tells the tragic experience of a soul in search of light, can be compared to those of the great Russian. Over half a million copies have been sold in Japan and in the nations of the Orient. In 1911, when he was barely twenty-one years old, Kagawa went to live among the destitute in a poor neighborhood of the city of Kobe. He lives there in alliance since then, sharing the life of the poor and working in their service, except for a couple of years when he went overseas to study. He is a socialist, and he has been secretary of the Japanese Federation of Labor. His passion is to reform the social conditions in his country, and he finds his inspiration and the norms for his work in Jesus, because Kagawa is a Christian in whom Christ has taken flesh. He has lost the sight in one eye, and at age forty-one, he makes efforts so that his Master will be reproduced in the life of his fellow countrymen, so that through the infusion of Christianity the national life may be revolutionized.

2

Whatever may be our opinions about religion, about Christianity, and about the Christian churches, we cannot deny that what we have here called Christianity, an emanation of the spirit of Christ, has been and is the greatest influence for renewal known in history. What is the essence of this superior force, and how can it be introduced into the heart of a man?

Christianity is what belongs to Christ. Perhaps the most revolutionary aspect of contemporary religious thinking is the movement called "back to Jesus." It has tried to climb through the labyrinth of Christian history, to penetrate beyond dogmatic creeds, further than ecclesiastical organization, until finding the pristine figure of the Galilean. The motto of this movement has been, "We want to see Jesus." In the year 1910 a professor of the University of Strasbourg, Albert Schweitzer, published a famous book titled *The Quest of the Historical Jesus*, in which he studied the efforts made, up until then, to find the teacher of Christianity. From that date hundreds of lives of Jesus have been published, and what is most interesting is that the authors of these lives of Christ are no longer clerics or professional religious, but men of letters, journalists, and sociologists. God has become secular in our age, José Ortega y Gasset has said. And at present, eminent figures of contemporary literature such as Emil Ludwig, Middleton Murray, Henri Barbusse, Giovanni Papini, Hermann Keyserling, and our Ricardo Rojas, have written either a life of Jesus or an essay about him. We could say that Jesus, also, has become secular. This is so universal that everyone finds in him different traits, according to their own character, so that each of his biographies turns out to be an autobiography of the author. But it is most interesting to observe the increasing fascination that the Man is exerting over the most representative men. It has been calculated that more than 50,000 monographs have been written about him in all known languages.

Moved by the same universal craving to know the Man, let us look at him on our own. Studying him in the pages of the gospel, we see one whose principal legacy to the world was not, as in the case of Buddha, his profound doctrine, but a perfect life, which, in the end, he allowed to be relinquished in obedience to the eternal law of spiritual progress. We do not see a "sweet

Rabbi" harmless, surrounded with flowers, incapable of hurting anybody with his word, but a virile Jesus, with manly gestures, who casts terrible anathemas against the hypocritical Pharisees, abusers of the poor and defenseless, one who throws out of the temple with a whip the despicable merchants exploiting popular religiosity. We do not see, either, a sad and listless person, who, in the words of Swinburne, "clouded the world with his breath." And as Ricardo Rojas states very well, Christ was not, as some have pretended, "an archetype of beggars, a sort of human wretch, a footstool for everybody, a summary of misery and a paragon of humiliation."

We see a glowing face of a leader who was attractive to all the sincere and yearning souls. We hear a voice that impressed all those who heard it by the authority with which he solved all the deepest and most contentious problems. His words opened the veil of mystery of the world, allowing us to see the friendly figure of the Father, to whom lilies and sparrows, children and the destitute, had a deep meaning. We feel a profound love, as no other who has lived on earth. It is a love that transforms the loved, because he loves them in spite of the mean things said about them, and in spite of the bad things the Lover himself knows about them. It is not a blind love but a creative love. It is the love with which Jesus transformed Zacchaeus, the dishonest tax collector, into a good man and the penitent Magdalena into a holy woman. It is the love that led him to say, during his lifetime, "Love your enemies, bless those that curse you, do good to those who hate you, and pray for those who insult and persecute you"; the same love that, at the time of his anguished death—the price of having loved—caused a prayer for his executioners to come from his thirsty lips, "Father, forgive them; they do not know what they are doing." It is this love, a love that knows no limits and that neither human ingratitude nor evil can extinguish and whose greatest glory is the cross, which constitutes the essence of Christianity and the only power that can rescue the world from barbarism. Rodó was right when he said about such demonstrations of love that Jesus was the true author of charity.

3

Christianity, as a creative force of love and not simply as a doctrine, is intimately tied to the person of Christ. In the admirable essay on Jesus with which Count Keyserling ends his book *Symbolic Figures*, the German philosopher makes the great point of connecting the renewing influence of Christianity, or, as we have said here, of what is Christian, through the centuries, with Jesus himself. This Man was more original than his doctrine, and for that reason occupies a more central place in Christianity, than the one occupied by Buddha, Mohammed, or Confucius in the religions that they founded. Keyserling gives Jesus the name of "Magician." He understands by this term that one *is*, and that this is not the mere process of becoming; one who *has* the truth, not just a seeker of the truth; one who uses his knowledge to radically *modify* his environment, and not a mere scholar who treasures his knowledge in the head. Jesus is, for Keyserling, the perfect and absolute type of Superior Being. He introduced into the world a new "meaning," fountain of all things the most pure, of all things the most vital, of all things the most creative that the world has.

How can we acquire this "meaning"? We come to possess it if we allow ourselves to be penetrated by Jesus himself. Our attitude has to be one of perfect receptivity to his influence, of absolute surrender to his sovereign will. We have here the greatest adventure of the human spirit, to place one's faith in the one who, according to all the evidence, is, and knows, and is able. In him we touch the eternal and the ultimate. Through him we enter into a relationship with God, the paternal archetype of whom Jesus is the perfect replica and interpreter on earth, and to whom Jesus, by now a spirit, will lead souls until the dawn of the day in which the whole humanity will have been redeemed from evil through and for love.[14]

What happens in our times when a man devotes himself in body and soul to the spirit of Christ can be exemplified in an epical fashion by the career of Albert Schweitzer, famous author of the book *The Quest of the Historical Jesus*. When he was writing that book, Schweitzer was a professor at the University of Strasbourg. Through his profound and prolonged studies to decipher the true personality of Jesus, he became so convinced that there was something so important, so mysterious, and so unique in this figure, that historical research was unable to define and classify, that he ended his book with these words,

> He comes to us as One unknown, without a name, as of old by the lake-side, He came to those men who knew him not. He speaks to us the same word: "Follow thou me!" and sets us to the tasks which He has to fulfill for our time. He commands. And to those who obey him, whether they be wise or simple, He will reveal himself in the toils, the conflicts, the sufferings which they shall pass through in His fellowship, and, as an ineffable mystery, they shall learn in their own experience Who He is.[15]

---

14. See Titus 2:11 and John 12:32. —Ed.
15. Schweitzer, *Quest*, 401. —Ed.

Prophetic words! The author realized upon writing them, that there is knowledge of Jesus and of Christianity that cannot be attained under a professor's guidance. The most profound knowledge cannot be communicated nor learned in the schools; it has to be felt and experienced on the road, following the Master himself. What was the task that the mysterious and overwhelming Master imposed upon Albert Schweitzer? He seemed to listen in the depths of his being to a commanding voice telling him to get ready to cancel the terrible debt that the white man had contracted with his black brothers. He began immediately to study medicine. Upon graduation, he said farewell to his chair and to the civilized world in order to enter into the virgin forests of West Africa. In this way, a Christian work was born among the indigenous Africans, in which Schweitzer already has the cooperation of other fine Christian spirits from various European countries who have gone to collaborate with him. But the most extraordinary thing remains to be said. How is this organization financed? Albert Schweitzer has the philosophical depth of a Raymond Lull, the humanitarian passion of a Bartolomé de Las Casas, and the musical talent of the great German masters. He has published the authorized edition of the works of Johann Sebastian Bach, of whose music he is the best interpreter.

Once in a while Schweitzer goes back to Europe. On those occasions he gives organ concerts in Paris, Berlin, and London, attended by the elite of those capitals. With the product of his concerts to white Europe, he maintains the work that he has begun for the redemption of black Africa. A few weeks ago Schweitzer won the Goethe prize for an essay on the great poet, and the money that he was awarded also goes to the cause to which he has devoted his life.

"Follow thou me!" The voice still resounds with the same accents that it sounded in the past at the shores of Gennesaret. It resounded this morning in the cloisters of Strasbourg. At these times it resounds in my ears and in yours, my friend. Silence! "Follow me, and you will be a man, and I will give you a vocation. You will get to know the truth, and I will be your friend. You will live as a son in the world of the Father, and with my loyal and permanent support you will fulfill your destiny."

2

At the Feet of the Teacher

"Lord, teach us to pray"

ON THE HILLSIDE OF the Mount of Olives and not very far from the Garden of Gethsemane, there is a Christian church called the "Church of the Our Father." This name has been given to it because around the wall of the patio one can find, in thirty-two different languages, the beautiful prayer which Jesus once taught to his disciples as a model.

With all the deep divisions that have split the disciples of Christ into different factions from the day when the teacher gave a familiar prayer to the first nucleus of them, this prayer has served as a spiritual bond among the diverse Christian groups. Repeating this prayer, they reveal the fundamental unity at the feet of the common Father.

According to what St. Luke says, the *Our Father* was Jesus' answer to the request of his disciples to be taught how to pray. Moved by the habitual practice of their teacher to devote a period of time to prayer every day, getting up quite often before sunrise to withdraw to some lonely place, they also wished to learn the supreme art of prayer.

In the immortal response that came from the lips of the Galilean, we do not have a magic formula from whose repetition we will wrestle favors from God but the expression of a filial attitude towards him, and at the same time a vision of basic needs that only the Father can satisfy, and for whose satisfaction we have to elevate our prayer as sons. The *Our Father* must not be interpreted, then, as a pattern or pigeonhole for our thoughts when we approach God, but rather as a candle that will illuminate us on the way to his presence. It has to serve to stimulate our interior life, not to mechanize it.

At the example of the Teacher himself, let us separate for a moment from the worldly bustle to enter into the inviolable safe of the soul. If we infuse ourselves in the petitions of the model prayer, we will learn to pray. And it will be much more than that. We will succeed in ascertaining the reality of the spiritual world around us. Our eyes will open up to new realities. We will see the present in the light of the eternal. And, if we were to have the mettle of real men, in our hearts will develop such anxious tension that we will not be able to avoid linking our fate to that of the kingdom proclaimed by Jesus.

Silence! . . . Let us meditate.

I. "Our Father who art in heaven"

We could say about Jesus, more than any other, that he was a "man inebriated with God." But his spiritual inebriation was not that of the philosopher. Supreme reality was not, in his view, a simple hypothetical being, fruit of a man's brain to explain the mysteries of the world, nor the personalized projection of the infinite anxieties of the heart. Jesus did not reason about the reality of God. He felt it. He did not seek him, because he knew him intimately, and how beautiful and significant the figure he uses to express to us his sense and knowledge of the Supreme Being! He calls him "Father." There were others in the ancient world who designated God by this name, but Jesus was the first who felt in his personal experience the divine paternity and drew the conclusions of this truth, experienced by the other people on earth.

Jesus possessed in this way, in a superlative degree, a homelike sense of the universe. He felt a paternal heart beating through the centuries, behind the veil of nature, and through the pain and mystery of life. The Father was concerned for his children, and wanted them to talk to him, expressing their worries and needs. Not a single petition by one of them for something needed in order to better achieve his vocation would be ignored in the workshop of his Father. No sob of a gasping heart could be lost in the surrounding emptiness that overwhelmed him, because he would be listened to by the One who, although in heaven, had counted the hairs of his children on earth. And do not forget that this Father "who is in heaven" does not imply physical distance from his children, but spiritual elevation over them.

Interpenetrated in this way by the celestial greatness and majesty of God, and meditating on his infinite tenderness as a Father that Jesus has revealed to us, let us join at his feet to say "Our Father" to Him, and pronouncing the word "Our" we should not stop feeling the solidarity with our brothers in all the earth, sacrificing over the common altar of the family whatever separates us from each other, and from the celestial Father.

II. "Hallowed be thy name"

"There is one thing," Goethe used to say, "which the child does not bring with him into the world; it depends, however, on the acquisition of it that he becomes much later a full-fledged man." He was referring to reverence. Whoever is incapable under any circumstance to feel reverence for something or someone is the most unfortunate, and an orphan on the earth.

As far as it refers to feeling reverence for what is above us, what is divine and holy, there are thousands who seem to lack such a sense. A young Peruvian, who was developing at that time a powerful work on behalf of the laboring masses of his country, declared that he could not mention aloud the word "God." It would seem that such name, instead of inspiring him with reverence, produced repulsion every time he pronounced it, because it was tied with the memories of his adolescence, to things and attitudes that he had come to repudiate. It may have happened that, in the environment where this young man had spent his early years, nobody had been concerned in sanctifying the sacred name of the Father.

And so it turns out to have deep significance that the prayer that Jesus teaches to his disciples begins with the desire that the name of "Our Father" be hallowed, that is, that it will be associated in such a way with all the highest values that men will feel an instinctive reverence for it. What is religious must be at all times symbol and source of the most pure morality.

And how can this happen? By the resolution, common to all those who call God "Father," to live in such a way, that the others "see their good works and glorify their Father who is in heaven."[16] Impressed by the ethical fruits, men will reach the point of becoming interested in the religious root. Seeing the reflection of God on earth, they will raise their eyes to heaven.

Hallowed be thy name, Father! Flood us with your light, strengthen us by your grace, so that, purified in our most intimate being and freed of any alliance with evil, we may dedicate ourselves, from now on, to start some activity that will lead the people to reverence you.

---

16. See Matt 5:16. —Ed.

III. "Thy kingdom come"

The Father is also king, and his lordship is great. This goes so far away from the frontiers of what is visible that not even the microscope or the telescope may be able to observe its limits.

Around all the spheres of nature, the sovereignty of the king Father is recognized. His kingdom entered into nature many thousands of years ago. So, already in his apparel or his workshop, his presence can be felt in the rhythms of the planet and in the red glows of sunset, in the return of spring and of the opening of roses in the garden. There is only one area in which the kingdom has not arrived yet: the heart of men.

Creation has thus remained unfinished. There is no cosmos yet, in the full sense of a word that means harmony, nor will there ever be as long as the kingdom does not penetrate the human heart. Mistaken are those then who adopt a purely esthetic attitude towards the universe, as if this were nothing but an exhibit of art with paintings for all tastes, without realizing that the masterpiece of the universal gallery has to be painted on the reluctant and soiled canvas of human life.

The heart of Jesus, so attuned always to the beats of the divine heart, perceived that the Father was anxious to perform a work among men, a work that would transform their insane egoisms to a cooperation of love with the Father and the brothers. Jesus knew that such was the end sought by the Father; and he also wanted to work towards the same end. The consciousness that the human sector of the universe lived in moral chaos by not recognizing the loving sovereignty of the Father produced in his soul such anxious tension that his thoughts, like his words and his deeds, reflected the never ending desire: "Thy kingdom come."

Together with the Teacher we should say also, "Thy kingdom come," kingdom of peace, justice, and love. We open our hearts, Oh most loving King! May all hatred and lies die in them when it comes. And upon establishing your kingdom in us, permit that, with the love of children and the loyalty of servants, we will be consecrated that it would spread out over the whole earth.

IV. "Thy will be done on earth as it is in heaven"

To follow one's own will all the time without consulting others at all is nothing but an aristocratic form of madness. The completely willful person with all his airs of an independent gentleman is possessed by the most tragic of all demons, the demon of "I." No one can be self-sufficient, nor can he perform a work that will last, if he has a selfish ambition as his only motive. Sooner or later the one possessed of the "I" will fall down in one of his reckless flights, encountering in the heights the wind contrary to the divine purpose. "The stars in their courses fought against Sisera," says the old book of Judges.[17]

It is sad to recognize it, but the history of this earth has been to a large degree that of a mad house. Men have wanted to build a world to their liking, either on so-called rational principles, or on economic or nationalist interests, or on the dominion of a caste or a race, and they have failed. And how tragic the human scene appears at present! What madness and misery darken the earth! Why should we not become disillusioned once and for all in the insidious lie of a natural law of progress? There is no such law in the human sphere. There is no authentic progress here, where the individual will does not subject itself consciously and joyfully to the eternal laws of God.

It is a good time to try a new attitude towards life. Let us say, then, looking up with fervor, "Thy will be done." Let us expect the commanding voice of the one who has been fighting through the centuries with the terrible moral inertia of the world, and that we may know at the same time that the one who becomes "to the divine Goodness what hands are to a man," he will be the arm of God on earth, to speed up the coming of the kingdom of love, that our selfishness delays.

But the will of God will not be done on earth without cost. What price will we have to pay to let us rest on his arms? We have to state that the cost will not be the reduction of our dignity as men, because we will never be more men than when we allow ourselves to be penetrated by the divine purpose. Looking at the Teacher we will get to know that. Each one of us will have to reach the shadow of Gethsemane. In our hands a chalice will be placed that will be full to the brim of the bitter immediate consequences of being loyal to the Captain of our lives.

After an anxious conflict, says the evangelical story, Jesus swallowed the contents of his chalice, and saying, "Thy will be done," he decided to go to the cross. From a bend in the road he turns his luminous face to us. His lips issue the words, "If anyone wishes to come after me, let him deny himself, and take up his cross daily, and follow me."[18] The road of progress is the road of the cross.

---

17. Judg 5:20. —Ed.
18. Matt 16:24. —Ed.

V. "Give us this day our daily bread"

With this petition we pass from the needs of a transcendental order to those of a human order. Having requested from God those things that we wish he will accomplish on earth, that is, the sanctification of his name, the acceptance of his kingdom, and the fulfillment of his will, let us ask from him the elementary things that we need from heaven: bread, pardon, and fortitude.

Although it is true that "man shall not live by bread alone,"[19] it is not less true that without bread we can only die. Bread is the symbol of everything that the human being needs for his physical wellbeing. Asking for bread, we ask one of the indispensable conditions to be able to seek the kingdom and to be arms of God on earth. But the bread has to be, like manna, for the satisfaction of daily hunger, and not to hoard it or to do business with it.

Someone who has not felt hunger is incapable of appreciating daily bread in its true value. Someone who has not seen any one else suffer hunger or has not had tomorrow's bread as his sole anxiety will not be able to offer this prayer from the heart. Someone who gives a free rein to a wild acquisitive urge robs God of his glory and his brothers of their bread. Irreligious and immoral at the same time are all those who go through life without recognizing their day to day dependence on God, while they devote themselves to amassing riches that they will not need for their own wellbeing, nor do they plan to use for their neighbors.

The attitude that Jesus proposes toward future physical needs is that of asking enough to be able to finish the journey. A journey may last twenty-four hours, or twenty-four days, weeks, months, or years. Telling the celestial Father, "Give us this day our daily bread," we are saying, "Give us today, at sunset, and at sunrise, when we start making plans to resume the search for the kingdom—give us the material goods that we need to be able to start the new day's journey well. Allow then, in this way, that, free from all preoccupations for material goods, we may be able to devote body and soul to the spiritual side of our work."

That we may have in this way—oh Father!—such awareness of your sovereignty over material things, that having consecrated ourselves to the work of your kingdom, we may not hesitate to have recourse to the promise that, seeking your kingdom, everything else will be given to us besides.

---

19. Matt 4:4. —Ed.

VI. "Forgive us our trespasses as we forgive those who trespass against us"

Every violation of a moral norm recognized by the conscience, that is when we are aware of the good but do evil, constitutes a double insult. It is an affront to our true self because it destroys its unity and harmony. It is also an affront to God, the source and personal custodian of the laws of life. The latter is above everything else. "Against thee, thee only, have I sinned, and done this evil in thy sight."[20] Here we have the authentic cry of a sick soul, of a soul without peace, of a split personality because he has committed some wickedness. In such experiential juncture there is only one thing that can bring back peace to the soul of a man: to recognize and confess his fault in order to be able to feel, later on, in the depth of his deranged being, the divine pardon. And the Father, always attentive to the voice of an anxious conscience that begs for pardon, will erase the debt with a kiss, returning peace to the soul.

But it will be useless to beg from God that he forgive our debts if we do not forgive those who have harmed us. "Be ye therefore perfect, even as your Father which is in heaven is perfect,"[21] is the norm of life that Jesus has given us. And recognizing that the most distinctive feature of God is his mercy towards the pain of those who have violated his law, we have to be merciful, also, towards those who have hurt us. We should not cry out for anything from God that we are not prepared to grant our brothers or that we have not bestowed already on them, friends or foes. The condition of our success to climb to the religious heights will be the daily descent to the black chasm of human wickedness, searching in it the good for our enemies, promoting our reconciliation with them in the spirit of Christ. Because there is a tight bond between religion and ethics, those forgiven by God must become in all the details of life, worthy exponents of the moral perfection of their Father.

Let us make, then, a sincere examination of conscience. Do we present ourselves as we are not? In some hiding place of the soul has some lie taken refuge, some hatred, some dishonest passion that paralyzes our spiritual life? If there is, let us ask pardon for it, subjecting ourselves to the searching light that shines from the luminous face of Jesus.

---

20. Ps 51:4. —Ed.
21. Matt 5:48. —Ed.

VII. "Lead us not into temptation but deliver us from evil"

Talent may be formed in a serene society, but character will be formed only by the powerful attack of a storm. Trees located at the border of a forest, accustomed from an early age to withstand the violence of winds, are much stronger and hardier than the ones that have always been under their protection. If you cut the hardened trunks from the border, the next hurricane will open up avenues through the forest.

Something similar happens in life. Those who have had to stand many trials, keeping their integrity in spite of everything, turn out to be imposing personalities and will serve as shields to the weak and inexperienced souls that have never lived at the mercy of the elements in their moral life. Thinking about the enormous value of hard trials to give temper to character, James wrote to the early Christians, "My brethren, count it all joy when you fall into divers temptations; knowing this, that the trying of your faith worketh patience."[22]

Perhaps Jesus did not want his disciples ever to find themselves in a difficult situation? Should they pray to God to keep them protected from the tests and temptations of life? By no means. What the Teacher wanted was that they, aware of their own weakness and anxious to behave in a way worthy of his Father, would ask him that they would never fall into a testing situation that could turn out to be greater than their moral resistance; that God would free them of the danger to succumb in the presence of the devilish forces of evil, either from the inside or the outside!

What is requested here, in fact, is enough spiritual force to help us to ride out the storms that may blow over our path. To the previous requests for bread and pardon we have to add this one for fortitude. In this way, the whole personality will prove to be equipped from this moment to take on the way of the kingdom.

Holy Father, having finished the prayer that your only begotten Son taught us, we want to live a life according to the petitions we have addressed to you. Allow, in your immense goodness, that the vision of your universal kingdom will never fade before our eyes, and that, having set our feet on the tracks of our Teacher, we may not lack on the way bread, pardon, or fortitude. And yours will be the kingdom, the power, and the glory, for ever and ever. Amen.

---

22. Jas 1:2–3. —Ed.

3

The Christian Response to Secularism

I

THE WORD "SECULARISM" APPEARED recently as a term for a phenomenon that today characterizes the spiritual attitude of many people. In a general sense secularism signifies the elimination of spiritual values and that which is transcendent in life and in the imagination. Secularism reduces life to an "alone dimension": it looks at the front, never at the top. Its watchword is "to evolve," although its perspective does not pass beyond the perspective of a frog in a puddle. It is proficient at only one activity, and while driving along the open road, it does not recognize the very edges of the road. It soon disappears.

A specific aspect of the present secularism is to find that man today has complete autonomy. Man is irritated with the divine, with the transcendent, and therefore he "needs" to emancipate himself from God. This secularism believes that "all is matter," believing that it has the capacity to pull the last secrets out of the universe. It considers itself in its very expression and achievement the supreme purpose of existence. This is exactly the essence of sin. In social life the tendency is to consider certain institutions and spheres of life without any other significance or end beyond the material element that they contain. It is very common to hear, "Yes, but this can't be. It may be true, but the freedom to spread your ideas does harm to the life of the state."

The modern church is the most tragic expression of secularism. Its life is found polarized between two extremes equally secularist in their appearance. In some places the church gave in completely to a type of philosophy entirely incapable of appreciation of the Christian facts or of supplying elements that would serve those truths as the basis of Christianity. In other places secularization has shut itself to what is passed in the world, interesting itself only in the perpetuation of living. That God is not the God of our days, because that God belongs to the past. A word of Christ would bring terror to that church. Christ receives the same treatment in it that Dostoyevsky gave to him in his story, "The Parable of the Grand Inquisitor."[23] "Be thankful," said the Inquisitor to Jesus in his prison, "since you left the work to us to take care of and finish in your name, go out now and be quiet." This form of secularization of the divine institution is the most tragic of all.

II

But what answer does one have to give to secularism? One looks to that very nature of matter and to the eternal moral order, and they suggest the answer. The secularism that is present now takes the form of a delirium. But the autonomous individual created by secularism, as someone has said, begins to feel uncertain in his autonomy. The number of men and women disillusioned and broken in spirit grows day by day. In comparing the days of today with the pre-war generation when men intended to banish fear, how little reason is found for congratulating William James and his contemporaries.

All society finds that it is in disequilibrium and great suffering. The situation today is a flood of paradoxes! Opulence and indigence; granaries of wheat are overcrowded, and hunger is at the table in a land that has such abundance. The seventh heaven of ecstasy crumbles on the side of burning warehouses of possessions, while the seventh heaven of misery rushes into the abyss![24] And still greater changes can come to the structures of society. The church, as institution, will not escape from these revolutionary changes. It is God's harvest. The snows of the little pines and the plateaus of society are

---

23. The story is found in Dostoyevsky's novel *The Brothers Karamazov*. The church in the parable no longer needs Jesus because the church is doing, in his name, the work that he began. Jesus leaves the jail in silence after kissing the Inquisitor. —Ed.

24. The two apocalyptic allusions are to the opening of the seventh seal in Rev 8:1–5 and to the pouring of the seventh bowl in 16:17–21. —Ed.

melted. Furious torrents run through the valleys, and they flood the plains. When the waters will have receded, we will see everything with another perspective: so that man should learn that he cannot do with the world of God whatever he wants. The very stars in the heavens fought against Sisera.[25]

III

And what should be the Christian answer to secularism? It seems that it is expressed in just one word—God. Not God only as an idea, not God as a simple projection of the mind, or even because of a sigh in our heart. Also, he will not be a God, a great prisoner of the universe, but the God, Creator and Architect, Father and Redeemer, the Beloved Father of Our Lord Jesus Christ.

It is very sad to see the consequence of God who was banished from human thought, to which he went and was an intruder, and as his name is found associated with matters that are desecrated. A young socialist said to me one time, "Whenever I pronounce the name of God, I feel nausea." I asked him why, and he answered me that the name of God is found associated with lies and for a long time with many evils and wrongs that he should battle all his life. Well may many young worthy Christian saints speak about "God," when the world questions them, since that name has not been reverenced by historical Christianity as Christ taught should be done.

However, with all of those defects, we answer secularism by God, and with God, and in the name of God. All thought should be guided under that light. Our life should be governed by God. To affirm God is to recognize that he is light, and he is life, and the life that inspires. Having this conviction, the job of the Gospel is to present a challenge and an answer to secularism from two points of view: first, by reinterpreting, in reasonable and vital terms, the true meaning of the personality; second, by reinterpreting, in similar terms, the exact significance of responsibility.

The personality does not belong to the mere individual, simple human atom, neither even to those who have enterprisingly carried out everything which their force of will has dictated. The solitary individual will become in reality a "person" when he connects with and attends to the requirements of God in his life, when he recognizes his nature in the light of providence and sees his fate related to the will of God. The personality only emerges when he himself is able to say, "You are my God." In that hour he is that man that

---

25. The Lord's victory over Sisera was won because a sudden downpour made chariots useless. Judg 5:20. —Ed.

stayed heir of everything;[26] the universe belongs to him, because all is from God, and God is his Father.

But, how is personality like this created? Jesus Christ, the man from Galilee, constitutes the divine ideal for our life. He is the eternal imperative. Christ is the dynamic power that transforms the sinner, the man atom, separate from God, into a Christian personality, in whom God inhabits. He is the indicative way by and for all in our life. Believe in him, in the complete sense, and accept him to be our all. In this way Christ becomes the center of the personality. It is the way that a unique, special individual is made truly Christian and is fulfilled in Christ. It is this way that God becomes the perfect objective for life, doing for him that which our feet and our hands do what they do so naturally for us.

The personality involves responsibility. The more a man discovers God, the more he recognizes he must serve those who are near him. No one will be able to say, "You are my God," without looking around and saying also, "You are him near me." The love of God itself drives us to obedience. The love that leads us to sympathy with men is this, "the virtue to suffer with others and for others."

Finally, the true demonstrations of responsibility involve inevitably the idea of the cross. Sensitivity to the divine call makes us attentive to Christ who suffers within men for their redemption.

The function of the church is to create, inspire, and guide Christian personalities. It must help to uncover the task that God gives for every man. Besides enlisting those that are broken, to be precise, the church must help its members understand the times in which they live, their problems, and prepare people to think clearly about everything in the light of God, to act in the spirit and under the direction of the Living Christ. To conclude, we are living in times when only by elevation of our sights will we indeed defeat secularism as a normative philosophy for life.

---

26. He is like the prodigal son who comes to the father. The son who was dead is alive again. Luke 15:11–24. —Ed.

4

The Profession of Being a Man

Dr. Gálvez, honorable Prefect, Ladies and Gentlemen:

Almost three months ago, as did the hero of the Eça de Queiroz[27] novel, I left the city suddenly to go to the sierra. I arrived in this valley of the Andes exhausted in body and soul, but your climate of hospitality, your eucalyptus forests, the green mountains with their spring mantle, and most of all your affection and your homes, have fully renewed my life. But, as I feel a new man, I must go back to my duties in the metropolis. The moment has arrived when I have to say farewell to you, and this makes me sad. The close perspective of my departure from Tarma makes me feel nostalgic, as I have seldom felt in my life. It is something similar to what I used to experience as a child when I had to leave the ancestral farm, where I used to spend my summer vacation; similar, also, to what I felt when I had to say farewell to Spain, the beautiful and beloved, the one that until now keeps a piece of my soul in the shade of the Guadarrama.[28] I know that as soon as I reach the gorge of the mountains, the day of my leaving, I will feel that another piece of my soul has remained in the ravines of this valley, as proof that, if it is God's will, I will come back for a visit.

If I had been a poet, I would have celebrated in verse my stay among you, and also the emotions and memories that it has awakened in me. I would have sung about the graceful eucalyptus where the doves rest, the hills tamed by the patient oxen, the Incan terraces with their splashes of shrubs. I would have sung about the local people: the shepherdesses who weave on the mountains and their sisters who spin the wool that walk

---

27. José Maria de Eça de Queiroz (1845–1900) was a Portuguese realist writer and diplomat. —Ed.

28. The Guadarrama mountain range is located in central Spain. —Ed.

barefooted through the valley; all the while carrying their loads are the Indian mule drivers, the patient donkeys, and the elegant llamas. I would have sung also the legends of long ago. But, not being a poet to compose one, I appreciate the elegance of one who is, and who invited me to talk about something else in this library.[29]

Someone has said, I believe it may have been Amiel,[30] "Each bud blooms only once, and each flower has only one minute of perfect beauty. And so, in the garden of the soul, each emotion has its bloom." You find me tonight in one of those blooming moments in my life. It is the feeling of responsibility that is opening its petals.

I have never appreciated an honor so much as this one that you have granted me to inaugurate the series of lectures that are planned for every month upon popular and vital themes. If I am not wrong, the town council of Tarma is the first in the republic to have promoted such a beautiful initiative. Considering that, it is not strange that the flower of responsibility may open up in my soul. Before it wilts, I hope to sow something that will last, and if at all possible, with unfading amaranth flowers. In this way, not being a poet, I will sow, and in this springtime I will cast some seeds for thought on the furrow of your minds. They will be the best memory I can leave you. I hope that they will germinate. But if they were to die, they could be the fertilizer that will feed your own thoughts.

The Universal Profession

I will talk, gentlemen, of man and his life in the most intimate and simple way. The phrase that forms the title of the ideas I want to present, was suggested by a line of the *Ariel* of José Enrique Rodó.[31]

I found myself deeply unhappy because I could not find the words to state everything I wanted to say in a neat phrase, I opened by mere chance that masterwork, and my eyes fell on that line, that I had underscored with a red pencil some time ago. "There is a universal profession, which is to be a man." Rodó had taken these words from a young French philosopher, Jean-Marie Guyau,[32] to reinforce with them the argument of his Ariel, and

---

29. As the conference should have been held in the local Adolfo Vienrich Public Library, the author put it this way, but given the amount of the public in attendance, he had to give it on the premises of the Provincial Council.

30. Henri-Frédéric Amiel (1821–1881) was a Swiss philosopher and poet. —Ed.

31. José Enrique Rodó (1871–1917) was an Uruguayan essayist. —Ed.

32. Jean-Marie Guyau (1854–1888) was a French poet and philosopher. In his short life he analyzed modern philosophy especially moral philosophy. —Ed.

I took them from the Uruguayan master, and the text of this lecture, "The Profession of Man," is the subject of our talk.

"The Proper Study of Mankind Is Man"

"The proper study of mankind is man." The English poet Alexander Pope, said this, and it would seem that science in our time has consecrated his famous saying as an axiom. The anthropologist, the physician, the psychologist, the sociologist, and the philosopher, each one of them has contributed in his way to our knowledge of the human being. All the questions related to the origin, constitution, life, and destiny of man have been the subject of the most detailed study. But the more this marvelous creature is studied in all the aspects of its nature, so many more problems come up that need an answer. The psychologist, and his cousin, the sociologist, not to mention other examples, are today in dire straits. The studies conducted by the Society for Psychical Research, together with the information provided by professional spiritualists, have taken him, in ecstasies, to the edge of a fairy tale world, while he has become almost dumbfounded by the latest social upheavals.

Who Is Man?

But there is a more significant problem than that of the psychic phenomena, and a problem prior to that of life in society: it is the problem of the personal life of man, which is at the same time the expression of results from the psychic phenomena and the key of the stirred-up sociological problem. It is the fundamental problem that can preoccupy the human mind. It has been considered through the centuries by the great poets, philosophers, and prophets of humanity, but the theme is still not exhausted. What are the characteristics of a true model of man, and what is the character of life that he ought to lead? In other words, what constitutes a true human professional, and when can it be said that he exerts his profession well? Here we have, gentlemen, the problem of centuries, and we will devote ourselves presently to its study. Attempting to guide and, if possible, to crystallize your thoughts on this matter, I will not talk as a poet, as a philosopher, or as a prophet, but, as one says in English, as *a plain man*, (a common man) who has been obsessed from his youth with the problems of life.

Men of Days Gone by and of Nowadays

I have said that the question of "the profession of being a man" is the problem of the centuries, and to be frank, the concepts of man and ideal life are as many and diverse as the historical eras and the schools of thought. Each new social revolution and the development of each new philosophical school have popularized a new type of man, pointing at the same time new directions for the exercise of the human profession.

To make a complete treatise on this subject, it would be necessary to consider all the main concepts that have been held concerning man and his life. We would have to examine, in this case, the mystic man of India, the man advocated in Jewish times, the philosopher-king of Plato, the stoic and epicurean types of Greek decadence, the roving knight of the middle ages, and the different ideals of man born within the sphere of Christianity, such as the friar and the puritan. We would also have to study the romantic man, the aristocratic and bourgeois types of modern history, and finally, the newest social phenomenon, the Bolshevik man. It would be very interesting, no doubt, to analyze all these types to see to what extent each one of them brings about in his life the true goal of the human creature. But, given the limitations of our time, and the character of the present study and lecture, I prefer to devote myself, not to a critical effort, but to establish in a positive way the fundamental principles that determine the dignified exercise of man's profession, then to sketch the different aspects of a full life. There is, notwithstanding, a theory of man that I would like to examine with care because of its attractive idealism and the prestige of its author; and also because the consideration of it will provide an excellent point of departure for the development of our own conception, I would like to examine it with some attention. I am speaking of the theory of Ernest Renan.[33]

"An Abbreviated Picture of the Species"

According to Renan's concept, one labors well at the profession of man by being "an abbreviated picture of the species." That is to say that the ideal man is the one who reveals in miniature all the human qualities. Such a concept is a reflection of the thinking of Plato who considered man as a microcosm of the society in which he lived. Moral excellence for Plato consisted in keeping a balance among the different elements of the soul and in developing the faculty of reason to the highest degree through a series

---

33. Ernest Renan (1823–1892) was a French intellectual famous for his *Life of Jesus* (1863). —Ed.

of dialectic exercises. The result of such a discipline was the philosopher, who was the only one who understood things well, given that he was looking at them under the light of the idea of the greatest good, so that he was the only one called to govern the state. From that idea comes the famous platonic saying that "the philosophers must be the kings," because they were a compendium of all virtues. This concept of Plato has the merit of not being purely intellectual, like the one of Aristotle, another Greek thinker, for whom the ideal man was the contemplative. For Plato, on the contrary, man has to do something more than to think: he must act, getting into practical and living contact with the society that surrounds him. But this theory, so attractive in its idealism, suffers from the following grave defects. It limits all human ideals to a very small number of people, that is, to those that God had given gold in their constitution. Only they could learn dialectic and get a glimpse of the good. All the other people, those who had only silver in their constitution, or copper, or an inferior metal, were fatally predestined not to see anything more in life than the shadows of things, or, to use platonic language, "the shadows of the shadows." And not only that: the theory mentioned could be realized only in a society like the Greek where social life was static and complete in itself, where the great mass of the people did not enjoy the rights of citizenship, where the existence of the state depended on the labor of slaves.

The Esthetic Man

But what does this have to do with Renan's theory? We will see it now. Renan was a modern Hellenic. He accepted the world in which he was born. He did not want to change it; but for himself, he built a separate world like an Athenian, a world that he embellished with all the monuments of human genius, and that he populated with beings that combined all the qualities that he himself, following the Greek fashion, determined beforehand as truly human. So that when Renan says that the ideal man must be "an abbreviated picture of the species," it is not difficult to see that "the species" which such type reflects is not the "human species" but the "esthetic species" whose members have been carefully selected according to the criterion of "good taste." An examination of the writings of Renan shows that he deliberately excluded from his concept of the human ideal many virtues that we hold as the most heroic and sacred. Such are the proper virtues of the reformer, the prophet, the missionary, of the humanitarian, of the simple Christian. The man advocated by Renan will be more a spectator than an actor in the world. He will not care for the pains of that twilight life of Paris, revealed by Victor Hugo, a contemporary of Renan, in *Les Miserables*. By adopting as a motto the famous saying of the German philosopher, that "what is rational is real," and accordingly, that what is not rational is not real, this hero of Renan will pass his life surrounded by "the rational," "the harmonious." His only interest in the world called "irrational," that is the world of injustices and human suffering, is the interest of the merely curious. In an essay titled "The Religious Future" Renan says, speaking from the point of view of one for whom the world is only an object to study, that even if "one could want to reform it, one might find it so curious that one would lack courage to do so." Concerning the problem of indigenous races, he says in the same essay, "Allow these latest children of nature to recline over the bosom of their mother, do not stop their childish games, their dances in the moonlight, their sweet brief intoxication." It shows that Renan did not look at the uncivilized world except through colored lenses of poetry, and that he did not recognize the noble role of the missionary, who in the last century has been the precursor of civilization in all the lands of the world. There are few who believe, like Renan, that there are races incapable of civilization and that the proper virtues of a Francis Xavier and of an Allan Gardiner, who gave his life for the aborigines of Tierra del Fuego, do not fit into his "abbreviated picture of the species."

Contemporary Greeks

But unfortunately there is no shortage in our present world of those who look at life with the eyes of Greeks, interested only in what is rational and beautiful, and remaining apathetic towards the irrational and ugly. They believe themselves superior beings, the cream of humanity. They live to enjoy esthetic sensation, and, like the Athenians of long ago, do not do anything but "Tell or listen to some news." For them nothing must be exaggerated; everything has to have its measure. The actual reality of things bores them, and the only contact they have with it is when they go up to their balcony to look, with a cynical smile, at the crowd that works and dies. It is said that when Dante walked through the streets of Florence, his forehead wrinkled in thought, the Florentine children used to say, "There goes a man who has been to hell." In the wrinkles of that face were reflected the problems and pains of his times, because Dante meditated about life in his time. But our Greeks spend their life in an artificial world, gilded with imitations and resounding with voices that have lost their sense. They do not have wrinkles in the forehead, for theirs is as placid as a statue of Phidias.[34] They have never been in hell, not even at its edge. They do not know what it is to live confronting reality, nor do they want to know. Therefore, they are not men but puppets, and even if, Greek like, they can be "an abbreviated picture of the species," posterity will relegate them to deserved shame and oblivion.

Ideal Qualities Do Not Make an Ideal Man

But it seems that I hear a criticism of what I have said. Assuming that the word "species" could be considered as encompassing the whole human species, would not, then, Renan's concept be a perfect definition of what man must be? Not so, either. In our concept a man could reach harmonious development of all his faculties under the aegis of reason, be a shining light of human culture, recapitulate in his own person all the virtues of all his ancestors since Adam, in a word, match perfectly Renan's ideal of being "an abbreviated picture of the species," and, in spite of it, be a poor, inept wretch for life in his own time and as sterile as a mule to influence life in the future. Or, stated in another way, to be a faithful reflection of all the ideal elements of human nature does not imply being an ideal man, a true professional man. It is impossible to avoid a somewhat pragmatic criterion when we look at human values. The only case in which the mentioned concept of an ideal man could be true would be if the world were a great athletic stadium, and life nothing else than running through an enclosed lane with all distances properly measured and posted. In such a case the ideal of man would not change much from one century to the next nor would the training necessary to attain victory in the human race. The athlete would always wear the colors of his country or his age, but nothing else would be necessary to carry the palm, if one were to have the traditional conditions of this kind of athletics. But the track of life will not always cover known places, and it will often go through many things, in some eras more than others, through mountains and valleys never stepped upon before and seas where an exploring keel has never ploughed through.

Man Is for His Times

The truth is that each stage of the long trajectory of history presents special conditions. Each historical age has had its own problems, and for the

---

34. Phidias (c. 480–430 BC) was a Greek sculptor whose statue of Zeus at Olympia was one of the seven wonders of the ancient world. —Ed.

solution it has not been enough to have men who were perfect types of generic humanity. It has been necessary in all occasions to find men suitable for the needs of their age. And if they have not been available, the civilization of that era has decayed. A sailor who has spent his life on tropical seas could go, if commanded, on an expedition to the North Pole to fulfill his duty, but it is very likely that, in those unusual conditions, his services would be of limited usefulness. The same would happen if we were to try to solve the spiritual problems of our age employing, for example, the monastic type of services of the Middle Ages. As Victor Hugo states in the work already quoted, "The monastic system, no matter how useful it may be at the dawn of civilization, to bring about the domination of brutality through the development of spirituality, is offensive when the nations have reached their maturity. The great monastic communities are to the great social community what ivy is to the oak, what a wart is to the human body." In other words, the monk is not the man adequate for today's world.

In Search of the Dynamic Man

Now, let us go back to our problem, to the point where we left it to examine Renan's theory. Who is the true human professional, and how can we recognize him? The great error of Renan, as that of many other idealist thinkers, is in attempting to determine what man should be by studying what man is. The best that such method can give is an esthetic ideal, and not a dynamic ideal. The right method to apply to the solution of the problem posed consists in studying first what the world is, in which man is called to play a role. It is the same method that would be applied to the question of an ideal physician. He is not an individual endowed with a number of qualities and abstract knowledge, but one who possesses those qualities and knowledge that entitle him to fight the diseases characteristic of his country and his time. In the same way, the true human professional is one who has the qualities required by life in general in his times, in his particular country. Surveying the universal aspects of life, we will come to know what man should be at all times. Studying the characteristics of our age and our country, we will be able to draw the sharp profiles of a man made for the current era.

Aspects of Life and Features of a Man

Let us cast a glance upon life, to see if we can determine its principal aspects. In our conception, they are three, namely, the principle of *evil*, the principle of *purpose*, and the principle of *adaptation*.

The life of the world is very far from what it should be. Nobody denies that. There are in man and in society pernicious elements that make it impossible to develop an ideal society in the world. It is not necessary to specify what those elements are, because I am convinced that no moral, sincere man living in a country illuminated by the light of Christianity will have trouble seeing with clarity what are the problems suffered in life. The real difficulty will not be in pointing to such evil, but in considering it seriously and correcting it. We have seen, for example, the type that finds the world so interesting that he does not want to reform it and rid it of its problems. There are others who think that evil is a purely negative reality, or that it is as necessary as is the good, or even, that it is a good and that its strange appearance is due only to our narrow vision. I reject this monism with all the strength of my soul. Monism sees everything in terms of an identity and purports to see in the devil just another name for God. I accept, at the same time, the doctrine of the disciplinary value of evil, in the spirit of the old Latin aphorism that states, "It is necessary to have heretics" (*Oportet haereses esse*). But if we were to look at things in the way that Spinoza says, "under the light of eternity" (*sub specie aeternitatis*) we will agree that evil serves to form the character of man. We have to agree, also, that the one who refuses to fight against evil, embracing it or laughing at it, completely lacks a true human character, given that character is formed in the fight. It is true that evil exists to defy us, and we must fight it without ceasing, relentlessly. And we should not struggle just to fight it, as one does with physical exercises. The fight is to win and to eliminate evil. In this case we cannot agree with the statement of Unamuno that, "The struggle is worth more than victory." In this case victory is worth more than the struggle and is the true goal of it. We know, then, the first element of a true human professional: *he will struggle against evil wherever and however he finds it.*

The second principle is that of the objective, the *purpose*. The establishment of the world and the course of history are not the result of any chance combination of atoms. The supreme law of the universe is the principle of teleology, meaning that everything is oriented towards a predetermined end, which is the true cause and explanation of everything that exists. As the poet Tennyson has said, "I know that a growing purpose runs through the centuries." As we are required to think in terms of the highest category that we know, that is, the one of the personality, we cannot but hold that the "growing purpose" mentioned by Tennyson is the purpose of a sovereign will that reveals the goal of history with growing clarity to each successive generation. What is that goal? Nothing less than the establishment of the kingdom of God on earth, the fulfillment of that prayer of the Master, "Thy kingdom come, thy will be done on earth as it is in heaven." The utopia dreamed by prophets, poets, and philosophers, that every good Christian and social reformer should struggle bodily to bring about, will one day delight the eyes of humanity. On that day injustice and ignorance will be no more, and all men will be united around the feet of God.

Given that the kingdom of God is the true goal of history, it is evident that those who wish that their earthly task may last and be worthwhile should identify themselves with the great cause, to bring the advent of the "Holy City." I know men of great talent that go through life groping along and stumbling simply because they do not possess a high ideal with which to identify. They are always afraid of appearing ridiculous to the public eye due to vested interests; uncertain at the edge of the great currents of life, on the shore never moving away from the bank. Meanwhile, God's waters go by, waters of renewal, carrying all men who have trusted them on the trough between waves to new horizons and noble tasks. While the rest . . . they play at living on the shore; they die and are forgotten. From this we find a second trait of the character of the true man: *he will consecrate his life to a noble cause related to the kingdom of God.*

The third principle of life is that of *adaptation*. To be able to survive all living beings have to adapt to their milieu. In dealing with human life, there are two very different ways that a man can fulfill this principle. He can adapt to his milieu in such a way that he becomes its slave, or he can do it in such a way that he turns out to be its master. There are those, for example, who adapt so perfectly to the environment in which they live, accepting everything good or bad, so that they lose their own individuality becoming mere puppets of a generic type without distinctive moral features. Slaves of routine, they always choose the path of least resistance and resolutely reject everything that does not suit their traditional models of behavior and thought. Every adaptation of that kind is deleterious to the best interests of society, since it tends to create a static, even rotten, social situation.

True adaptation consists in seeking points of contact with the present society with the goal of transforming it, bringing it closer to the vision that one may have of the City of God. This is the way that a teacher adapts to the world of a child, the humanitarian to the life of the proletariat in the poor neighborhoods of a great metropolis, the missionary living the life of the indigenous tribe. And this is how the God-Man adapted himself to life in time. It is an adaptation that generally requires sacrifice. I have said already that a man has to be a true child of his country and of his time. In such a case, if he is going to adapt to the life of the one and the other, as advocated with the aim of carrying out the work of civilization, he will have to sacrifice in one way or another. He cannot be selfish. He may discover other countries more pleasant than his own because of a higher culture or an easier way of life, but he will not abandon his native land as long as its national life is not well settled, unless he may be going to a foreign land to learn or to bring back something useful for the motherland. Even when he might want to live a quiet life separated from the world, he will not fail to answer the calling of his country in times of deep political, social, or religious crisis. Denying himself, he will carry the cross of his native land. He will place its interests ahead of his own. In the noble words of Wordsworth he "will choose for his scepter the thistle of duty, while his forehead is crowned with the roses of youth." In this way he will save his country from ruin and himself from shame and oblivion. Here we have the third feature of a true man: *he will reveal a sacrificial spirit.*

Our Times and Their True Children

At this moment let us stop looking at life in general, and let us fix our gaze on *our age*. The current age is characterized by two principal notes, which determine the type of man adequate for it. They are *its importance* and *its tragedy*.

Unquestionably we live in the most *critical* moments since the foundation of Christianity. Civilization has reached the crossroads. It has also its "Isla del Gallo."[35] An invisible sword draws a line on the sand of time, and a fateful voice, that of destiny, can be heard. "This way to the kingdom of God and to happiness; this other way, to chaos and to ruin: a worthy human has to choose." At the time of the French Revolution the poet Wordsworth, filled with enthusiasm by the new doctrines of equality between men, wrote, "It was happiness to live at that sunrise, but to be young was heaven itself." And in spite of the shadows cast by bolshevism, the feared failure of the League of Nations, the storm clouds rising up in the Asian world, we have to congratulate ourselves for our luck to live in our present times. For the same reason this moment is solemn, and the destiny of humanity is in the balance; it is possible that a man may give his life a weight that his grandparents would not be able to imagine. Although it is true that we think, with Carlyle, that the hero is the main motor force in a historic movement, we have to agree, also, that the hero is just the product of his times. Living in a remarkable age and identifying himself with a noble cause, even mediocre men can become heroes.

The true servants of their generation will be *men of vision*, of as much vision but of more sublime things, than the vision possessed by the men who

---

35. This refers to an episode in the life of Francisco Pizarro in which he challenged his followers to a heroic decision by drawing a line on the sand. —Trans.

followed Pizarro in the Isla del Gallo. As Ruskin wrote in one of his books, "the greatest thing a human soul can do is to see something, and to tell what it saw in a plain way." Those who glimpse an important truth connected with the reconstruction, proclaiming it to their companions and incarnating it in their lives, will be true human professionals in our current world.

But if our time is more important than other eras, it is also much more *tragic*. In past times the world was much more static; the movement of civilizations was slower; behavioral norms were more stable. But at present, for good or for evil, everything is in vertiginous flux. We have witnessed the dissolution of old dynasties, and now we can feel the foundations of our civilization cracking under our feet. Politically, we live over the boiling crater of a volcano, while from a moral point of view we are drifting, wrapped in a fog that hides the sun and the coastline. It is not so easy for a young man to say, "I will get this or that job" or "this or that is what I believe." It is not rare to suffer the greatest disappointments in search of one's ambitions, and such a person may see himself obliged to break with the customs, the ideas, and even the religion of his parents, not finding in them all the goodness and peace that his soul longs for. Utilizing the title of a book by a friend, a poet, we could say that ours is the age of "thinking pain." Today's man has to think in a different way than his ancestors did, or in Unamuno's words, he has to think with his head, his heart, and his guts. The lack of signs on the roads of life, and even the lack of roads themselves, makes it necessary for the traveler to think, to question, to have recourse to a compass.

How many souls are completely disoriented at present, resting at the bottom of an abyss, wrapped in the "dark night." They seek light about the moral problem, about the mystery of life, and do not find it. They are sincere men, and they do not abandon the search. Agnosticism does not satisfy their burning spirits. They need a solid base for their faith and action. Is there hope? Is there something unchanging in the midst of the flux? Listen. "God gives songs at night," said the prophet Elihu.[36] I am going to teach you one of those nocturnal songs. A soul had lost his way in the recesses of life. He could not see a point of light anywhere on the horizon, so he looked down to earth. But even if the traveler "does not look at heaven, heaven looks at him" and teaches him a song. The song goes like this, "It is better to be generous than selfish, better chaste than licentious, better loyal than false, better brave than a coward." To the music of such song that soul, feeling that there was something immutable in worldly things, lifted his eyes and looked at heaven, seeing there the first star to bless his eyes since he lost his way.

---

36. Job 35:10. —Ed.

That star turned out to be the morning star, and the traveler got ready to emerge from the abyss, and he did it singing:

> When you guide, the night is bright
> And I will cross
> Valley, mount, cliff, and stream
> With steady foot;
> Until the day will rise,
> And I will find the warmth of my sweet hearth.

There is nobody that can live the human profession in our times, as well as the person who has felt the sensation of despair in his soul, and who has struggled towards the light. He, only he, will be able to become a leader because he knows what he believes and why he does believe it. The only ones who will serve in a tragic and disoriented age like ours will be the *men of conviction*.

The "Underground Forges" of America

But we are already carried on the currents of our thought to contemplate our America, to inquire next into the character of the men that she demands.

I have said "our America," because, even if that Celtic land, the old Caledonia, is my unforgettable mother, the Colombian lands have adopted me already. I will not talk about the whole of America but only about the Andean countries. Allow me to read a few lines taken from "The Epic Poem of Artigas" of Juan Zorrilla de San Martín.[37] "This region," says Zorrilla referring to the Andean countries, "is in continuous ignition; it is a rosary of active craters like no other on the planet. The Cyclopes are still at work in those underground forges with their devilish bellows and their stentorian hammer blows and take away the dreams, more than once, of those men of the earth's crust. It is a world being built."

The author of this epic poem wanted to describe the physical conditions of the western coast of the continent, but who would say that the description is not the symbol of the social and political condition of that region? The mention of the "Cyclopes," who, with "devilish bellows" and their "stentorian hammer blows that take away the dreams more than once," reminds us what another author has said about these countries, that is, "that the principal products are minerals and revolutions." Be that as it may, it happens that Peru and neighboring countries are countries that, in a special sense, are being

---

37. Juan Zorrilla de San Martin (1855–1931) was an Uruguayan poet and diplomat known as Uruguay's greatest poet. La epopeya de Artigas was published in 1910. —Ed.

formed. Thanks to the "underground forges" and the "perpetual ignition" that they maintain, the social structure of these countries is more malleable than that of older countries. Who knows that among us the only fixed thing is the republican form of government? At this moment the craters are not throwing smoke, but it would seem as if our ears could hear a distant sound, like the infernal shovels of Cyclopean stokers, heating their underground forges in a hurry. It seems difficult to postpone for a long time the social, moral, and religious crisis that has already shaken so many countries in the world.

Impressionist and Structural Men

In one of his famous writings, the great Catalonian author, Eugenio D'Ors,[38] distinguishes between *structural* men and *impressionistic* men. Forgive me if I say that Peru has had a surplus of men of the impressionist type. If they had been the type of impressionists that reproduce in words or on the canvas the noble contours of the Peruvian landscapes, or the sadness or the aspirations of the people, we would applaud their patriotic efforts; but unfortunately this is not a common type, while the other, the bitter critic, proliferates like poison ivy. There is nothing more repulsive than to listen to a man cursing his own country, although there is nothing as common in Peru or in Spain. In Spain it is almost a traditional custom. Fígaro satirized it brilliantly in his famous article "Features of this country." And in Peru, what foreigner does not hear almost every day of his life, "I am Peruvian, but I think like a foreigner," or "I am Peruvian, but I cannot stand life in this place," and more of the same. Enough! Enough! Have you never heard, you traitors, the following words?

> Can he exist, a man with such a dead soul
> That has never told himself:
> This is my Country, my Country!

The motherland does not want to be cursed, she wants her children to be *structural* men, that will consecrate themselves to build, on the Incan land, something worthy of its past. I do not know words that translate so faithfully the feeling of the true structurals, than those of William Blake, in which, talking about England, he says,

> I will not cease from mental fight
> Nor shall my sword sleep in my hand,
> Till we have built Jerusalem
> In Albion's green and pleasant land.

38. Eugenio D'Ors (1881–1954) was a Spanish Catalonian essayist. —Ed.

I know that you are tired. I cannot abandon the subject, however, without having applied the principles already discovered to concrete daily life. If we already rightly understand the *qualities* that a sound human professional ought to possess, the professional needs to know how those qualities will *apply* in the different aspects of life.

Every man is called to act in three spheres, namely, the sphere of *nature*, the sphere of *ideas*, and the *transcendental* sphere, or *that of God*. I want to consider in brief terms, how a man should behave in each one of them. Of course, the time I have will only allow me to suggest topics for your thought that you may be able to develop at leisure on your own.

Man in the World of Nature: Worker and Citizen

When I mention *nature* I mean not only the fields and the farming life, but the whole world external to man. We cannot accept the distinction implied in the familiar saying, "God made the countryside and man made the city." Not at all. The city and the state, and all institutions of the one and the other, to the degree that they represent necessary aspects of the human spirit, are integral parts of nature, and so much God's work as the forests and the mountains. Everything that is truly human is also *natural*, in this sense. Man has to play a double role towards nature, that of a *worker* and the role of a *citizen*.

Every man has to be a *worker*, a craftsman of some kind. It is true that it would not be bad if everyone were to know how to work with their hands. All the Jewish youngsters in the past were required to learn a manual trade, in addition to their vocation. It did not matter if their parents were rich or aristocratic. Does the idea exist in anyone's mind that manual labor is not honorable, not a job for a gentleman? Whoever thinks that way is lost. There is a line of Hesiod which says, referring to the primitive times of Greece, "Work was not shameful for anybody." According to Plutarch, the great legislator Solon did business in his youth, while Plato was able to afford the expense of a trip to Egypt by selling oil. It is the same spirit that inspires many European or American students to do menial work to pay for their studies. But there are also intellectual or artistic works. Whoever meditates, works, and whoever projects an idea on a canvas does the same. The important thing is that all men, aristocratic or plebeian, rich or poor, should not be idle or parasitic, but produce something that benefits the community.

The second role that man is called to play in the sphere of nature is that of a *citizen*. Every true man has to love his country with a *sentimental* and a *civic* love. He must love with enthusiasm and with pride the native soil and the country that has made him what he is. I will never stop preaching love of the motherland and everything that it has. The country that is not interested in its history and its antiquities, making of them the subject of songs, still lacks a true nationality. Similarly, the province and the town that do not know about their history and their legends, and whose rivers, forests, and mountains do not evoke any memories or arouse any emotion, do not have a proper individuality. There is a refrain that says, "Let me write the songs of a people, and let anyone else write its laws." And really, the songs and not the laws are the powerful factor to attain greatness in a country, and those songs can only begin to flow when a breeze of sentimental love blows in every corner of the motherland.

Civic or public spirited love arises from sentimental love and consists in a complete identification of the citizen with the life of the motherland. On some other occasion I would like to talk, at greater length, about true public spirit, but at this moment the limitations on my time do not allow me to do any more than to point to the features of a good citizen. He will never stay away from his country any longer than what may be necessary for the good of it, will cultivate a receptive but independent spirit, be respectful but also a reformer, be dignified but optimistic.

Probably the feeling that is most oppressive for a good patriot in a country like ours is that of the apparent uselessness of every effort, no matter how well intentioned. There are so many contrary forces that seem to cancel out every good initiative. On the slab that marks the grave of Jean-Marie Guyau, the author of the heading of this conference, the following words are engraved,

> "Our most noble efforts appear to be precisely the most useless, but they are like the waves that, having been able to reach us, can go even further. I am convinced that my greatest occupations will survive me. Not only that, perhaps not a single one of my dreams can be considered lost. Someone else will pick them up, although they may appear as mere ghosts in the night, until they may one day reach perfect fruition. Thanks to the waves that die continuously in its bosom, the sea has the power to carve the beach and the huge ocean bottom over which it moves."

No sincere effort is completely vain, gentlemen, as the Master said, "One sows, someone else reaps." There is no room for discouragement or for pessimism. The world does not know its greatest benefactors. England and France last year began to pay homage to the unknown soldier, a symbol of the unknown crowd that gave their lives for the motherland and whose feats no one has praised. The only thing that should matter to a man is to live a life worthy of his ideals, fulfilling his duties without thinking of rewards.

Man in the World of Ideas: Educator and Reader

Let us then consider briefly man in the world of ideas. The cult of nature is what we call *patriotism*; the cult of ideas is what we call *culture*. We have already considered, when dealing with Renan's theory, a culture completely divorced of the throbbing reality of life, and there is no need to repeat. The only thing I will do is to speak superficially about the two great means by which we attain citizenship in the world of ideas. They are education and books. Education provides the working instruments. The books are the soil that we cultivate. In the world of ideas men are educators and readers.

The true educator will take care of three particular things, namely: to sow ideas, to develop minds, and to discover souls. No one denies that true education consists in the double process of providing the child with matter for his mind and helping him to express his true self. But an educator has to do something more, he must be at all times in search of souls, of talents that will be able, later on, to be of service to the country and to humanity. I will explain. It is told of the famous English chemist Sir Humphrey Davy, that when he was asked what his greatest discovery was, he answered, "My greatest discovery has been Michael Faraday." This Michael Faraday was a poor child who was hired by Davy to work in his laboratory. The skilled eyes of the great chemist did not take long to discover the incipient talent of his young aide, talent that he tried to cultivate by all means, until the young Faraday became a scientist even more distinguished than his master. This, gentlemen, is nothing but a parable. You will remember that Mexico discovered an Indian, Juarez,[39] who became one of the greatest men in the history of Mexico. Peru has some three million unknown Indians. I have no doubt that, once their souls are discovered, you will find that there is a Faraday and a Juarez among them.

Thomas Carlyle, the great Scottish thinker, said on one occasion, "Today's real university is a collection of books." I congratulate the municipality of Tarma for having a library for the people like this one, which even Lima did not have until now. I hope that the books that fill those shelves may be the best companions of the readers that gather in this room after their daily work. Cultivate the friendship of books, and so that you may do it more

---

39. Benito Pablo Juárez Garcia (1806–1872) was a child of peasants who left him an orphan at the age of three years old. He was raised by an uncle. Later he served five terms as president of Mexico. —Ed.

properly, I will give you the three rules, the practical advice of Emerson about reading. "First, never read any book that is not a year old. Second, never read any but famous books. Third, never read any book that you don't enjoy." But never, never should you read a book that will leave a stain in your soul. Do not ever read a book that may suggest to your mind the question of the young man that we find in one of the comedies of Terence, "If Jupiter did it, why not I?" and allow me, in addition, to express my hope that at no time will one or more copies of the Holy Scripture be missing from the shelves of this library. It is a sad fact that this book, commonly called the Bible, may be among books what Artigas was, for some time, among men, "the great slandered of America."[40] But Artigas has been vindicated already, and I trust that the day is not far off when this book, whose text has been the source of light and civilization in so many countries, will be vindicated in all the libraries and homes of Latin America, as it has been for centuries in the Anglo-Saxon world.

Man in the Transcendental World

We are coming now to the last item of our talk, man in the *transcendental world of God*. I cannot conceive that one could reach the highest degree of the human profession without having religious sentiments. "Why do you go to church?" someone once asked Oliver Wendell Holmes. "Because God has placed on my chest a small plant called reverence, and it has to be watered at least once a week." Reverence is the fundamental attitude that a man has to have with respect to the spiritual aspects of life. All nature is permeated by the Divinity, and it must inspire reverence. We do not need to be pantheists to believe in the immanence of God in the world, and what is even better, to feel it: in the majestic temple of nature it is possible to attain communion with an eternal Presence, better even than in the gothic or Byzantine cathedrals.

> Earth's crammed with heaven,
> And every common bush afire with God:
> But only he who sees, takes off his shoes,
> The rest sit round it and pluck blackberries.

This was the lyric of the sweet poet Elizabeth Barrett Browning.

But feelings are not all that is to be found in the transcendental world. On this I disagree profoundly with numerous authors who have written on this subject. Religion is more than a mere sentiment: it is life, energy, the

---

40. José Gervasio Artigas Arnal (1764–1850) was a national hero of Uruguay. —Ed.

highest energy. It is the greatest creative force that we know. It is *love*, but not only sentimental love, but dynamic love, the love of a supreme personality whose presence fills the huge emptiness of the soul and whose commands are obeyed. I am also convinced that the captivating skepticism of Ernest Renan, whose highest religious merit is "to have talked about the gods in beautiful language," has never filled with enthusiasm, and much less transformed even one soul, while a simple devotion to the person of Jesus Christ has changed the face of the whole world. There is no energy as powerful as the "expelling power of a new affection."

When we are dealing with religious values, we cannot disregard, either, a pragmatic criterion. Culture diffuses sweetness and light, but religion gives fire and strength, and the world requires fire and strength even more than sweetness and light. I think like Francisco García Calderón[41] and Lord Bryce[42] that the supreme need of these countries is the possession of true religious sentiments. One needs a religious faith to be at the height of one's human vocation.

But where can we find a man's faith, a faith that will satisfy his intellect, inspire his heart, and strengthen his will? A few days ago, reading some comments of Eugenio D'Ors, I found the following words in the section entitled "The Christian Note." "Who is Christ? He is the Man-God. In other words, history together with eternity." The historical Christ is at the same time the eternal Christ. Now, to overcome the contradiction between the eternal and the historical, means, in short the application of a formula: "Establish everything in Christ." Pay attention to the phrase: "Establish everything in Christ." It makes us remember another phrase of a deeper thinker than this Catalonian, Paul, the Jew of Tarsus, who says: "The apostle and pontiff of our profession, Christ Jesus."[43] Here we have also a synthesis of the eternal and the historical. Just like the apostle, Christ places God in contact with men, and as a pontiff places men in contact with God. Faith in that exalted figure is what best empowers a person to exercise the *Profession of Man*.

---

41. Francisco García Calderón (1883–1953) was a Peruvian lawyer and diplomat who played a role at the Paris Peace Conference and wrote on topics of foreign affairs. —Ed.

42. James Bryce (1838–1922) was a British jurist, historian, and Liberal politician who served as British ambassador to the United States (1907–13). —Ed.

43. A translation of Heb 3:1 using the term pontiff in lieu of high priest to make a theological point to his listeners. —Ed.

Part Two

The Message and Education

5

Young Students

IN THE ABSENCE OF an official definition of the subject of my report, I will take it in the most obvious sense that occurs to me. I will interpret "young students" as a synonym for "university students." With respect to the geographical range of this understanding of youth, I imagine that it refers to a study of university students of all Latin American countries, not only those around the Caribbean. If it were otherwise, I would not have a right to deliver this report, since the knowledge I have of this region is insufficient to allow me to prepare a study devoted exclusively to the young students of this region. The only thing I can do is to sketch, and that with broad strokes, the principal aspects of student life in the ten or eleven Latin American countries that I have been able to get to know up to now. But even in that case I would have lacked the courage to start such a study, were it not for two special circumstances, namely, that the countries I know are representative of the ones I do not know, and that student life in all of Hispanic-America presents more than a few generic features.

I have to add, also, that the reason why I have willingly answered the invitation of the Committee of the Evangelical Congress of Havana to deal with this subject was my wish that the participants of the congress could take a close look at the university world with the goal of understanding its problems, to take the pulse of the studious youth, and to become aware of the new winds blowing in the old cloisters. In this way you will be aware of the directions of the intellectual youth of these countries and perhaps will be inclined to help the wayfarers in their pursuit of the truth.

Now, without further introduction, we will get down to business.

I. The University Environment

Let us take a quick look at the milieu in which the young student will pass from four to nine years of his life.

The Goal of University Education

What is the goal of the Latin American university? Its traditional goal is to prepare professionals, that is, lawyers, physicians, engineers, and in some cases, teachers. This means that culture is not recognized in the classrooms as an end in itself. And even as a means, it does not exist with the goal to train the student for life, but for the exercise of a specific profession. There is nothing that resembles the North American college or the arts faculty of some European countries. In general, the faculty of letters or of humanities of our university is nothing other than the vestibule of the law faculty, as the sciences faculty is to medicine. Fortunately, in several countries there are a few hints of the perceived need to give university education a different cultural goal than merely a professional one. The distinguished Uruguayan intellectual, Carlos Vaz Ferreira, the new rector of the University of Montevideo, has just presented a plan to establish an Institute of Advanced Studies in that university. The humanities faculty of the progressive University of La Plata is positioned towards a cultural objective. The same tendency may be noted in the University of Mexico. But, in general, up to now the Latin American university has not endeavored to form men but to hatch professionals.

The Teaching Staff

Who are the university professors? The vast majority of them are professionals, that is lawyers, physicians, engineers, men of letters, or journalists who hold a chair at the university, to which they devote a minimal amount of time. This means that the university lacks a teaching staff devoted exclusively, or at least mainly, to it. How shall we explain this phenomenon? It could be argued, of course, that the salaries received at the universities do not allow the professors to devote themselves exclusively to higher education. There is, however, another reason of a psychological order that we consider more fundamental than that. It is that university professors in general resist specialization, wishing to do more than one thing at the same time. Most of them also lack the sense of vocation as professors.

As the teaching function is nothing more than an incidental in the life of men absorbed by multiple interests, it is impossible to develop the cordiality necessary between a professor and his students so that the instruction would be fruitful. Only in a small minority of these teachers have the university students been able to discover the prototype described by José Enrique Rodó in his *Ariel*, and it is said that Uruguayan youth could not find even in Rodó, the university professor in Montevideo, the character Prospero, advocated by Rodó, the essayist. But in every case when the young have found an authentic Prospero, a man on the model of Don Francisco Giner de los Ríos, the young have responded to his words. But how often in my ventures through the universities of the continent, have I heard the young saying, "What we need are real professors."

The Students

A university devoted to training professionals, served by professors who are not professionals in the teaching arts, has left tragic imprints in the life and attitude of the student body. How many illusions have been brought by the youngsters entering the halls of the university! And how great has been their disappointment! They expected to find an alma mater and they ended up finding a harsh aunt. For that reason they do not sing praising the university during their stay, nor do they feel the tender bond of memories after graduation. Lacking the constant stimulation and camaraderie of their professors, the students do not have the necessary orientation and encouragement to organize cultural societies within the university. Once in a while such organizations appear. But, in general, their life is ephemeral. In each student generation one or more magazines are born which rarely survive the graduation of their founders. Once in a while a burning issue of national or university politics appears, producing a rebellious agitation among the students. The youths will go on strike, if it is an internal issue, or they will organize demonstrations of protest against some measure or attitude of the government, if it deals with a national issue.

II. The University Revolution

In the year 1918 a movement arose in university life in Latin America that has had all the features of a university revolution. In that year the academic heavens in Argentina became dark with threatening clouds. The deep dissatisfaction of the student youth towards the traditional university finally manifested itself in an unusual and violent way. Several causes contributed to the outbreak. The world war had familiarized the youth with the spectacle of sudden and radical changes in many secular institutions. The success and ideals of the Russian Revolution suggested to them the need to apply new norms to the valuation of all the people and public institutions. The writings of the great Spanish thinker, Don Miguel de Unamuno especially that magnificent work of glowing prose, titled "The Sepulchre of Don Quixote," which appears as the prologue of his *Life of Don Quixote and Sancho* awoke in the souls of the students the spirit of crusaders. On the other hand, under the influence of José Enrique Rodó's *Ariel*, in whose pages the youthful spirit is idealized and continuous renewal is proposed as the ideal in life, the university youth attained full awareness of their own meaning and mission. The same youth had to be the means of renewal and of justice. A new social class had been added to those that already existed. It was the hour of youth. At the foot of the Andes, in the old city of viceroys, a shout resounded in their youthful hearts, that of González Prada, the great fighter of the prior generation, "Old men to the grave, young men to the task at hand." But it was in Argentina, in the conservative and cloistered city of Córdoba, where the first battle between the youth and the old university took place.

The Movement of Córdoba

Following sterile negotiations with the university authorities and an intervention by the federal government that did not satisfy the aspirations of the students, they took over the university buildings by sheer strength. Because they had the support of the president of the republic, Mr. Hipólito Irigoyen, the youths carried the day. At once a revolutionary wave began to sweep the other Argentinian universities, and then the movement extended to all Hispanic America. Brazil and Mexico were the only countries that escaped the swell in the placid waters of the university cloisters. Brazil did not feel the student revolt in part because of the way higher education is organized in that republic, and in part because of the limited response there that ordinarily meets movements that originate in Spanish Latin America. Mexico did not feel it because of the simple reason that revolution in all orders of life, including education, was already going on in that country. A Mexican, Licenciado Vasconcelos, became the prototype of the new educator for the reform minded students of South America who named him "Master of Youth." In Mexico, in 1921, an international congress of students took place with representatives from the United States, many Latin American republics, and some countries of Europe and Asia.

A Historical Manifesto

But returning to the Córdoba movement, what goals drove the students to open up an insurrection against the university authorities? Immediately after the university assault, the youngsters published a manifesto addressed to "the freemen of South America." It is worthwhile to pause for a few moments to examine this document, since it reveals some of the wounds of our university life, and at the same time it shows the ideals and illusions of the revolutionary youth that planned it. Here is the essential portion of this historical document.

> In the twentieth century men of a free republic have just finished breaking the last chain that used to bind us to the old monarchic and monastic domination. We have decided to call everything by its real name. Córdoba has redeemed itself. From now on we have one fewer shame and one more freedom for the country. The pangs that remain are the freedoms to come. We believe we are not mistaken; the echoes of the heart confirm our ideas; we are undergoing a revolution; we are living an American hour.
>
> Up to now, the universities have been the secular refuge of the mediocre, the income of the ignorant, the secure hospitalization of the invalids and— what is even worse—the place in which all the forms of tyranny found a chair to express themselves. The universities have thus become the faithful image of these decadent societies which attempt to offer the sad spectacle of a senile immobility . . .
>
> Our university regime—even the most recent one—is anachronistic. It is founded on a kind of divine right: the divine right of the university professors. It creates itself. It is born and dies in itself. It keeps an Olympian distance. The university federation of Córdoba rises up to fight against this regime and understands that we risk our lives. We demand a strictly democratic government and affirm that the university *demos*, its sovereignty, the right to form a government, lies mainly in the students. The concept of authority that corresponds and accompanies a director or a professor in a home of university students cannot rest upon the force of disciplines unconnected to the substance itself of the studies. The authority in a home of students is not exercised commanding, but suggesting and loving: teaching. If there is no spiritual bond between the one who teaches and the one who learns, all teaching is hostile and, as a consequence, sterile. All education is a long labor of love to those who learn. . . . The souls of the young must be moved by spiritual forces. . . .

We are accused, now, of insurrection in the name of an order that we are not debating, but that has nothing to do with us. If that were so, if in the name of order we are going to continue being deceived and brutalized, we proclaim loudly our sacred right to insurrection. In that case, the only gate that remains open to hope is the heroic right of youth. Sacrifice is our best stimulus; the spiritual redemption of American youth our only reward because we know that our truths are those—and painful ones—of the whole continent. . . .

Youth always lives at a heroic moment. It is disinterested; it is pure. It has not had time yet to become contaminated. It is never wrong in the election of its own teachers. Dealing with youths, there is no merit in flattery or bribes. It is necessary to let them choose their teachers and directors, confident that success is going to crown their decisions. From now on, the only possible teachers in the future university republic will be the builders of souls, the creators of truth, of beauty, of goodness.

The Meaning of This Document

Some phrases scattered in the text of this manifesto have an extraordinary interest, inasmuch as they crystallize different aspects not only of the psychology but of the ideology of the university students in the last decade. The young addressed the document to *the freemen of South America,* and they had the intuition of living *an American hour.* We have here an expression of a new sense of American solidarity born during the war, when they began to think that the American continent would have to be the hope of the world. Consequently, the American countries that had until then remained remote from each other ought to declare their solidarity to fight against the evils suffered in common.

The goal of the movement was redemptive. *Córdoba has redeemed itself,* shouted the crusaders, who sought as their only reward *the spiritual redemption of the American youth.* The beautiful messianic spirit is a feature shared by the Córdoba youngsters with the youth of many countries in the period after the war. This messianic fire, this quixotic passion, burning in the hearts of these youngsters who wanted to redeem every chained galley slave and right all the wrongs of the world, was to receive its strongest expression soon after in the developing movements by the Peruvian youth on behalf of the proletarian classes, the workers, and the indigenous people of their country.

The traditional university was not satisfactory for the student youth because of its *senile immobility*. It did not march with the times. Professors, whose appointment had been influenced by politics, who had jobs in the classrooms but not a vocation, who were absorbed by too many interests outside the professorship to remain up to date in the matters of their teaching specialty, clearly were reluctant to address the troublesome innovations in their cloistered monotony, as defenders of order, authority, and discipline.

It was precisely the Olympic and thunderous concept of authority that was most opposed by the young students. They felt like prisoners in a jail, or conscripts in a barrack, while what they wanted was to be citizens of a republic, or children of a home. How cleverly they applied the rights and principles of democracy to the university regimen, trusting in the pure, selective, and accurate instinct of youth! It did not occur to them that on some aspects of competency of the teachers the students are not competent to judge. But they exaggerated the note of their own capacity, sovereignty, and purity just because they wanted to secure teachers that would be affectionate, that would exercise their authority *not . . . commanding, but suggesting and loving: teaching*, who would move their souls by *spiritual forces*.

We want master teachers! We want master teachers! Here we have the basic and primary note that inspired the student movement in Latin America. In some sense, there is no more orphan and tragic class than the youngsters in our universities. When will we see fulfilled the dream of the Córdoba youngsters, of a true cultural home in which *the only possible teachers . . . will be the builders of souls, the creators of truth, of beauty, of goodness*. Holding the floor are those citizens and institutions who maintain spiritual values are supreme. Realizing that the problems of higher education, like all human problems, are really ethical problems, they must devote greater vision and effort to form men, so that master teachers will develop.

Later Influence of the Reform Movement

The history of the reforming movement in the rest of the Latin American universities is recorded in Volume VI of the work titled *The University Reform* (*La Reforma Universitaria*) published in 1927 by the University Federation of Buenos Aires. It is interesting to notice how, little by little, this student movement stops occupying itself with university problems in order now, in preference, to occupy itself with social and political questions.

In November 1918 the Argentinian University Federation expressed itself on the Pacific dispute, and in October 1920, "Against World Imperialism." Agreements in 1920 between Argentinian and Chilean and

Argentinian and Peruvian students established that the students of those republics ought to work for intellectual interchange between their respective countries; for reform of education; for a more intensive culture of the lower classes and the organization of popular universities sustained by the youth; for an effective ideal of Americanism, seeking the rapprochement of all the peoples of the continent; and for the exchange of students of the institutes of higher learning.

A document called "Organization and Declaration of Principles agreed upon at the First Chilean Student's Convention of 1920" includes some extremely revealing articles on the spirit and tendencies of the Chilean university students at that time.

Referring to the fundamental principles and means of action of the student federation, the document states:

> It is one of the highest aims to fight against all forms of immorality.

On the social question it states the following:

> Viewing the real needs of the present time, it is considered that the social problem should be solved by the replacement of the principle of cooperation by the principle of competency, the socialization of the productive strengths and the consistent common distribution, and for the effective recognition of the right of each person to live fully his moral and intellectual life.[44]

> It is declared, finally, that all real social progress implies the moral and cultural improvement of individuals.

Concerning international problems it states, among other things, the following:

> In international conflicts it will subject at all times the interest of the individual, of the family, and of the mother country to the supreme ideals of justice and human fraternity....
> It condemns wars in general, which are violations of the rights and of the freedom of the peoples.
> It will work towards the ideal of the simultaneous abolition of armies of all nations, for the application to international law of the rules of private law, and for a continuous interchange of ideas and sentiments among the different peoples.

Thus it happened that a movement that began claiming new teachers in the cloisters, ended up in a few years asking for a new humanity on earth.

---

44. The communist party in Chile was founded in 1922. —Trans.

So that the students meeting in the Mexican International Congress in 1921 began the list of resolutions with this statement:

> The university youth proclaims that it will fight for the advent of a new humanity, based on modern principles of justice in the economic and in the political order.

III. Results and Consequences of the University Revolution

Let us attempt to strike a balance of this movement. Where did it lead? How shall we evaluate it?

Academic Reforms

The early results, as could be supposed, were of an academic type. The students of several countries, notably those in Argentina and Peru, obtained modifications in the national university organization. But it must be recognized that in both cases the voice of the students was listened to by their respective governments for political rather than educational reasons. In Peru, for example, the student strike at the beginning of the reform movement in that country coincided with the ascension to the presidency of the republic of Don Augusto Leguía, who did not highly esteem higher university authorities at the time.

In those cases in which the students' efforts were successful, the main reforms introduced were the following. First, those professors that the students considered incompetent were fired. It must be noted that the government and the university authorities took the students' "right to dismiss" very seriously only at the time of the reorganization of the university. Second, the university professors had to be chosen by a competition, able to retain their chairs for ten years, after which they had to give in to a new competition. Third, free attendance was established, abolishing the attendance list. The students' idea behind this proposal was that they would not be required to attend the lectures of the bad professors. It was clearly understood by all that the students would willingly attend the lectures of the good professors. Fourth, the students got the right to be represented by a number of delegates in the university council. In some universities these delegates had to be professionals, former delegates of the university; in some others, like the University of La Plata, they could be students.

One could almost say that of all these reforms not one remains in Latin American universities, except student representation in the university councils, and, to some extent, free attendance. Concerning the first, it has turned out to be an improvement, even when, at the time of choosing the delegates, it encourages political games; with reference to the latter, that is, voluntary attendance, it has turned out to be a serious evil. Instead of increasing the enthusiasm of the students to acquire knowledge, it has contributed to intensifying the traditional practice of not studying during the whole year and to cram for the exams in the final few weeks.

From the point of view of the academy, life at the university remains as it was ten years ago. True reform will have to begin from the inside. Neither the government nor the student body can reform the university. One or the other can identify poor teachers and fire them, for example, but neither one nor the other can replace them with better ones. Let us repeat it once more: the problem of the university is, above all, a problem of men.[45]

Social Aspects

In the field of social services, on the other hand, the students' movement had beautiful results. The deep human passion which inspired the young revolutionaries was expressed in the consecration of many of them to an effort of university extension. Here and there popular universities were born. Cuban students meeting in Havana at the end of 1923 expressed the duties of the students towards blue collar workers in the following terms. "The student has the duty to spread his knowledge throughout the society, mainly among the manual proletariat, because this is the closest element to the intellectual proletariat, and in this way men have to become brothers in their work, to form a new society, free of parasites and tyrants, where people will live only by virtue of their own efforts." No one who reads these words will fail to realize that this is not the mere altruistic diffusion of culture, but of preparing the masses for their later participation in a crusade destined to modify the existing society. This was the reason why many governments looked with suspicion on the cultural work developed by the students among the masses of workers.

---

45. A human problem. —Trans.

Initiatives of Peruvian Students

The González Prada Popular University of Lima, Peru, no doubt offers us the best example of a work of university extension initiated and maintained by students. This work was founded in January 1921 by the student Haya de la Torre, who two years earlier had headed the movement in favor of university reform in Peru. Backed by a group of students of advanced social ideas, this young man was able to win the confidence of the proletarian masses. In addition to giving lectures on elementary culture, the youths gave talks on diverse subjects, simultaneously starting anti-alcoholic and sanitary campaigns. They also directed artistic evenings and picnics. The life of an industrial town called Vitarte located about twelve miles from the capital was transformed. In the town each year the Day of the Tree is celebrated. In all some six hundred trees were planted there, whose care became the responsibility of the workers. This neighborhood, that had been a terror for the police, became more and more moral. The young Haya de la Torre became the idol of the people. Everything went fine until May of 1923, when the relations between students and workers took a political turn that brought about the government's intervention.

Political Aspect

With this we come to consider the political aspect of the university revolution. The heads of the movement were, in the main, as we have been able to notice, students with advanced ideas in social and political matters.

In liberal countries like Argentina, Uruguay, and Mexico, in which legislation is already very advanced and where socialist ideas have for years been a power regulating legislative activities, the leftist ideology of the students had barely any public repercussion. But it did not happen the same way in the countries of the Pacific, Chile, Bolivia, and Peru, where the social problem is always found in a delicate situation. The formation of a united front of students and workers in Chile in 1920 led to some bloody encounters with government forces, resulting in the death and jailing of some students and the deportation of others.

In Peru the conflict between the student-worker group and the government took place in May 1923. Following a mass meeting that took place in the university to protest the consecration of the republic to a brass image of the Sacred Heart of Jesus, the armed forces attacked the students and workers who attended the meeting on their way out to the street. One student and one worker died. The demonstration of mourning, organized two days later at the funeral of the dead companions, was impressive, with at least thirty thousand men of all social classes, and on that same night a decree was issued by the government, suspending the ceremony that had motivated the protest. But from that day on the government began to take steps to crush the student–worker entente. In September of that same year, Haya de la Torre who had been the soul of all that had happened, was taken prisoner and exiled from the country. His deportation was followed by that of numerous other Peruvian students.

The APRA

Now a new political influence of the reform movement appeared. The exiled students of Latin American countries, especially the Peruvian ones, took the initiative in the formation of a political entity called Alianza Popular Revolucionaria Americana[46] or APRA as it is usually known. This new group was organized in Paris, in 1924 by Haya de la Torre, who has acted since then as its general secretary.

An article he published in *The Labour Monthly* of London in December, 1926, reveals the program and organization of APRA. The article states:

> The APRA which has become the anti-imperialist, revolutionary Latin American party is a new international organization formed by the young generation of manual and intellectual workers of several countries of Latin America. It already has a vast division in Perú and divisions in México and the Argentinian Republic, Central America, etc. and with a division in Europe whose center at present is Paris, where a sufficiently numerous nucleus of students and workers is organized, with subdivisions in Germany, Spain, and England....

Its program consists of the following five points that we quote verbatim from Volume VI of the opus *The University Reform*: first, action against *yanki* imperialism; second, for the political unity of Latin America; third, for the nationalization of lands and industry; fourth, for the internationalization of the Panama Canal; fifth, for solidarity with all the oppressed peoples and classes of the world.

According to the data that it has been possible to collect, the program of this party does not enjoy high prestige or support either among the current generation of students or even among the socialists and communists of Latin America. The latter ones fight APRA because it has drawn inspiration

---

46. American Popular Revolutionary Alliance. —Ed.

more from the programs of the Chinese revolution than the Russian one, while the socialists and the students, in general, do not take it seriously. At the present moment each Latin American country is more and more concerned about its own problems than concerned with a Latin American movement. It seems that the members of one of the main cells of the party, Peruvians in the majority, have recognized the situation and have addressed the other cells in the following terms:

> In the meantime, companions, we must not continue spending energy on a continental campaign that threatens to die of lack of understanding, divisions, intrigues, and bluffs. We must peruvianize our action.

Here ends a whole cycle of youthful idealism, that sought to involve the whole world in its flight, with all its human problems. Now it has returned to its nest to die in it or to attempt a new flight. Just a small number of the old revolutionaries continue struggling to realize their juvenile daydreams. The new student generation appears apathetic in general to social and political problems, and even to the university ones. In some cases chauvinism has followed internationalism in the atmosphere of the cloisters. All this shows that institutional life is like individual life, that it will never revolutionize itself by violent peripheral action, but only by the presence of ferments.

IV. New Ferments in University Life

For the time being, as we have said, neither the social nor the political nor even university problems excite the student youth. If something moves them, or at least a growing number of studious youths, it is a new metaphysical concern. Perhaps later on this will be the source of the true university revolution.

Spiritual Awakening

A new cycle of concerns is arising in the old cloisters. It may be said that materialism as a philosophical system has been toppled in the majority of the Latin American universities. Comte, Spencer, and Haeckel have found refuge in a few law and medical faculties, but they have been completely eliminated from the faculties of philosophy and letters. A hot stream of spiritualism has found its way through the hard positivist crust. The universe does not appear as a mechanical and closed system, as it appeared to professors and students a little more than ten years ago. Neither is the hegemony of the intellect considered the only discoverer and standard of truth. It is recognized also that the heart has its reasons and intuition its accurate visions.

New Philosophical Influences

Diverse influences have contributed to the spiritual awakening. Primarily we must mention the influence of Henri Bergson. As soon as the creative evolution of the French philosopher got into the university environment, positivism started retreating; Boutroux,[47] Höffding,[48] Eucken,[49] and Otto contributed to reinforce the victory of the new spiritualist orientation.

The South American visit in 1925 of the eminent Spanish thinker, José Ortega y Gasset marked an era of new influence on the philosophical thinking in Argentina. He was the one who brought to the Rio de la Plata the new German currents, especially the one emanating from Marburg where the new generation of Spanish intellectuals had been educated. Later on, Ortega y Gasset founded the *Revista de Occidente* through which he has disseminated throughout Latin America the new orientations of European thought. He also worked in cooperation with several other intellectuals in producing translations of numerous contemporary philosophical works, especially German ones. In this way books that have turned out to be classics were published in Spanish, like the *Decline of the West* by Spengler, *The Idea of the Holy* by Otto, and *The World in the Making* by Keyserling. The first and last of these works appeared in Spanish long before they were published in English, which demonstrates that as of today Latin America is in closer contact with the sources of contemporary ideology. The French influence is ebbing, and the German is increasing. In all likelihood the most influential contemporary thinker among the young intellectuals in Latin America is

---

47. Émile Boutroux (1845–1921) was a French philosopher of science and religion, and an opponent of materialism in science. —Ed.

48. Harald Höffding (1843–1931) was a Danish positivist philosopher. —Ed.

49. Rudolf Christoph Eucken (1846–1926) was a German idealist philosopher who won the Nobel Prize for Literature in 1908. That same year his book, *The Meaning and Value of Life*, was published. —Ed.

Count Keyserling. When we consider the dominant trends of this thinker, for example, how he places the ideal of spiritual perfection above the ideal of progress, and that in one of his last books—up until now translated only in French under the title *Figures Simboliques*— he dedicates a special study to Jesus, whom he considers the most powerful spiritual personality of all times and the source of all the dynamic that can be found in Western civilization, it is not difficult to foresee that a complete reevaluation of Christ and what is Christian is going to begin in these countries.

Literary Influences

There have also been literary influences that have predisposed the Latin American intellectuals to favor spiritual values. In this sense the disquieting works of this great Christian thinker, Don Miguel de Unamuno, have had a profound influence; similarly, Romain Rolland, especially through his lives of Tolstoy and of Gandhi. The writings of Tolstoy, and even more so those of Dostoyevsky, have opened a new world of Christian values to the contemplation of our intellectuals. This is so clear that one does not exaggerate in saying that, in the moral sense of the most leftist of them, the figure of Christ has been etched and has come to represent the highest value known. How could it be otherwise, when the French Communist Henri Barbusse, whose books have had an enormous circulation in the Hispanic countries, wrote a book recently titled *Jesus*, and on the title page states, "I have seen Jesus, too. . . . I love him; I have him attached to my heart, and I will debate others, if necessary." Not only that: an indigenous author, the most cultivated poet and historian, Don Ricardo Rojas, has given us a book on Jesus. Who can measure the significance of the fact that for the first time in the history of Latin American letters, a front rank man of letters has written with love and depth about Jesus Christ, calling himself Christian at the same time, and stating that in the gospels he had found at last the satisfaction that for a long time his head and his heart had desired?

Religious Influences

In addition to these philosophical and literary influences, we have to point to some strictly religious influences that have been felt recently in the university world of Latin America. Here are some of them. Facing the reigning religious indifference, the Catholic Church has adopted a new tactic in recent years. She has made an effort to add prestige to religion, that is, the Catholicism among the university elements, in the presentation of the

Christian message, dispensing with the traditional liturgical vestments. Some three years ago a young Spanish Jesuit showed up in Montevideo and Buenos Aires who called himself a disciple of the famous histologist Ramón y Cajal. After having given some biological lectures in the universities of both countries that were very well received, he returned to Spain. He came back one year later, and after just one lecture in the university, he threw himself into an evangelical campaign in the churches of his order. Night after night an enormous crowd of men, among which there were many university students, remained hanging from his burning words. The greatest novelty was that there was no ritual of any kind either before or after the sermon. The discerning evangelist realized the hostility of the lay public towards rituals, so that he eliminated them in favor of greater attention to his message.

Theosophy has also expanded among the university element. The phenomenal progress this oriental system has achieved is an additional indication of the present spiritual hunger. Toward the end of 1928 a distinguished Hindu philosopher, Dr. Jinarajadasa[50] passed through South America giving lectures. In Montevideo, Buenos Aires, Santiago, and Valparaíso the theaters where this theosophist was lecturing were packed every night with a very exclusive public.

But even more significant has been the success of the lectures of that ecumenical and independent Christian, Don Julio Navarro Monzó, mainly in countries like Chile, Peru, and Mexico. Navarro Monzó, born in Portugal and a naturalized Argentinian citizen, is a highly cultivated man who underwent a deep religious experience in the year 1916, when he was a member of the Orthodox Church in Buenos Aires. In 1922 he abandoned an important government position, and another position in the editorial offices of the great Buenos Aires newspaper, *La Nación*, to bind himself to the South American Federation of Young Men's Christian Associations. From that year on he has written several important books on religion in general and on Christianity in particular and has carried out several tours through Latin America. This personality, with a powerful intellect and extraordinary erudition united to deep personal mysticism of a Johannine type, has done more than any other man to confront the continental intellectual circles with the religious problem and the Christian solution.

We could add to the prior influences the one exercised by the Young Men's Christian Association by means of student camps, which take place

---

50. Curuppumullage Jinarajadasa (1875–1953) was a theosophist born in Sri Lanka, skilled in western languages, who founded branches of the Theosophical Society in Latin America. —Ed.

in several countries of the continent. The life of many a student has been completely transformed by attending one of these camps. The Young Men's Christian Association, through its non-sectarian and non-ecclesiastical character, occupies a very strategic place to work among the university youth. Its dais has high prestige, and it offers one of the best platforms for the Christian lecturer. This was fully demonstrated by the South American tour of Dr. Stanley Jones. In all the cities visited by that great apostle, the association organized the best gatherings. This visit must be added to the constructive spiritual influences in recent years, but there was little that Dr. Jones could have done if he had not found an environment well prepared for his words.

As to the direct influence of the Evangelical churches on the university class, it has been limited so far. But since a growing number of the children of evangelicals are pursuing higher education, and since the number of pastors who have a university career grows, it can be expected that they may leave a deep imprint on the morality and ideology of intellectual circles. The truth is that no prior moment has been as suitable as the present one for the eternal truths of the gospel to ring out on the ears of the studious youth and in the higher spheres of thought.

6

The Philosophy of the Red Triangle

THE LAST CENTURY GAVE the world two new emblems that in war as in peace have symbolized twin aspects of Christian altruism. One is the red cross of the association of that name; the other is the red triangle of the Young Men's Christian Association. The first has become the symbol of a new concern to alleviate the physical suffering of the wounded on the battle fields; the second is the symbol of a new concern for the strengthening of the total health of those who participate in the battle of life. The former takes care of invalids, attempting through its efforts to bring them back to health; the latter deals with healthy individuals, trying to strengthen and guide their present health.

The Red Cross Association was founded to deal with abnormal situations of life, like a war sowing death or a natural cataclysm producing identical effects in the life of peoples. The Young Men's Christian Association was born instead to deal with the perennial conditions of youth in which the bursting of a war or the presence of any catastrophe is only an extraordinary calling to everyday labor. We have here the emblems of two eternal goals of the Christian spirit: to retrieve the health of those who had been deprived of it, to guide the health of those who have it.

We have met in this room to witness the graduation of five young men who, after four years of preparatory technical studies, will be initiated into a new career. Two of them as secretaries and three as directors of physical education will devote themselves from now on to interpret in the screen of their lives the symbolism of the red triangle of the Young Men's Christian Association. It seems timely to offer, in the name of the technical institute of the association, our interpretation of the sacred emblem that decorates the walls of our buildings and the lapels of our members.

Our Shield

Our shield is rather simple but not less original and suggestive. It has an equilateral triangle upside down, which, through the bottom and parallel to the base, has a bar on which the initials of the institution are written. Each side represents and carries the name of one of the constituent aspects of the human person: spirit, mind, and body. It is an excellent synthetic figure, a diagram that proclaims by its form that life is more than a group of lines and angles. It announces an ideal in which all the legitimate directions of the human personality, and also its unavoidable angles, concur to form a symmetrical whole under the tutelage of the spirit. Our triangle contains some of the symmetry of the ball and the angularity of the cross.

But we should not sin in symbolism, nor shall we do so! The red triangle is not, fortunately, a parabola containing esoteric meanings understandable only to those already initiated. It is, rather, an outline carrying its own interpretation printed in itself. The Young Men's Christian Association seeks the goal of contributing to the development of the human personality in the physical, the intellectual, and the spiritual, attempting to form men that will consecrate themselves to pursue the same ideal in their lives and those of others.

Now, no longer speaking in abstract terms, let us ask two concrete and fundamental questions: first, how should we interpret each of the three aspects of the human personality whose full development constitutes the whole ideal of the association? And second, how should we formulate the relationship that must exist among them, not only in the life of the institution, but in the life of each one of its members? The answer to these two questions will be our philosophy of the red triangle.

I

Physical Department

Let us start by asking what do we mean by physical development? Although the side that symbolizes the body does not occupy a preeminent position in our symbolic triangle, we will take it up first because, after all, the body constitutes the basis of life, even if not its crown, as could be imagined by the preferential attention given to it by the majority of men, even within the Young Men's Christian Association itself.

In thousands of gymnasiums and athletic fields innumerable young men carry a red triangle on their chest, live witness to the enthusiasm with which the athletic and sports activities of the association have developed. The association is leaving a very deep imprint on the sporting lives and ideals of our continent. It has introduced some games that are already very popular. In addition, it has promoted sports arenas for children in several South American republics. In at least two of them men prepared in institutes of the association have been appointed by their governments as national directors of physical education. Of the four athletic teams that participated in the South American championship that took place in Montevideo in 1926, two were coached by physical education directors of the association. We could also add that the association has contributed greatly, in some republics more than others, to the creation of a new spirit and new sports norms. Based on data like these many people have reached the conclusion that the Young Men's Christian Association is a sporting club, no more, no less. This was the opinion Dr. José Ingenieros expressed to me on one occasion.

But between the ideal sought by the physical department of our association and the ideal of an athletic or sports association, there is the whole difference between a total physical ideal and a partial physical ideal. An athletic association attempts to form men that will stand out in competitions that will test their physical aptitudes as individuals. A sports association goes further: it attempts to develop and train the physical aptitudes of its members so that they will stand out in team activities or games, as we call them. But the department of physical education of the Young Men's Christian Association seeks, above all, to develop resolute physical aptitudes, and from the success of its teams in the different competitions in which they take part, the ideal is to train its members physically for life itself. The ideal of this department is physical life, and not physical prowess, an ideal that it tries to achieve not through a program of physical training but through a program of physical education. Whatever may be related to athletic or sport's accomplishments do not constitute, nor will they ever constitute, the goal of the physical activities of the Young Men's Christian Associations, only its separate accompaniments. If the day were to arrive in which the physical department of our association were to exist only to win trophies and medals and not to guide all our efforts toward the complete physical health of its members, creating around them an environment that strengthens their nerves and drives away a thousand gnawing concerns, instilling and forming healthy habits, it would have failed in its sacred mission to place sound bodies at the disposal of the mind and of the spirit that will respond to a higher way.

Cultural Work

Interpreting in this way the concept of the association with respect to the physical, let us move to interpret the side of the triangle that carries the name of mind. What is the meaning of mind? We will not drown in psychological or metaphysical analysis. We will take the word in its familiar sense as the equivalent of the capacity of man to think, of setting up goals and attaining them. By virtue of their mental activity, men can propose problems and solve them; they choose a line of work or a career and dedicate themselves to it; they create in their environment a culture of works and thoughts.

What does this side of the red triangle symbolize for the Young Men's Christian Association? What kinds of activities are understood, in speaking of intellectual work? The association states, on the one hand, the common place that each man has the duty to develop his mind, and on the other, it offers certain facilities to the members for the development of theirs. It places libraries and reading rooms at their disposal; it offers lectures on subjects of interest to its members; it organizes conference cycles and, on occasion, artistic evenings. Those associations that have developed great growth of the intellectual department offer their members such privileges that would have to be sought at public libraries, athenaeums, or at an academy or university.

Unfortunately, there are some associations that have given a very narrow interpretation to the intellectual activities that take place in them. They have confused the intellectual work with the organization of commercial courses. There are associations where these courses have turned the building where they operate into a kind of school, monopolizing an amount of time and energy that does not have a proper relation with their importance. In such cases it has been decided to follow an opportunistic policy that ends up misrepresenting the true concept of intellectual work in the Young Men's Christian Association.

There are other associations whose lectures follow no definite plan, in which the air of the library smells of moths, where no breaths of intellectual curiosity can be felt, where one finds only bourgeois youths who live at the margin of life and of ideas. The mere mention of a conference or a debate is enough to terrify them. In the meantime, in the cities where such associations are located, there must be hundreds even thousands of youngsters thirsting for ideas who up to now do not find in the milieu of the association what may satisfy their curiosity for knowledge or their desire for solutions. Should the association have something in its program to attract such youth to its interior? If they are not interested in commercial clubs, nor feel enthusiasm for old books, comfortable seats, baths, sports, and cheap meals, should the association offer them something that will attract their interests?

It is necessary, obviously, to think again about the concept of "mind," and to formulate anew the class of activities that expresses it best within the association. I dare to suggest some norms that will help us to determine the significance of this concept. In the first place, every local association has to start from the immediate needs of its own members in matters of education. It follows that it will not be possible to completely forgo the utilitarian aspect in the interpretation of intellectual work. In dealing with members who want to study some matters for the immediate goals in their lives, it is a duty of the association to offer its help—but with this caveat, that in doing so, it will not be duplicating facilities available to youths in equally favorable conditions in some other quarter. In the second place, it is appropriate for each association to awaken a lively interest in its members for the great manifestations of human genius, for the great problems that have roused humanity, and in this way, as it were, also for the problems and principal stages of life in our age. It is necessary that our members live the life of their time intensely, and the association has the duty to put them on the right path toward it.

But at the same time we should not forget that the intellectual department of the Young Men's Christian Association cannot exist only to discuss problems but also to solve them. It must offer all the advantages of an open forum without becoming one. It will tend to search for truth without forgetting that it possesses a truth worthy of being known. It will reveal to its members the most beautiful manifestations of universal genius without forgetting that it is a work of Christian genius. In other words, one of the goals of this department consists in interpreting and showing objectively the association as one of the great creations of the spirit and its triangle as the symbol of a saving truth of contemporary civilization.

The Concept of Spirit and Spirituality

With this we have arrived at consideration of the third side of our triangle, the one that has the name of spirit. Historically it is the base of the triangle, and it is its logical summit, the sun that illuminates it, the starry sky of its ideals.

The words "soul" and "spirit" are synonymous in the terminology of the association, as in popular language. I prefer "spirit" because it is a more comprehensive and suggestive term. Without preoccupying ourselves particularly with the psychological geography or the metaphysical identity of the spirit, let us say that this is the inviolable safe of man, the seat of ideals that move him, the hidden room where he can look eternity face to face and have communion with the eternal one. The character of a man is determined by the gods that he adores in the sanctuary of his spirit, and, over all, by the character of his preferred god, that he worships as the lord of his life.

All the great human movements have started from the inviolable certainty of a given man. From time to time through the centuries new prophetic voices have sounded; clean springs have flowed; shining flames of fire have appeared; hurricanes have been unleashed—all of them emanations of the spirit for the renewal of the world. They have transformed the life of entire generations.

The Ideals

A man begins living at the moment in which, amazed in his interior sanctuary, he catches a glimpse of an ideal of life that will grab his heart. And he will have the right to call himself a free man from the moment in which, having gone out from safety to daily life, he proclaims his ideal and lives according to it. It may be necessary, perhaps, to live a lonely and ridiculed life, to fight in a minority at all times, but, all in all, he will be a free man, a spiritual man in the widest sense of the word. He will be one because he saw a truth and had the daring not to silence it. On the other hand, those men who ignore the existence of an interior sanctuary, who will be afraid of staying alone within themselves, that lack their own convictions, will not be free men but windmills or automatic toys. They will start moving by the gusts of loud popular voices or the influence of their particular interests.

Just as the mind deals with ideas, the spirit deals with ideals. So that the spiritual man, in the widest sense of the word, is the one who, like the pearl merchant of the gospel parable, discovers something of such great value that he immediately sacrifices everything to own it.[51] Spiritual ideals are not obtained by inheritance, but each person has to discover his own in the sanctuary of his soul and make himself the full owner of them, embodying them in the daily fight.

But the connotation that the Young Men's Christian Association gives to the top side of the triangle, although it includes all the elements already mentioned about spirituality, is infinitely richer and more concrete. The red triangle symbolizes a specific form of spirituality. It advocates, not ideals in general, but a particular ideal; not an abstract principle to lead life, but a concrete personality that transforms souls. The Young Men's Christian Association, in the selection of the symbolic triangle, and giving the name of spirit to its upper side, wanted to proclaim, not just the existence of and

---

51. See Matt 13:45–46. —Ed.

the preeminence of ideals, but also to state clearly its conviction that Christ embodies concretely in his personality and in his ideas the highest conceivable ideals, and that the solution of all human problems, be they personal, social, or international, consists in the acceptance of him and his teaching, by each and every person.

The New Search for the Christian Ideal

The popularity of an ideal proves nothing—I know that well. I cannot, though, avoid calling attention to the reaction that has occurred in recent times on behalf of a new study of the personality and the teachings of Jesus. Contemporary intellectuals have begun a pilgrimage to those olden times when the Galilean lived on the earth. One can find them marching, Mahatma Gandhi, Henri Barbusse, Bernard Shaw, H. G. Wells, Miguel de Unamuno, and an additional hundred crusaders who are trying to rescue the sepulcher of Christ from the exclusive possession of the "bachelors, curates, barbers, canons, and dukes" of traditional ecclesiasticism. The Christian search has become secularized in our times. Every honest man, every being who is agonizing to find new paths for the current apathy wants to look for himself at the uncovered face of Jesus. He studies, then, with infinite anxiety, the gospels, those four poems in prose about Christ, as Oscar Wilde called them from his prison, where he read them with renewed interest. In the Hindustani city of Ahmedabad, Mahatma Gandhi is currently delivering a course on Jesus and his ideas to the students of a nationalist college, at their own request. Last September Henri Barbusse, upon ending his new book titled *Jesus*, wrote on the cover, "J'ai vu Jésus, moi aussi" (I have seen Jesus, too). So, people want to see Jesus as much in the East as in the West.

Christophiles

There is no lack of people who, although not Christians in the ecclesiastical sense of the word, call themselves "Christophiles," professing a limitless love for Christ. The truth is that there is no more highly important current phenomenon than "Christophilia," if I may be allowed to coin such a word. And so who will dare to call the attitude of our association anachronistic or archaeological for consecrating the name of Christ in its official title, advocating in this way a specific Christian spirituality?

How can we describe, then, the spiritual ideal of the association? It consists in being a loyal disciple of Christ. It has its roots in a deep spiritual satisfaction and its blooms in a life that will give off the aroma of the Master. It unites the most tender religious sentiment to the most pure moral activity. The disciple of Christ loves his Master and lives in spiritual communion with him, inspired at all times by his example and his teachings, so that the principal manifestations of his spiritual life will be love and goodness. He passionately loves the Lord of his life and loves and serves his neighbor with altruism.

The feeling of love by which a man feels attracted to Jesus and becomes a "Christophile" can have different hues according to the motive that inspires it. It will be a kind of esthetic love, in which Jesus is loved for the unmatched beauty and poetry of his life. He is loved as one could love a poet, whose life was also a poem. "I had said of Christ," said Oscar Wilde in *De Profundis*, "that he ranks with the poets. That is true. Shelley and Sophocles are of his company." And later he adds, "Christ is just like a work of art. He does not really teach one anything, but by being brought into his presence one becomes something."

One can become a "Christophile" also through a sentiment of intellectual love, that is, love for the ethical values that the life of Jesus incarnates, and by the sublime principles that he announced. One loves him for his beautiful abnegation, for his absolute fidelity to his cause, for the sublime adventure of the cross. Or one falls in love with him for the idea, the most revolutionary of history, that behind the veil of matter and deeds lives a being with the heart of a father.

Furthermore, who would not be enthusiastic, like Tolstoy, for the concept of the kingdom of God, for the principles of non-resistance of turning the other cheek to the aggressor, and would stop feeling deep affection for its author? Intellectual love is what a man like Bernard Shaw feels for Jesus; he who believes deeply that the principles of the Galilean contain the only remedy for the problems of civilization, and who, in view of the last European conflagration, said, "The only gentleman who has come out of the war with his reputation unharmed is Jesus of Nazareth." With this love many great revolutionaries and reformers of society have loved, and still love, Jesus.

The Christophilia of the Born Again

Nevertheless, another shade remains in this rich concept. There are Christophiles whose affection for the Master has been born in the experience of an interior transformation worked in their souls by their contact with him. They resorted to him at times of deep moral malaise, when they were anxious to find peace and purity. Face to face with him, they experience that feeling of the "luminous" mentioned by Otto in his already famous book *The Idea of the Holy*. They felt as though in the presence of God himself, who would talk to them through Christ. Overwhelmed by a feeling of sovereign love that embraces them, they deliver their personality to that other one. Afterwards, they enjoy an ineffable peace, while the new love that inspires them begins expelling from their insides all vile affection and all dishonest tendencies. The dramatic scene which ended that banquet that St. Luke mentions in his gospel is repeated time and again with the colors of our time. A man called Zacchaeus, a tax collector, had invited Jesus into his home. During dinner he felt so strongly moved in the presence of his guest and—realizing that he could not enjoy his affection and appreciation if he were to remain in his vile deeds—said, "Behold, Lord, the half of my goods I give to the poor; and if I have defrauded anyone of anything, I restore it fourfold."[52]

Analogous experience moved the founders of the Young Men's Christian Association to call Christ "Redeemer," because they found out that he redeems every man, who subjects himself to his influence, from the power of evil and from all selfishness. In addition, they called him "Divine" because in him, and only in him, they were able to find the infinite God with enough concreteness as to be able to love and trust him. Our personal witness should reveal that, for a restless soul seeking a transcendental satisfaction, there is nothing better to escape from a cloudy and sterile mysticism, than through the throbbing personality of Christ. For this reason one loves him with infinite devotion.

Beyond Virtue

The second element in this spiritual ideal of becoming Christ's disciple is kindness. This kindness must be distinguished clearly from something usually called virtue. A person is considered virtuous when he lives in agreement with certain ethical norms, either the norms established by an absolute law that commands human life, or norms originating in the social conventions of his time. But it happens very often that a virtuous person, in this sense of irreproachable character and conduct, completely lacks any human warmth. His virtue is limited to keeping some precepts and not transgressing the frontiers of correctness. His only concern consists in knowing what his duty is and fulfilling it. Everything that remains outside of the sphere of his explicit duties does not interest him. His favorite motto is the "just mean," a watchword of the old Athenians. And, as for those, their ideal in

---

52. See Luke 19:8. —Ed.

life is more esthetical than ethical. All the beauty of his conduct will be that of a Greek statue, and it will be equally as cold.

But the kindness of our Christian ideal lies in a quality superior to mere virtue. It is an attitude toward life that is not ruled by precepts, not even by principles, but from an instinctive love. Without ignoring virtue, when this coincides with general principles of morality, it is especially characterized by going beyond what is required by the law and by conventions. There will be no frontier that such a disciple of Christ will not cross, nor social convention that he will not be willing to get around, each time that it may become necessary to do so in favor of a humanity in need. He considers it, not only as personal duty, but on the basis of someone else's needs. He will not ask, "Who is my neighbor?" But, "Of whom could I be a neighbor?" In the life of a true disciple of Christ, the selfish and whimsical "I" disappears, while in its place acts a new personality loved by Christ, modeled on Christ, and consecrated to express, through all the actions of life, that sublime human passion that Christ described in the parable of the Good Samaritan.[53]

Here we have the concrete and throbbing ideal symbolized by the upper side of the red triangle.

II

Our explanation of the meaning of "spirit" may perhaps seem excessively long. But its length will make it much easier to discover the ideal relationship that must exist between the physical, the intellectual, and the spiritual in the work of the association.

The Ideal Relationship Is Not Mechanical

Needless to say, the relationship between the three aspects will not be of a mechanical nature. They do not represent three independent spheres of life, each one complete in itself that are juxtaposed only to form a mosaic. They do not represent, either, elements of equal importance to be installed in the cogwheels of the institutional machine so that it can operate. The reason is not difficult to find. The physical department, for example, cannot be looked on as a complete sphere in itself. It could very well happen that many of its most distinguished and perfect constituents were nothing but strong and healthy animals, some of them completely ignorant, and some others certified egoists. Many members could exist, whose principal interests were in

---

53. Luke 10:30–37. —Ed.

culture in all its manifestations, but they could be just contemporary Hellenics, spending their whole life in perfumed balconies, loaded with flowers, away from any real contact with the people. To the sinful and desolate they would at best offer a book, a song, or a musical piece that they could very well give without leaving the balcony, while the need of those poor souls is friends of the road.[54] And it would not be unusual that some members could interpret the essence of the spiritual so narrowly that their interest in the association would be limited to the celebration of pious gatherings, without making of them a field in which the spiritual will realize itself in works, without giving in love of neighbor what they receive in the contemplation of God. In this way, any attempt at isolating one or another expression of the physical, the intellectual, and the spiritual within the life of the association, keeping them independent, creating around them the interests of a club, would end up destroying the symbolism of the red triangle.

It Is Not of a Biological Order

The relationship between the three aspects symbolized by the triangle is not of a biological order either. In biology the vital phenomena undergo an evolution passing through successive steps in a gradual ascent to its final and perfect form. Thus, in the passing of time, and by a natural process, a stalk will sprout from the seed of the rose; from the stalk, new shoots will grow; from these, leaves, and at last, the buds that will perfume the garden. But the most intensive cultivation of the physical department will not be able, through any natural law, to awaken interest for culture; nor will the conversation of the association in a kind of athenaeum or academy be able to create an altruistic and Christian spirit in the members. More likely it would happen that the inordinate and myopic concentration on physical life would end up turning the association into an athletic or sporting club, while a unilateral enthusiasm on culture would produce a kind of dilettantism that would always be talking of light and beauty when the world would be demanding fire and strength. And it is no exaggeration to say that the exclusive concern for cultivating the interior life, as an end in itself, would unavoidably lead to a bastard spirituality, selfish and barren.

---

54. See "Two Perspectives: The Balcony and the Road" in Mackay, *Preface*, 27–54. —Ed.

One Can Find It by Analogy with Life

Not by analogy with mechanics or biology will we have to interpret the symbolism of the red triangle but through an analogy taken from life itself. Two decisive factors determine the life of a man or of an organization: the ideals it holds and the moral strength that it possesses to develop them. Both factors are concerned with the spiritual terrain. Therefore, life is happy when the spirit dominates it. Thus it must be, also, with the Young Men's Christian Association; it will work well, and it will fulfill its mission in the world only by living fully under the hegemony of the spirit. Let us not forget that the institution that develops its activities under the aegis of the red triangle is, above all, a Christian spiritual organization. It was born from an ideal of service to youth. This ideal was inspired by Christ and carried to fruition in some fifty countries by men who called Christ their Master. Since these men believed that what the world needs most is that men may be true disciples of Christ, they wished that the association that they founded would contribute to the realization of that end. Convinced at the same time that the sole guarantee that the association would follow in the altruistic path that they drew up was that every man who, not happy with the selfish enjoyment of the privileges that it offers, would, in addition, want to cooperate actively in the propagation of her spirit and supervise her fate, and would sign a personal declaration of principles stating his loyalty to Christ and to his cause.

Toward an Ideal Association

An association in which the three departments maintained an ideal relationship among them would be one in which all the members were interested in all three. Each department would have its windows and doors open wide to allow free access to the influences of the other two, and also to be able to attend the calls from the others. What happens now would not occur if some members were to go to the premises exclusively to exercise, others to eat, some to read or listen to a lecture, and a few to pray, each withdrawing into the shell of their particular interests. All members could find something in the three departments that could contribute to the development of their personality. In the physical department they would strengthen their health, in the intellectual they would broaden their knowledge and would exercise their minds, and in the department of moral and spiritual education they would find the inspiration and the power necessary to help them to lead a saintly and altruistic life worthy of Christ.

This ideal will be realized only in so far as the members experience the transforming influence of Christ in their lives. His enthronement in the place that corresponds to him, in the life of the institution and in the life of each member, is the key to our success. And success, how will it be judged? Not by the magnificence of the buildings that we may be able to build here and there around the continent, nor by the social prestige that we may attain, but by the number of our members that will leave, in the length of the path they walk, unmistakable traces that will be reminders of the world of the Master whose instructions they carry.

Young friends, new colleagues, comrades in the holy crusade of placing the red triangle on the chest of youth, may your initiation in this race be a new starting point for an interpenetration of South American life with the influence and ideals of Christ the Renewer.

7

Is There a Relationship between the Young Men's Christian Association and Religion?

To SUPPLY AN ANSWER to this question, I will examine first the principal terms in it, that is, the concept of "religion" and the organization known as "Young Men Christian Association." Before we attempt to discuss seriously the relationship between them, it is necessary to work out the meaning of the first term and to understand the character of the second. In this way we will avoid the sterile effort to develop an opinion on the relationships between two entities whose essence is not known. This preliminary study becomes indispensable in this situation, where so many contradictory opinions exist about the essence of the one and the other basic terms.

Two Common Opinions about Religion

Two opposing opinions can be heard concerning the meaning of religion. For many religion is understood as an institutional or ecclesiastical loyalty. It consists, according to this point of view, in the total surrender of ones personality to an established authority who will then satisfy all spiritual concerns.

Maurice Barrès in France, and Manuel Gálvez in South America, not to mention others, have proposed a religious ideal that identifies religion with compliance with a venerable authority consecrated by tradition and age. By accepting a fixed body of thought and obeying detailed rules one can, in the phrase of Barrès, "reach agreement with life." Gálvez states that only in this way can one discover the unity of ones being. At the same time he praises a religious doctrine that accepts no argument. In this way, the Argentinian author states, students will get a norm for life that will avoid the torment of uncertainty and will insure them the recovery of peace.[55] In his last book, *The Agony of Christianity*, Unamuno mentions this educational ideal. Don Miguel tells of a friend of his who saw in some school a painting representing St. Michael, the archangel, who had the devil satan under his feet. "The rebellious angel had in his hand a microscope! The microscope is the symbol of hyperanalysis!"

The opinion of those who consider religion a synonym for spiritual slavery is very different. They identify it with obscurantism, with intolerance, with lack of progress, and with all kinds of superstitions. Or they think, with Comte, that every religion involves an anachronistic attitude towards the universe that nowadays is to be replaced by science. Or they state, as the Soviets, that "religion is the opium of the people." They reject the idea that a man could possibly be an intellectual and a religious person.

In Peru I met a young university student, a superior and idealistic spirit, who was fully consecrated to the service of his fellow human beings, for whom the mere name of God was repellent. He refused to mention it, saying that in his experience it was a word so bound up to hypocrisy and social injustice that the mere sound of the word gave him serious disgust. The same point of view has inspired, certainly, the extreme radical government of Uruguay, to attempt to wipe out from the calendar any name with a religious connotation, calling the day of the Nativity "Family Day," and turning Holy Week into "Touring Week."

Wrong Opinions about the Young Men's Christian Association

There are similarly opposing opinions, and not less mistaken, about the true character of the Young Men's Christian Association.

There are those who insist that the association is an ecclesiastical institution, a church, or the appendix of a church. They are mistaken. It is a lay organization, founded by a lay person and governed by lay directors. In it there are no hierarchy, no sacraments, and no rites. It does not attempt to replace the church in the life of its members, nor do they have to change one church for another. A young man joins it, not as a member of a church, but as a personal decision if he wishes to be an adherent member [*socio adherente*] or through a personal statement of principles if he wishes to be

---

55. Gálvez, *Solar de la Raza*, 257.

an active member [*socio activo*]. The personal basis is a condition for admission, and it is already universal even in the United States where last year it was substituted for the ecclesiastical basis of Portland.[56]

Its principles within the framework of Christianity are not sectarian. They do not attempt to separate people, but to join them together, given that members from all confessions are found within the wide and liberal bosom of the association.

But in any case it may be stated that it is a Protestant institution. If this means that it is a daughter of Protestantism in the ecclesiastical sense of the word, that is, in the sense that it has been founded by a church or a group of churches, then certainly not. Neither does it obey the control of any church or group of churches. On the other hand, if it means that the founder was Protestant, and that it advocates the principle of freedom of examination, that is, the right and inevitable duty of every man to think for himself—including upon religious matters—then yes, it is Protestant. But if such is the case, where but in the bosom of Protestantism could a free and autonomous organization like this be born? Because autonomy is one of the most sacred attributes of the Young Men's Christian Association. The World Committee, with headquarters in Geneva, does not recognize any ecclesiastical control, and each national movement, each local association, is equally autonomous.

So, then, the Young Men's Christian Association is not a church or a sect. To become a member one does not have to belong to a given church, nor is one required to associate with any church after becoming a member. The least and the most that is required of an active member is that he should be a Christian in his personal attitudes toward Christ and his teachings.

There are some who say, on the other hand, that the association is a sporting club. This was the opinion expressed by José Ingenieros[57] in a conversation several years ago. And a number of people have this same belief. Yet, there is a deep and radical difference between the association and a club. A club, be it political, equine, sporting, or whatever, is based on the pleasure of its members or their particular interests. The members will not concern themselves except with what interests them or their group. But the Young Men's Christian Association has not been founded on the interests or desires of a small circle but on human ideals. It advocates and pursues

---

56. The personal basis meant that membership in a church is not a prerequisite for membership in the YMCA, but, as noted in the text below, a member "should be a Christian in his personal attitudes toward Christ and his teaching." The ecclesiastical basis of membership meant that church membership was a prerequisite for membership in the YMCA. —Ed.

57. José Ingenieros (1877–1925) was an Argentinian psychiatrist, author, and rationalist. —Ed.

the superior ideal of human perfection. It attempts to form dynamic men of integrity who will consecrate their physical strength, their clear intelligence, and their moral virtues to the service of others in the hope that in due time the beneficiaries may get to represent and pursue the same ideal of service. Having finished these preliminary observations, let us consider in a positive way how the religious problem is looked upon in contemporary thought and what is the attitude of the Young Men's Christian Association towards this problem.

The Religious Problem in Contemporary Thought

One of the characteristics of our times is the extraordinary interest in religious studies. Religion is no longer seen as an anachronistic concern or as the proper study for archeologists. Distinguished authors in all the countries in the forefront of intellectual development, philosophers and scientists, poets and fiction writers, all of them devote ample space to the consideration of that subject. Since the times of Tolstoy and Ibsen, religion has been one of the favorite subjects of the great European authors. Looking at two countries as different as England and Spain, we find that, in the first H. G. Wells, G. K. Chesterton, and Bernard Shaw, and, in the second, Unamuno and Ramiro de Maeztu,[58] will not go for a year without touching the religious problem. Chesterton and Unamuno published new books in the last year. The book by the first is called *The Everlasting Man* and studies mainly the personality of Christ; the second one, published in French, is entitled *L'Agonie du Christianisme*. A few weeks ago I received a book in English with the title *Science, Religion, and Reality*. It has an introduction written by Lord Balfour, the most distinguished philosophical thinker in England, with such articles as the following, "Science and Religion in the Nineteenth Century" by Antonio Alitta, Professor of Philosophy at the University of Naples; "Mechanistic Biology and Religious Conscience" by Joseph Needham, Professor of Biochemistry at Cambridge University; and "Religion and Psychology" by William Brown, Professor of Philosophy at Oxford University. And what a surprise I had last year when one of my students at the University of Lima showed me a Spanish translation of the most famous book on religion of recent years written by the German professor, Rudolf Otto, published in Spain by the group of the *Revista de Occidente* with the title *The Idea of the Holy*! A translation of the same book had appeared in English less than one year before. And one of these days a new book should appear by the

---

58. Ramiro de Maeztu (1875–1936) was a Spanish, journalist, political theorist, and literary critic. —Ed.

distinguished Peruvian thinker Mariano Ibérico Rodríguez titled *The New Absolute*. Also in South America the same concern begins to throb. I believe it is not necessary to say any more to prove that the religious problem is on the table and that it deeply preoccupies contemporary intellectuals.

What is the reason for this new and growing interest in the religious problem? It springs from the conviction that religion has had, and now has, an importance of the first magnitude in the life of man, constituting a necessary and inseparable feature of his experience.

What is the attitude of science? Today's science, being more profound, is also more humble than yesterday's. It is obsessed by the deep mystery of things. The study of matter and of organisms pushes it through many old barriers and leads it to the edge of mysterious abysses ignored in times past. The materialist tradition that attempts to explain all things in terms of a single category, the quantitative, has been broken. Vital elements, mental and spiritual, that have been factors even in the evolutionary process, cannot be ignored. Not only that, the flower and the fruit of things have as much or more right to provide the principles of interpretation as the roots do. Science has now recognized completely different spheres of reality that have to be studied through their own categories. And it has also been recognized that religion is one aspect of total reality that has its own sphere and involves its own categories that have to be discovered. It has been established, furthermore, that the first requisite to be able to study religion in a scientific fashion is to be religious, just as it is necessary to be a mathematician to study a mathematical problem.

The lectures of William James, the American psychologist, at Edinburgh University in 1901 and 1902, published later with the title *Varieties of Religious Experience*, marked an epoch in the psychological study of religion. This book has been the source for thousands of books written afterwards about religious experience. James applied a pragmatic criterion to the study of religion and stated the thesis that the religious man, the mystic, was through the centuries the great creator of new and brilliant impulses, carrying life in his age to higher levels. Psychology following James has accepted religious experience as a constitutive element of human nature and attempts to investigate its origin, its laws, and its essence. No matter how many different explanations are proposed, it definitely has had influence.

The new science of sociology studies religion as the main force that creates and cares for social values. The psychological point of view has been well expressed by the American sociologist Elwood, who states in a remarkable book published three years ago, "A social world without religion would be an uncertain social world, devoid of enthusiasm and vision, reduced to the dead level of individual coexistence. It would be a social world in which harmony or good will could not prevail very long." Aware of the enormous potential of religion as a social force, practical and shrewd politicians, even if they themselves are not religious—men, for example, like Mussolini or Charles Maurras, the French monarchist—advocate the strengthening of Catholicism in their countries as a necessary bastion against the numerous forces that threaten to break up those societies. Those politicians have recognized a great truth even when they prostitute the goals of religion and make it cooperate with chauvinism.

We still have philosophy remaining, and every student of it knows that contemporary philosophical thought knows of no other more controversial problem. A treatise on the philosophy of religion represents the acme of the philosophical efforts of great thinkers. Among our contemporaries, Höffding and Eucken have published their treatises; Bergson's work is still pending, and his system will remain truncated until he completes it. Because there is no problem more fundamental than the relation of man and the cosmos to which he belongs, there is no higher consciousness than of a man who feels a full citizen of the universe.

In this way science admits the existence of the spiritual world. Psychology recognizes the reality of religious consciousness; sociology determines the social value of religion; and philosophy, led by the totality instinct, attempts to interpret the religious experience of the individual in relation to the whole universe.

Religion as Life and Friendship

Now, if all the fundamental disciplines of thought are concerned with religion, how should we interpret it? The trend of looking at religion in terms of life and friendship accelerates all the time. Religious life, according to this interpretation, must be the highest expression of life in general. It must create superior personalities whose character and whose activities present in human terms the perfection of God. "Be perfect," said Jesus, "as your father in heaven is perfect."[59] Religion is, then, a quality of life. It is something quite superior to the simple acceptance of a system of fixed ideas, or the blind faith in an institution, or the detailed compliance with a code of rituals; all of these lead to spiritual stagnation. Religion is the conscious union of man and God in such a way that the life of God will palpitate in the human life, and his designs for good for humanity may be fulfilled by means of men

---

59. Matt 5:48. —Ed.

who live the sublime adventure of being controlled by God's sovereign will and not by man's own selfish whims.

Such a life is superior to mere culture, be it social or individual culture, because, in truth, culture can be something as exterior and artificial for a man as his money, his properties, and his social class. It lacks interiority. This is the thesis of Eucken in that remarkable book, *The Meaning and Value of Life*. Social culture, according to Eucken, is insufficient as a life ideal because it attempts to improve the conditions of life without affecting life itself. These are his words.

> Well-being, that is, a life devoid of cares and full of satisfactions, is not enough to make a man happy because as soon as we rid ourselves of enemies such as need and pain, a different one develops in us, perhaps even more pernicious, in the emptiness and the boredom of our life; and whatever mere social culture can supply against it cannot be accepted fully. In reality, all culture that limits itself to man's cares and satisfactions of present and immediate existence carries necessarily the seal of loneliness and emptiness; concern for the means in life smothers life itself. Such culture cannot produce an interior change, reach the fundamental dignity of man, but has to be accepted just as it is found; it can only utilize existing strengths.

Individual culture is not enough because it reduces life to a succession of states, without integrating them into a spiritual whole. Eucken states:

> Social culture tends to occupy itself preferentially with the conditions of life, but in that effort, it forgets life itself; individual culture aspires to consider it in itself, but given that it cannot be concerned merely with particular situations and instants of life, it cannot become fully integrated. It is not capable of attaining any interiority, no interior world, and we notice here the absence of a true spirit, remaining relegated to having a superficial character for every action and every tendency.

The ideal of life, then, is a spiritual creation, an interior life that will transcend all the changes and vicissitudes, lived in view of eternal values and in communion with the Supreme Being who rules the world.

But if the essence of religion is life, the essence of religious life is a friendship in which man goes in the company of a friend. A most beautiful example of how a transcendental friendship becomes the essence of religious experience can be found in a portion of Unamuno's masterpiece, *The*

Tragic Sense of Life, in which the great author bares the depth of his Christian soul. The words in which he gives witness to the reality of a fellowship in his own life are deeply moving. He says:

> I believe in God as I believe in my friends, because I feel the breath of His affection, feel His invisible and intangible hand, drawing me, leading me, grasping me; because I possess an inner consciousness of a particular providence and of a universal mind that marks out for me the course of my own destiny; and the concept of law—it is nothing but a concept after all!—tells me nothing and teaches me nothing.
>
> Once and again in my life I have seen myself suspended in a trance over the abyss; once and again I have found myself at the cross-road, confronted by a choice of ways and aware that in choosing one I should be renouncing all the others—for there is no turning back upon these roads of life; and once and again in such unique moments as these I have felt the impulse of a mighty power, conscious, sovereign, and loving. And then, before the feet of the wayfarer, opens out the way of the Lord.[60]

The Centrality of Christ in Contemporary Religious Thinking

Another characteristic of contemporary religious thinking is giving to Christ a central place.

In the world of today he has no serious competitors for the admiration and devotion of men. Someone has stated that in our times it is easier to believe in Christ than to believe in God. The religious studies of the last century are, in the main, the story of the search for a "historical Jesus," and we can state that the research that has been done allows us to contemplate, as in no century since the first of our era, the pristine image of the founder of Christianity. Christ's personality, his life, and his teachings are captivating the imagination of the best men from the West and from the East. In India, for example, they already know to distinguish between Christ and the civilization called "Christian"; they no longer confuse him with ecclesiastical institutions and ideological systems that carry his name. They want to know Jesus and nothing else. They define a Christian saying that he "is a Christ," that is, an imitation of the Master.

In a recently published book with the title *The Christ of the Indian Road*, Stanley Jones, the author, cites a number of very interesting cases

---

60. Unamuno, *Tragic Sense of Life*, 194–95. —Ed.

which indicate the extraordinary influence that Christ and his doctrine exert in that country. Some textual quotations are as follows. "When India, a non-Christian nation, wanted to pay the greatest homage to the most noble of its citizens, it searched for the highest term that they could know, and called Gandhi a Christ-like man." An Hindu gentleman stated on a certain occasion, "Is it not our Christian duty to help our Muslim brothers in their troubles?" And—what a shame!—another Hindu once told Jones, "If you call one of us a Christian man, he will feel complimented, but if you call him Christian, he will consider it an insult." This would mean that not all Christians, unfortunately, are Christian men, as they should be. But it is interesting that Christ is not blamed for the faults of those who call themselves by his name.

I hope that I will have the opportunity in the near future to talk about the influence of Christ on contemporary thought. On this occasion, given the brief time that I have, I can say simply that religious thought becomes more and more christocentric. We are witnessing, without doubt, a neo-Christian movement destined to renew current Christianity. It is a movement that professes a total loyalty to Christ, and that tries to begin the great adventure of applying the teachings of the Master to all the problems of life and society. The new crusades are convinced that the symbol of the cross can receive a deeper and more dynamic interpretation than the one we associate with the "Spanish Christ."[61] The cross becomes, then, not a symbol of tragedy, but of victory, a victory reached living one's life on the altar of the eternal principles for human redemption. The cross teaches that ill will is vanquished by undergoing its attack and, in spite of everything, continuing to love the evildoer. Because "Force generates nothing; only love is fertile," as a South American president has stated,[62] only when the principles of the cross, of the "second mile," and of the "other cheek" are applied to the practical problems of life, including the political ones, can we expect the advent of a better world. A non-Christian author, Bernard Shaw, thinks the same, and has said, "I am not more Christian than Pilate or than you, distinguished reader, however, like Pilate, I prefer Jesus over Caiaphas by far. And I am ready to admit that after contemplating the world and human nature, I do not see an escape hatch from miseries of the world but for the way Jesus would have chosen if he had become involved in the task of a practical statesman."

---

61. Compare Unamuno, "Spanish Christ," and Mackay, *The Other Spanish Christ*, ch. 7–8. —Ed.

62. Arturo Alessandri (1868–1950) was President of Chile from 1920 to 1925 and from 1932 to 1938. —Trans.

In this way we are reaching the point where we can answer the question that has given rise to this whole discussion. What is our answer? Can we suppose that the Young Men's Christian Association may remain at the edge of a reality that the whole world is discussing, that has a supreme importance for contemporary thought, the essence being life and friendship, and whose center is Christ, and the goal a better world?

By no means. This association is tied to religion, as it has been interpreted, by two eternal bonds. When those break down, the association will have lost its reason for being. Those bonds are a purpose and an experience.

The Pair of Bonds that Ties the Young Men's Christian Association to Religion

The Young Men's Christian Association is not a church or a sect; yet it follows a religious goal which is to form Christian men. A Christian man ought to develop all the capacities that God has given him. The symbol of our triangle should be a reality for him. He has to be a man of integrity, not only in the harmonious development of his personality, but also in that which concerns his moral character. He will be an uncompromising, virtuous man. But he will not become a Christian man solely because of the harmonious development of his personality nor his untarnished virtue. He will need a life lived in plenitude, that will overflow the margins of conventional virtue and will express itself as a redemptive passion that will know no limits of caste, of country, of race. The Christian man will remind the world about Christ. He will seek the good of others ahead of his own and will sacrifice for it. He will place the cross in life and life on the cross.

Secondly, the Young Men's Christian Association treasures a religious experience that it wishes to share with everyone. It is the experience that comes to a man who meets Christ face to face and surrenders to him. The association has proved through the personal lives of thousands of its leaders and members, since the time when George Williams[63] fell in love with Jesus and wanted to embody his experience in a new movement, that the love of Christ and an absolute faith in him transform the whole personality of the man in love, the man of faith. In the presence of the expulsive power of this new love, evil desires and disastrous habits that enslave the soul yield and lose their strength. The Galilean vanquishes now as always, and the man that will experience such deep change in his inmost self will walk through

---

63. George Williams (1821–1905) of Somerset, England was the founder of the YMCA. He was knighted by Queen Victoria in 1894. —Ed.

the paths of life, no longer alone, but in sweet and strengthening company. Whoever dares to try it will realize that what I have said is true.

In this way we have arrived at this conclusion. The perfection of man and the establishment of a better world are closely tied to religion and to Christ. The Young Men's Christian Association recognizes this relationship. Far from being embarrassed by it, it binds this to its own fate and proclaims in a loud voice that the future of civilization also depends on the recognition of this very principle.

Part Three

The Message and
Intellectual and Literary Life

8

The Intellectuals and the New Times

LADIES AND GENTLEMEN:

In the current week I have seen my long desired dream realized. When I was just a lad, I read the historical classic Prescott's *The Conquest of Peru*. It sowed in me a strong desire to see and to set foot on the old square of Cajamarca, immortalized in that book. And now, after long years, and following a visit to mother Spain, after having visited neighboring countries and other regions of Peru, after a quiet life in Lima—all of this has done nothing but to keep my old desire burning—I have been able, at last, to relive the past and dream again of the future at the foot of these mountains.

Legendary Cities

And "What do you see in Cajamarca?" you ask. I will answer your question with the same words I used to the friend that came with me, when, after going over the *Cumbe*,[64] we reached the point where the city, the countryside, and the mountains appeared for the first time to the eyes of the travelers. "I have never seen a city," I told him, "as similar to Granada as this." And now I can state that whatever I have seen and experienced during the recent days has fully confirmed my first impression about the similarity between your city and the famous and beautiful city in Andalusia.

Thus, through its topography and history, Cajamarca is a memory of Granada. The green countryside seems like a piece of the fertile Granadan

---

64. The word is from the Quechua term *kumpi mayo* (well-made water channel) located twenty-three kilometers from Cajamarca. —Ed.

valley. Saint Apolonia,⁶⁵ dominating the city and the valley, is the Rock of the Alhambra in miniature. It is true that it does not have a legendary palace on top, but it has a chair carved in the rock, symbolizing the royal power. The Baths of the Inca⁶⁶ have their counterpart in the luxurious baths of the Moorish kings, while the peak of the Sierra Nevada, standing like a watchman behind the last Arabian capital, can be seen reproduced in the frozen range that watches over the destinies of this city. And lastly, there is a place near Granada called the Sigh of the Moor where the last Arab king, Boabdil the younger, cried over the loss of his capital, the same as the site in this square where Atahualpa, the last prince of the Dynasty of the Sun, exhaled his last breath. If Granada is to Europe the symbol of the fall of the Arab empire and of the definitive retrieval of their own land by the Spaniards, Cajamarca is the symbol in the history of the New World of the fading of the last native civilization and the beginning of the colonial empire of Spain in South America. Granada and Cajamarca, legendary cities, one by its nature the other by its destiny, I salute you, and in you, to the race that conquered them.

But, having invoked the past, we have to proceed to contemplate the present and greet the future. At the request of my Mercurial⁶⁷ good friend who has just introduced me with adjectives that I do not deserve, I will share with you about the age in which we live. If what I will say were to offend good literary taste here and there, soiling the language of Cervantes with barbarisms, you will forgive me, attributing it to the fate that made me to have been born "gringo." But, with respect to the concepts that I am going to express, I will not apologize or expect applause. I will not ask for your pardon, because I believe them, and I will not ask for applause, because they overwhelm my spirit, and I cannot keep quiet about them. They are like prophetic voices sounding in the depths of my soul that cannot be kept quiet. Therefore, gentlemen, I will only ask for your cultivated attention.

The New Epoch

From half a century prior to the last world war, it became evident to all thinking men from the large number of new discoveries, new ideologies,

---

65. Cerro Santa Apolonia is a hill overlooking the city of Cajamarca from the southwest. From the carved stone, the Seat of the Inca, near the top, the Inca is said to have reviewed troops. —Ed.

66. The Baths of the Inca are natural hot springs six kilometers from Cajamarca. —Ed.

67. The reference is to a colleague connected with the periodical, *Mercurio Peruano*. —Ed.

and new social phenomena, that a new era in history was looming. The war blew up, and immediately all the elements of the old civilization were thrown into the crucible of Hades. Legendary shores experienced this hurricane. The ship of civilization that had been anchored on quiet waters had to turn around and go out to sea. It is already in the middle of the ocean, and we cannot see new shores in the distance, not even know if there are any shores. There is only one thing we know for sure: that our civilization has definitively broken with the past. Behind it, under the light of the setting sun, there is no safe haven; we have no other solution than to move ahead in spite of the night and the storm. But, we, men of this hour, should know that even if the abyss were to swallow us all, we are starting on the greatest adventure ever confronted by humanity. The only similar occasions in the past were the advent of Christianity and the Renaissance and the religious Reformation of the sixteenth century.

Allow me to state exactly the most striking characteristics of the current times. Today's world is characterized by the presence of a double series of contrary forces, that is, destructive forces. Contemporary history is the result of the reciprocal actions of those forces.

The Destructive Forces

Let us look at the destructive forces. There are three. The first one consists of disputes over frontiers. They have their origin in the nationalistic spirit and so-called patriotism. Thus, in Europe, Asia, and America there are interminable fights over territorial questions. What belongs legitimately to this or that people? Such is the problem. Fiume, Ulster counties, Silesia, the Yap islands, and Tacna and Arica are places that have become violent clashes of opinions between nations, and at times they are fated ghosts of future wars.

In prior times the danger of a war between nations was due, almost always, to the presence of an imperialist spirit in one of them. But we do not recognize the imperialist spirit any more that has become anachronistic in contemporary politics, because imperialism, if it exists, does not dare to show its face in these times. The new danger presents itself on the side of nationalism and arises from the attempt of each nation to keep what it has acquired, and in legitimating its titles to territories that it possesses or pretends to possess, in the name of a putative right.

The second destructive force is found in racial hatred. In these times that hatred has entered into a new phase. Each race places itself on the defensive. It is not unlikely that in coming times effective political union will be not so much the nation as the race. What else is the meaning of the sudden appearance of so many "pan-isms," Pan-Latinism, Pan-Iberianism, Pan-Germanism, Pan-Slavism, and we could almost say Pan-Saxonism? The racial federations announced by those names exhibit the possibility of serious divergences in the future between the different peoples of the white race. Now Pan-Americanism, which is an impersonal "ism" inspired in geographical unity, is threatened by Pan-Latinism, inspired in racial unity, that is, in the blood.

On the other side, the yellow, the black, and the coppery skinned rise successful and challenge the secular hegemony of the whites, while they are waiting the day in which they will be able to settle their old accounts with them. Lately in Peru the uprising of the indigenous in the south of the country has been very surprising. These, led by former members of the national army, have tried to eliminate the white people, whom they see as their natural enemies, like the sparrow looks at the hawk, and, under the impulse of the idea of power, they hope to reestablish the old empire of Tahuantinsuyo.[68] We have here a concrete and local example of the danger that may threaten civilization under the growing consciousness of race, with its load of hatred, if it is not subordinated to some idea higher than skin color, common origin, and blood bonds. It is also the time for the white race to examine its conscience about all its ideas of superiority, and also about the way it has exercised its administration of the world through the centuries.

But, undoubtedly, the main problem that we have to confront in the contemporary world is that of class strife. If the dangers raised by the exacerbation of nationalism and racism may be warded off by international conferences, it is not the same for the problems of the relationships between the different layers of society. In this case, to become aware of the problem is not the question but to accept the fact of a war declared, that will, in all likelihood, be a war to the death. The proletarian classes believe that it is their turn to lead the destinies of the world, after the control of human affairs has been successively in the hands of the aristocracy and the plutocracy from the dawning of our civilization.

The greatest danger threatening civilization at this time is that the government can be taken over by an ignorant and unscrupulous proletariat, without any other ideal than to take revenge against the bourgeoisie, with no other goal than to establish an iron hard dictatorship. Power at all costs, blood and fire, and cheating, such is the motto of the new proletarian imperialism, according to its most authorized spokesman, Lenin himself. He said, in a speech delivered in March 1919, "It is necessary to resist all of this (opposition of the unions to the communists), to make every sacrifice, use

---

68. The name the Incas gave their empire. —Ed.

all the stratagems, adopt illegal procedures, keep quiet at times, hide the truth, with the only goal to enter into the unions, own them and fulfill, in spite of everything, the communist work."

Notwithstanding, the most terrifying aspect of bolshevism as a destructive force is not so much in its creed nor even in its revolutionary program, but in the moral confusion of the enormous majority of their current adherents, and also in that unknown crowd of proletarian elements in all countries, who are always a threat of being potential Bolsheviks. Looking at bolshevism through their principles, the system has two phases, at least, that are not bad, the principle that "if one does not work, one does not eat," and the principle of a functional system of government. And concerning the revolutionary program, one has to admit that there are currently such inhuman conditions that justice will only succeed through a veritable cataclysm. We have to look at things in the face. This old civilization in which we have been born, that is now adrift in the middle of the ocean, has been, in the end, more pagan than Christian. The pagan principle of competition has taken primacy over the Christian principle of cooperation. Given that Christianity has not been tried as a solution of the social problems, we find ourselves now confronting bolshevism, which is nothing but the greatest protest that has arisen against the iniquity of the traditional system. And let us not deceive ourselves, believing that we, in this continent, can look from the balcony as mere spectators of the imminent catastrophe. Do we not know that there are red flags fluttering all over between Moscow and the Chicama valley?[69] One does not have to be a prophet to make the prediction that, in the next ten years, South American life will be shaken by a strong storm. It is necessary to think now where our port will be. But I have to say, gentlemen, that what worries me in this red bolshevism, is not that it may precipitate a worldwide social revolution, leading to the disappearance of social classes, private property, the current ecclesiastical institutions, even the state, but that its final victory may introduce anarchy in ethical values, and the emptying of the concept of good of all its transcendental aspects. In a word, I am afraid that the social revolution that we can foresee may take place before a true "revolution of spirits," before man may be morally qualified to carry out the dangerous experiment of a government in which "all will give according to capacity, and take according to need."

---

69. A port and coastal town in northwestern Peru. Peru's largest sugar cane plantation is in the valley of the Rio Chicama. —Ed.

The Constructive Forces

Fortunately the forces of disintegration are not the only ones operating at this moment in the world. There are other forces, of a constructive tendency, that operate to save a civilization that is close to falling down. From concern about total catastrophe, from the desire to straighten the problems of our social and political system and to build on this earth a real home for mankind, a new series of constructive forces has been born. The League of Nations; the disarmament conference in Washington; ecumenical congresses and missionaries of all the churches; international associations of physicians, of women, of students; societies to fight alcoholism, opium, trafficking in women—all these represent different forces that have been unleashed to counter the contrary forces and to set civilization on a new basis. In Geneva alone there are the main offices of eighty-eight international organizations, most of them pursuing elevated and humanitarian goals. Such organizations carry out in the whole world a truly apostolic message destined to settle the differences between nations and among the social classes, to create a new environment of international fraternity, and to eliminate all the causes of political friction and of social unrest.

But perhaps the most powerful constructive force, whose effects can already be felt in the world, is a new norm of public opinion. Those who are truly concerned about the fate of civilization are adopting more and more a new moral perspective. They have developed a new pragmatic criterion to judge things. According to this criterion, that, and only that is good, if it serves the true interests of man. It does not matter how venerable an institution may be, how wealthy a man may be, how prestigious an idea may be; if it does not contribute at all to the enrichment of life, it has to disappear whatever the cost. Everything has to be judged by its fruit, and a man, or an idea, or an institution will have the right to exercise some control over life, only when their fruits have a high moral value. "Even now the axe is laid to the root of the trees; every tree therefore that does not bear good fruit is cut down and thrown into the fire." (Luke 3:9).

"There is one thing," Victor Hugo said, "that is more powerful than all the armies: an idea whose time has come." Now we have a new idea in the battlefront, a new moral force that will become suddenly irresistible. From now on each thing will have to justify its existence by its beneficial results; and for the same reason, every man, every idea, every institution that can prove its capacity to purify and elevate human life should be helped in its beneficial work. If this norm had been applied to all human things in prior times, the world would be a very different place than the one in which we live. But as this has not been done, many things that should have been done during the light of former centuries have remained undone until ours, and they have to be done in a hurry so that they will be finished in this twilight, before the sun sets.

The Role of the Intellectuals

Such is the current situation of the world: on the one side, everything is dangerous; on the other, we find elements for hope. How can our desires for success become permanent reality with a better order of things? Shadows will disappear; truth and justice will come to this earth when the intellectuals of all countries recognize their role and fulfill it. The midpoint between our problem and its solution lies in a new kind of intellectual.

Now, what is the type of intellectual required by these new times, and what is the role that they should play?

Rarely have the intellectuals of the world been given an opportunity like the one presented to them at this time. The masses hunger for ideas, for guidance, and they will not listen to anybody with so much attention as to the men whose only interest is the truth, and who are not tied up with any system of exploitation. "Philosophers should be kings." I do not mean that all thinking men must be authorities, but I do mean that they should be the kings of public opinion. They have the sacred duty to guide the people on everything concerning their spiritual life and politics. They have to make it humanly impossible for their countries' destinies to be tied to unscrupulous and heartless politicians. They must stand vigil so that ideas deleterious to public morality will not prosper. They have to be the champions of social justice. All good initiatives must come forward from them. And whoever has constructive ideas should feel called to exercise an apostolate.

Intellectuals of the Mausoleum

And yet, how few intellectuals there are in our national environment, who identify themselves with architectonic ideas that they fight for to apply in life, ready to sacrifice themselves for the truth they contain! Among some of them the preponderant idea is esthetics. What interests them in life is the "beautiful thing," the "interesting thing." They may be enthusiastic about a sound, a color, a landscape, an elegant concept, a resounding verse. The life of man interests them only as drama, as a drama with entire and harmonious development, in which falsehoods, baseness, and evil are elements as important as truth and virtue. Everything is needed to produce an "interesting" or "curious" effect. They wish to be spectators in the universe, to have the world as their field of research, and if at any time they considered reforming it, "they would find it so strange," in the words of Renan, "that they would not dare to do it."

Some others devote themselves to bookish erudition. Their main concern is to know what Tom, Dick, or Harry has thought or what they have done, not to learn how to act or think, but with the only goal to fatten the brain with such knowledge. Subtle theories are attractive, but they flee from the disquieting conclusion. Just like worms who share their interest for old tomes, they burrow and crawl, but they never develop wings. Unamuno has stated it perfectly, "Faintheartedness of thinking leads many to erudition, a sleeping pill for restlessness of the mind, or the occupation of mental laziness." H. G. Wells was also thinking of them when he wrote in one of his latest books, "History and political philosophy are found in the modern world as timid partakers in a banquet; they make small balls of bread, and speak quietly to their neighbor, terrified by the mere idea of talking to the whole table."

Furthermore, what will we say about historicism? If I am allowed to criticize the Peruvian contemporary intellectuals, I would say that it has overrun them excessively. On this point I am completely in agreement with the opinions on the subject of my distinguished friend, Doctor Ibérico, in his admirable article in the centennial issue of *Mundial*.[70] Starting from the well founded concept that it is a duty for every civilized country to know thoroughly the smallest details of national life, a large number of our young intellectuals, privileged intelligences, devote themselves almost exclusively to historical investigations of more minute details and recondite nature. But there is something that those companions forget, something really fundamental. In other countries these studies are performed when most of the serious problems of the nation have already been solved. Among us these problems are studied when our nation confronts cultural problems of great transcendence. "We are trying to form a national spirit!" is their reply. Fine: the goal could not be higher. But keep one thing in mind: if in an older country the national spirit is preserved through the constant remembrance of the past, in a young one it has to be done watching the future. After all what matters in the life of a people is not where it came from but where it is going. And it will go where it wants to go, not flitting here and there as a butterfly through mausoleums and museums, but starting to work in the present moment, listening to the dynamos of our ideals. Sooner or later, the whole country becomes a cemetery, as has happened already in old

---

70. *Mundial* was a Peruvian weekly magazine that had modern graphic design and content. It was published between April 1920 and September 1931. —Ed.

Europe, where every name, every piece of land has some history associated with it, and a corresponding monument.[71] Europe, if you will, can live out its memories and spend its glorious old age pacing its huge cemetery, reading epitaphs from thirty centuries ago. But it makes no sense that in a young American country, so many young and competent leaders can devote themselves entirely to deciphering the past, when they should be forging the future, more so when their country and the whole continent finds itself looking at an unavoidable cataclysm.

But perhaps the most tragic condemnation of historicism, this intellectual isolation from the throbbing reality of the world, all that I dare to call intellectualism of the mausoleum, is that it generates a morbid attitude in the end, a repugnant cynicism, an indifference, a self-absorption, a sickly analysis of national defects, a hopeless pessimism. Those who spend their lives in pantheons or mausoleums of people, of facts, of institutions, or ideas, end up becoming true cemeteries themselves. A day will come when, in the evening, a frenetic voice will break the silence, "By God! Another cemetery. My heart is nothing but another sepulcher . . . Who has died in it? Horrible sign! Here lies hope."[72]

Intellectuals in Campaign

Just as in the modern age when a religious ideal replaced the asceticism that used to bury divine light in the darkness of a cell, a religious ideal that demands that the religious spirit must drench and transfigure all aspects of human life with its light: in the same way the intellectual ideal must change in this our age from narrow interest in those studies called the Humanities to a wider interest, as broad as true life and nature are. If, during the Renaissance the humanists came to replace the old scholastics, substituting the original texts of the Hellenic culture for the worn Latin translations, it is time now for modern intellectuals to open the original text of true life and study man and his vital problems, not with the old goal of doing literature, but with that of finding solutions. Now that the cannons of war are silent, we may see on all fronts a war of ideas, and it may not stop until the whole world has become a cemetery! . . . but a cemetery of evils and lies that have harassed man's welfare through the centuries.

---

71. The preceding lines in the paragraphs of this section ending at this superscript were published under the title "Intelectuales de Panteon" in the journal directed by V. R. Haya de la Torre, *Claridad: Organ de La Juventud libre del Peru* (Año 1, Núm 1) (May 1923), 17. —Ed.

72. Mariano José de Larra, "El Día de los Difuntos" ["All Souls Day"].

Fortunately, the truth is already on the way. New recruits are added daily. They are all men who take as their motto, "the plain truth," who dare to "stare at the sun," who have resolved to "cooperate with the real trends of the world." They will not make from literature a mere field for amusement, nor from history, a museum of antiques. They will read the classics of human thought, like the ones who enter an armory to equip themselves for the fight. They will study history to learn their situation in the world and the role of their tongue and their pen in the definitive strife for justice and truth. Their goal will not consist of being called men of talent, but of being called men of character. Whenever they will write or speak, they will not try to please, but to convince. And their will is not going to die through empty words, but their writings will be imperishable, having wet the pen in the red ink of their blood. With a real architectonic view of life, they will not start rebuilding the world by covering old walls, to turn them into ballrooms and theaters while providing other rooms to store rare things suitable for museums. First of all and over all they will live and work to turn the old house of civilization into a worthy home for authentic daily life.

Some French intellectuals have recently given a beautiful example to the whole literary world, forming a group with the name of *Clarity*, tending to develop an active intellectualism of the type I have just sketched. Recently, they have called on the intellectuals of all the Latin American countries, asking that they support their effort. No matter how much one could disagree with some of the articles of the creed of *Clarity*, as stated by Henri Barbusse[73] in his book, *Light from the Abyss*, it is the duty of every educated man to support the noble campaign started by him and Anatole France[74] to wake up the sleeping conscience of the intellectuals of the world, and face up to the actual problems of society.

Roving Knights with a Divine Look

"Knight errantry," said Don Quixote on one occasion, "is like love, that makes everything equal." Gentlemen, we need a new roving knighthood, a body of knights of head and heart, great levelers and redressers of wrongs, who will never scorn to address "all the goatherds," except that they will not

---

73. Henri Barbusse (1873–1935) had been editor of *Clarté* and an associate of Romain Rolland, French Nobel Prize winner in Literature, 1915. He joined the French Communist Party in 1923. —Ed.

74. Anatole France (1844–1924) won the Nobel Prize for Literature in 1921. All his works were placed upon the *Index Librorum Prohibitum* May 31, 1922. —Ed.

talk so much about a golden past but of a future golden century that will come with strife and prayer.

I know a few knights of this type. They are still young squires, but they have a lot of practice in the use of weaponry and make occasional efforts to speak to the "goatherds." On a given night they will carry out the vigil of arms, and the following morning they will start the campaign for the kingdom of heaven. Gentlemen, a nation that can give rise to a kind of young intellectual, whose enthusiasm leads him to give a lecture against drinking at two o'clock in the morning to some hotel employees, will have a future among the nations of the new era.

On a brass plate on the bridge of the *Quest*, Shackleton's ship, have been sculpted the verses of Kipling, depicting the qualities of an intellectual on the move.

> If you can dream—and not make dreams your master;
> If you can think—and not make thoughts your aim;
> If you can meet with Triumph and Disaster
> And treat those two impostors just the same;
> If you can force your heart and nerve and sinew
> To serve your turn long after they are gone;
> If you can fill the unforgiving minute
> With sixty seconds' worth of distance run,
> Yours is the Earth and everything that's in it,
> And—which is more—you'll be a Man, my son![75]

Having already considered the current situation of the world, the urgent need of the intellectuals to get involved, and also the type of intellectuals whose intervention will prove effective, I would like to use the time I have left to direct attention to three new senses that must be cultivated by the errant knights of the new era if their labor is going to be useful.

A New Sense of Humanity

We must cultivate, in the first place, a new sense of humanity. It is not enough to support an abstract doctrine of the value and inviolability of the individual. It is not enough to sing the triumphs of the conscious "I" over inert matter. We have to love man, all men without exception, listen to their concerns and soothe them; to believe in the feasibility of the redemption of the other unfortunates, and work actively for it, inspired by the vision of

---

75. Rudyard Kipling (1865–1936), an English author, won the Nobel Prize for Literature in 1907. Mackay's text excerpts lines 9–12, 21–22, 29–32 from Kipling's poem, "If." —Ed.

the kingdom of God. A passion for man more than for all ideas will be indispensable to any intellectual who wants to be of use to the current epoch. And no one can forget that "a little bit of help is worth more than a full load of compassion."

We have one aspect of this new sense for humanity in the new cult of the "unknown soldier." This is the unknown man, symbol not of the generality of the citizens who sacrificed themselves in war, but of the plebeian who gave his life for the nation. In prior epochs Tom, Dick, and Harry and all their plebeian parentage had no more interest for the government than to serve as instruments to build pyramids, or roads, or to make war. In other words, they only had an utilitarian value, an imperialist one. They were desired not for what they were, but for what they could do. Once the war finished, the monuments and songs were for the heroes, the live or dead warriors, who distinguished themselves in the battles.

But now we have made a hero of one that nobody knows, one whom we do not know if he was brave or a coward; one whose only title to immortality is to have been a representative of all those plebeians who lost their lives in the Great Tragedy.[76] The nation has taken a great step forward. It has come to recognize the value of the anonymous people when they sacrifice themselves for the nation in a war. Another step is necessary: that the nation will recognize the value of the same people when they sacrifice themselves daily, in civil life. It is fitting for true intellectuals to feel, and to make others feel the value of the millions of human beings who work and die in the stifling cellars of our civilization.

The cultivation by intellectuals of that sense of humanity would produce in them a double effect. On the one hand they would lend their strongest support to every project destined to facilitate the free development of the human being; on the other hand, they would throw themselves into the fight to eliminate those hindrances that impede a man from being everything that he can and should be. This means that they would be the champions of popular education and the protagonists of social justice.

This double duty of intellectuals to cast the light of truth and remove the obstacles from the road of progress brings to mind that beautiful parable of Christ. On one occasion the Master said, "What woman, having ten drachmas, if she were to lose one drachma, does not light a lamp and sweep the house and seek diligently until she finds it?"[77] The lighted lamp was a condition to start the search, but the light alone did not reveal the coin covered by dust in a corner of the room or hidden under the bed or in the

---

76. World War I. —Ed.
77. Luke 15:8. —Ed.

closet. She had to sweep the floor, and for that she needed a broom. But once it was gripped and, after moving all the furniture to do a better job, and after all the disorder and the temporary dust cloud, she finally found the coin. Popular education is like the lamp casting light and guiding a person to work; but, unfortunately, there are human beings so covered by dust, and so hampered by the heavy furniture of an antichristian civilization, that light does not reach them. Some other action is needed: that of the broom. The perfect intellectual for the campaign is the one who not only bathes the world and souls with light, but the one who searches all the hiding places where one can find lost souls, kneeling, if necessary, to find them and to save them. In one word, gentlemen, let us not forget, advocating popular education, that man needs redemption as much as education, and occasions present themselves when our main job must be to attack everything that appears in society as responsible for the malaise and backwardness of man.

A New Sense of God

The intellectual in campaign must cultivate, in the second place, a new sense of God. One of the characteristics of our epoch is the appearance of a new religious spirit. For example, José Ingenieros[78] has said, "As in the first phase of Christianity, of the Reformation, or of the French Revolution, the new consciousness of humanity has assumed the character of a true mysticism, indispensable to serve an ideal." It has been recognized that the religious spirit is a constitutive element of human nature, so that the normal man is the religious man. It is recognized at the same time, that religion may be the highest moralizing force, or, to the contrary, the most demoralizing of all forces that move man. Religion makes the man a saint or a devil. It all depends on the religion that he has, what it means, of the idea it has of the Supreme Being, and how the person senses God in his life. Religion is in part concept and in part sentiment. Advocating a new sense of God, we want to say that we have to change our idea with respect to the Divinity, and at the same time, open our hearts widely to his influence. God is love, and as such, all his being throbs with the deepest, the most divine compassion. To think of a God who is impassive, not interested in the sins, the fights, and the sorrows of man, is impossible. "An affectionate worm in a lump of earth is more divine than a God without love." Thus spoke Browning, and he was right because the least we have to think about God is that he has at least as

---

78. José Ingenieros (1877–1925) was an Argentine physician and positivist philosopher who played a prominent role in university reform in Argentina in 1918. He published *El hombre mediocre* [*The Mediocre Man*] in 1913. —Ed.

much interest in human things as the man that loves his equals most deeply. But God is more: a force, a presence, a companion, if you wish, because he acts through the lives of those who feel him, fighting, molding, establishing his kingdom in the heart and in the world. God loves, and God works, and true life consists in being aware of his love, and being voluntary agents of his action. Then yes, it is possible to "cooperate with the true tendency of things"; then, yes, man is invincible.

But, where and how can we cultivate this sense of God? In the Bible, and by the total interpenetration of our spirit with Jesus Christ. The Bible is the epic poem of God's love for man. That is the historical movement in which, through the centuries, God revealed himself to humanity. In the Bible we find the discovery of man by God and the discovery of God by man.

The pith of the Bible is in the Gospels, those four poems in prose about Christ. Reading recently the *De Profundis* of Oscar Wilde, a book written in jail where the author reveals the wounds of his heart, I found the following paragraph, "Around Christmas I happened to find a New Testament in Greek, and every morning, after having cleaned my cell and the dishes, I used to read a little of the Gospels, a dozen verses taken by chance from anywhere. It is a delightful way to start the day. Everybody, even if they live a turbulent and undisciplined life, should do the same." If the author of *Dorian Gray* had taken this custom in his youth, to read the Gospels and placed himself in touch with Jesus Christ, far from finishing his life in the abyss of shame and pain, he would have placed his dazzling talent to the service of virtue.

It is marvelous how the intellectual's gaze turns anxiously towards the figure of Jesus Christ. The Man from Galilee has never had such prestige. Over the rough waves appears once more that figure approaching calmly and majestically the ship of humanity. So many times it has been considered an illusory ghost in the night. And there is already a disposition to listen to him when he says, "It is I . . . do not be afraid."[79] But what can Christ do in the middle of the turmoil?

> Who will be able to calm
> this turbulent sea?
> Who can order the irate wind?
> If You are hidden,
> who will guide the ship to port?

The voice of the Master has now the same authority as before; there is no commotion that he cannot calm. But it is necessary that its dogmatic

---

79. Matt 14:27. —Ed.

accents can reach the ears of forsaken peoples and hearts. It is necessary that this voice resound anywhere there are violent, passionate winds. When the teachings of Jesus Christ will be seriously applied to the solution of individual, national, and international problems, the life of man will issue such a sweet and harmonious music as the legendary one of the spheres. All men will live in a sacred communism. It will be a theocratic communism, of love, because the petition of the Our Father will have taken place already, "thy kingdom come, thy will be done, on earth as it is in heaven." Then everyone will know what so few know now, that the secret of life is in loving and feeling God, that is, in the interpenetration of the personality of man with that of Jesus Christ, as expressed in the words of St. Paul, "It is no longer I who live, but Christ who lives in me."[80]

A New Sense of Duty

One more sense is missing, the sense of duty, the one that turns ideals and feelings into action. "I was asleep," Kant said, "and I dreamed that life was beauty; I woke up and noticed that it is duty."

The first duty of the militant intellectual, once the eyes are already fixed on the ideal, and the heart throbs with holy enthusiasm, is the duty of having no shadows. As soon as the new errant knight goes out to face life, the shadows of things start watching his steps and bringing terror to his heart. There are all kinds of shadows. There are huge giants and charming dwarves. Now it is the shadow of public opinion, of the ridicule that may befall. Now it is the shadow of the loss of prestige or of a job. Now it is a possible conflict at home. Now, a possible failure.

So that the shadows will not scare him, there is a remedy: look at the sun. When Alexander the Great observed that the reason why the famous steed Bucephalus did not allow anybody to mount, it was because it was afraid of his own shadow, he turned the head of the horse towards the sun. The spirited horse calmed down immediately, so that young Alexander could jump on its back. That is it, gentlemen: looking at the sun there are no scary shadows.

The second duty is that of steadfastness. Victory is not attained in a day. The journey is long, and the road, difficult. Temporary failure must be but a spur to force us to greater effort. It is better to die than to yield or turn back. Hope is never lost.

The strife after truth is like a relay race in which all the runners cooperate. Each one covers his segment, while the testimony goes from hand to

---

80. Gal 2:20. —Ed.

hand always ahead. The last one crosses the line and gets the applause, but the race was not won by him alone but by the constancy and common effort of all. In this way we have to advance being strong errant knights for truth!

At times the heart becomes dismayed and the head says: enough! At such times what a pleasure it is to find companions! Recently, at a moment of discouragement, I found a verse taken from a poem by the American poet van Dyke,[81] which strengthened my fighting spirit once again. The poem's title is "Hudson's Last Voyage." All his life Hudson had dreamed of finding a passage in the northern part of America that would join the Atlantic and the Pacific Oceans. His exploring ship was riding the waves of the bay that now carries his name when the sailors rebelled, and after having cast into a small boat Hudson, his small child, and an old pilot, John King, who remained faithful to his captain, they turned around towards the open sea. Finding himself in this desperate situation, abandoned and without resources, in the middle of the ocean, Hudson did not bend, and addressing King, who manned the rudder, told him in words that could well be the password of a true intellectual:

> So point her up, John King, nor'west by north.
> We'll keep the honour of a certain aim
> Amid the peril of uncertain ways,
> And sail ahead, and leave the rest to God.

---

81. Henry van Dyke (1852–1933) was a graduate of Princeton University and Princeton Theological Seminary. A Professor of English at Princeton University from 1899–1923, he was a widely published poet and hymn writer who served as U.S. ambassador to the Netherlands. —Ed.

9

Don Miguel de Unamuno
His Personality, Work, and Influence

I DEDICATE THIS HUMBLE essay written with a trembling hand and in an alien language—a respectable task imposed by a brave resolution of the Faculty of Philosophy and Letters—to a memory from Castile.

Traveling through the land of Spain about two and a half years ago, I found myself in the medieval city of Salamanca. During a short stay in that place in old Castile, where the banks of the slow river Tormes give breath to memories of rogues and mystics, and where innumerable buildings even retain traces of the piety and culture of olden days, I had the good luck to call on the illustrious Basque author, Don Miguel de Unamuno, in his own home. To those moments spent at the feet of this outstanding teacher, whose phrases turned me into a fervent admirer and disciple, I dedicate the following, unworthy lines. Because, in this special hour of my life, when unaccustomed emotions cause my heart to throb, given that the first and most illustrious daughter of old Salamanca has deigned to recognize me, crowning my poor brow with the laurel wreath of its superb traditions, how could I hold the attention of this august assembly any better than by speaking about the personality, the work, and the influence of the aforementioned rector from Salamanca, who has inspired souls and has been a shining star of contemporary Spanish literature?

Whoever has had the rare privilege of going through the rooms of that treasure house of art, the Prado Museum in Madrid, will never forget the emotions felt contemplating the paintings of Velazquez. Those paintings are, by and large, portraits of men, of full-fledged men, filling up the whole canvas. Is it not symbolic that the most classical and representative of all

Spanish painters, could be a painter of men? Is it that the painter of the *Christ Crucified*, *Phillip IV*, and *The Drunkards* would know how to penetrate the deepest expression of the Spanish contribution to literature and history, not about ideas but about characters; not to systems, but to facts; not to codes, but to conquerors? Instead of a *Divine Comedy*, Spain has given the world a *Don Quixote*; instead of a *Critique of Pure Reason*, a Saint Teresa; instead of a *Magna Charta*, Hernando Cortes and Francisco Pizarro. Very well, the subject of this study, rector, critic, philosopher, poet, mystic, and politician, is, first of all and above all, a man. Don Miguel de Unamuno is far from being a mere widely read man, or a professional wordsmith. Through all the lines of his pale Basque skin, as in the accents of his sonorous voice and the throbbing paragraphs of his writings, one can discern, as if engraved with capital letters, the word *hombridad*, a word coined by the Portuguese writer Oliveira Martins, and that has been taken over by Unamuno to crystallize what in his thought are the qualities of an ideal man. This sturdy image whose constant longing is to flesh out, with passion and thought, the idea of a true man, could very well glorify a canvas of Velazquez. And as a consequence of the development of this *hombridad* in the character of Unamuno, it turns out to be impossible to read what he writes and avoid forming a definitive opinion about him: either you believe him and venerate him, or you hate and reject him with all your heart.

Now, before examining the objective work of Unamuno, let us look more closely at the personality of the writer who provides life and passion to that work.

His Personality

There are three constitutive elements that we can identify in the literary personality of Unamuno, his race, his culture, and his individualism.

Race

Don Miguel de Unamuno is a native of Biscay, and his native town is Bilbao, a port on the Bay of Biscay, where he was born on September 29, 1864, as he states in his book *Memories of Childhood and Adolescence*. Time and again in his books he returns to mention his native soil, to which he feels indebted. The statement in his masterpiece, *The Life of Don Quixote and Sancho*, is highly moving. "O land of my birth, of my parents, of my grandparents, and great grandparents, land of my childhood and adolescence, land where I took the companion of my life, land of my love, you are the heart of my soul! Your sea and your mountains, my Biscay, made me what I am; of the soil that kneads your oak trees and your beeches, your walnuts and your chestnuts, of that land you have kneaded my heart, my Biscay!"[82] In that land of Biscay a group of famous men saw the light in the era of Spanish greatness. Ignatius Loyola was born there and also Francis Xavier, roving knights of the divinity, spiritual conquistadores of broad lands. From Biscay Don Alfonso de Ercilla y Zúñiga, soldier of Almagro and singer of the conquest of America, also originated; and on Biscayan soil grew up the grandparents of Simón Bolívar, who was to liberate the lands that his forebears enslaved. Speaking in their own language, an extremely difficult one and of meager literature, and limited in their usage of Castilian Spanish, the inhabitants of the Basque provinces have led an isolated life. The traditional Basque, although not an epicurean, has been an energetic man, ambitious, restless, and permeated with a vague and inconsistent romanticism. He has lived up to the portrait drawn by Tirso de Molina—"short in words and long in works." As could be assumed, the type of mysticism that bloomed on the Cantabrian shore has been different from the Castilian in some important respects. Castilian mysticism was passive, serene, and contemplative; the Basque one, active, muddy, and uneasy. The former was limited to the monastic life in Spain; the latter jumped into the world, crossing oceans and exploring the virgin forests, attempting to impose the catholic faith and morals on the pagans.

Unamuno is of this lineage, cream of a race of mystic fighters. In him the spirit of Biscay, renowned in the past for its works, has found a voice that can sing and explain the world. After long silent centuries, Biscay, like Russia, has been able at last to express itself. It already has some distinguished authors and painters of great originality who can represent it in the arts with vehemence and mental independence. Outstanding among these compatriots of Unamuno are Pio Baroja, who has given new directions to the Spanish novel, and Zuloaga, a marvelous colorist, who has been able to delineate tragedy better than any other Iberian painter.

Culture

If Unamuno owes his fighting spirit of a restless mystic to this lineage, he owes other personality traits of similar importance to his ample and varied culture.

---

82. Unamuno, *Vida de Don Quijote y Sancho*, 87–88.

Although he refuses to refer to himself this way, he is a true sage and scholar in the widest possible sense of these words. He has been the head of a department in the University of Salamanca for many years. In this department he has studied in the original the great Greek classics and also the New Testament. This latter volume, as I was able to hear from his lips, is one of three books that is never missing on his desk, the other two being *Obermann* from the French author Senancour, and *The City of Dreadful Night* of the British author James Thomson. The books that fill up the simple shelves in his office are a wonderful assortment of wise selection. There are books in some twenty languages. Next to volumes with austere binding, revealing their Spanish origin, there are books in Hebrew, Greek, Latin, Italian, Portuguese, French, English, German, Basque, Catalonian, etc., etc. And then, when we believe we have noticed all the treasures of the library, two additional ones are removed, and he reads for us, in expressive tones, paragraphs of Ibsen and Kierkegaard—the latter a tragic Dane, the former a Norwegian playwright.

The energies that the forefathers of Unamuno concentrated on crossing new seas in the conquest of unknown lands for Castile and the faith, he has concentrated in a desperate and perpetual struggle with the mystery of life. What has led this Basque to dominate grammatical forms of so many languages—as it were to cross the barren plains of lexicographic research—has not been a mere linguistic study, nor even the urge to swell up the head with encyclopedic knowledge, but the desire to discover thoughts that would cast a light over the byways of life, and also to encounter spiritual companions for the trip. He has always been an enemy of translations, since in them it is extremely rare to be able to reproduce the soul of the author or the most accurate and subtle of his thinking, while the most representative authors of a people— those precisely with the greatest interest for Unamuno—almost never get translated into other languages.

Aside from the old Castilian classics and perhaps the New Testament, the literature that has left the deepest marks on the personality and work of Unamuno has been English literature. A good portion of his library is composed of British authors, many of them barely known in the Hispano-American world. Unamuno does not speak English, and when he attempts reading it, his pronunciation is terrible, but he can translate with the greatest ease even the works of the most difficult authors. Although the knowledge that he has of English perhaps is not such that would allow him to make a living in a South American department store, such is the control he has acquired of the literary language of England that it has allowed him to become steeped in the profound philosophy of life of British poets like Shakespeare, Tennyson, Browning, and Thomson. He recounts that upon reading a great

Scottish romantic poem at fourteen years of age, something like "a morning breeze" blew over his spirit. Remembering that time of this life, he writes in his *Memories of Childhood and Adolescence*, "Happy is the one who can revive in his memory the innocent expression of his romantic years, those days when I made efforts to cry without reason, in which I believed myself victim of a premature mysticism, when I enjoyed kneeling to prolong that discomfort, when I went to los Caños,[83] with Ossian in my pocket, to repeat his sorrows of Morven, to Rino and to the children of Figal, applying to old Aitor and to Lecobide, the fantastic creations of the inconsistent Basque romanticism."[84] At that time he read the beautiful Tennyson poem "Enoch Arden" for the first time; reading it impressed him deeply. From the blowing of "that morning breeze" until now, the English poets have been the ones who have provided daily bread to the spirit of Unamuno.

But it is still necessary to mention the English writer to whose influence Unamuno owes more than any other, and whom he resembles, not only in his ideas but in his literary style. This author was the eminent thinker, Carlyle, author of *On Heroes*, *Sartor Resartus*, and *The French Revolution*, this latter book Unamuno translated into Spanish. At times reading the works of the Spanish author, it seems as if the creator of the *Philosophy of Clothes* had been resuscitated, dressed in old Basque clothing, without a tie, while he intones his preferred catchphrase from *Heroes*, thundering once again against the mechanical and positive theories of life, praising love of work, pointing to the path of duty, and, with brush strokes and lively apostrophes, rescuing the individual from the social whirlpool, lifting the soul of the most insignificant bootblack over all impersonal institutions.

Enough has been said to be able to understand that Unamuno owes as much to the atmosphere of his library as to his Basque heredity. Let us return to deal lightly with the third element of his personality, that is, his individualism.

Individualism

It may be said that the individuality of a man is that in which he is distinct from all others, being then something that can be acquired by an analytical process of differentiation. Or, on the other hand, his personality means the collection of his qualities, either distinctive or universal, that make him the social being that he is. Individuality rests on the bosom of the personality

---

83. A seaside town. —Trans.

84. Unamuno, *Recuerdos de Niñez*, 147. [Literary references are to *The Poetical Works of Ossian* by James Macpherson (1736-1796). —Ed.]

in the same way that the personality rests in the structure of society, both contributing in their place to the routine functioning of life. But when the distinct elements that constitute individuality become exaggerated to the point that they obscure those traits that a man has in common with others, we find the case of moral individualism, and that man is an individualist.

There is no doubt that Don Miguel de Unamuno can be an individualist of this kind, and were it not for the malign associations of the word, we would say "egoist." But whether it is called "individualism" or "egoism," the result is that he is a unique and lonely figure in the Spain of today. And not only that, but Unamuno is proud of his spiritual isolation to such a point that sometimes he becomes unpleasant. How can we understand why Unamuno stresses his individuality to such an extent? How is it that he thinks and acts like no other person in Spain, becoming a most singular character, and leading many people to call him "crazy"? The explanation is not difficult to find. The individualism of Unamuno is the unavoidable consequence, on the one hand of his deeply rooted conviction that he was born to fulfill a definitive mission, and on the other, from his philosophy in which he affirms that the end of man is to become eternal, which is the same, so to speak, as to become conspicuous and stand out.

On different occasions Unamuno leads his readers to recognize what he considers to be his mission in life. He exists, as he says in his *Monologues and Conversations*, "to sow in men the germs of doubt, of distrust, of worry and even of desperation."[85] He wants men to worry, so that they make an effort to think, so that they do not remain subject to traditional idiosyncrasies, that they form sacred guilds to confront the mystery of life. He looks forward to the day when the Spanish spirit, having broken its old ties, will stand up as an unchained Prometheus, over all conventionalisms, conquering intellectual freedom and enjoying with it the exquisite pain of thought. The mission of Unamuno is that of an alarm clock, a purely negative mission, utilizing rough paradoxes, intimate contradictions, outlandish dances like Don Quixote, any and all means that will force the dozing minds to end up listening. This explains why he does not care about being disliked, nor much less jeered at. He embodies in his own being the doctrine that he never stops recommending to others, namely, that they learn to face ridicule. The only thing that saddens him is indifference, frightening him that his mission may be in vain.

---

85. Unamuno, *Soliloquios y Conversaciones*, 55.

His Work

Publications

The greater part of the works of Unamuno consists of collections of articles that appeared from time to time in Spanish and American magazines and periodicals. He began his literary career at age twenty-two with an article that he wrote for a periodical from Bilbao. Since 1885, when that article appeared, until the present, Unamuno has been writing articles on a great number of subjects—literary, topographical, linguistic, sociological, political, philosophical, and religious. Those articles have been collected on occasion by the author and now form the volumes entitled *Landscapes* (1902), *From My Country* (1903), *My Religion and other Essays* (1910), *Through Lands of Spain and Portugal* (1910), *Monologues and Conversations* (1911), *Against This and That* (1912). In addition, five collections of articles have been published by the Students Residence of Madrid, an institution that incarnates the spirit of Unamuno and attempts to spread his ideas.

Although Unamuno is better known to the public as an article writer, he has played on different occasions the role of novelist, poet, and philosopher. In our opinion, his novels, three lengthy ones and a collection of short ones, are the part of the author's literary work that gives the least brilliance to his fame as an author. They are, like the half-novel written by Carlyle, too didactic and moralizing to be able to satisfy the popular criterion of a work of fiction, that is, "that makes time pass without getting seriously involved." The poems that Unamuno has published are very characteristic of the man. They are, perhaps, the best mirror in which we can look at his soul in all its nakedness and anxiety. In spite of their high poetic qualities, Unamuno's poems will never attain popularity given their extreme metaphysical character. They free the soul from its worldly ties to leave it then in the abyss of doubt, without ever providing wings with which to fly to heaven. We find the most original and lasting of Unamuno's work, no doubt, in three of his books, which are *About Authenticity*, a very profound study of the spirit of Spaniards, *Comments about the Life of Don Quixote and Sancho*, considered by the author as his best work, and *The Tragic Sense of Life* which is the most systematic and philosophical book that he has written.

With regard to its literary value, the work of Unamuno is very uneven. Many of his articles are loaded with collateral associations and digressions, and they are written in a less than careful style. But one has to keep in mind that Unamuno has the highest contempt for literary professionalism, for all those who "think to write." The idea, for him, is to "write because one has thought," and even to write *as* one thinks, *as* one feels at the moment of setting down the pen. Because of that his articles are frequently nothing but collections of "beads without string," which end up, often, with a promise to deal more carefully with this or that point at a future date. In the majority of cases it would seem that the "other occasion" that he mentions constantly has never come around. But all of this is so human and so sincere that it is charming. Nonetheless, when Unamuno tries honestly to expose his ideas on a subject that burns his heart, he rises right away to the top of the highest and most polished language. His vocabulary is most extensive. He is a great coiner of new words and habitual enemy of the Royal Spanish Academy.[86]

With this brief note of the writings of Unamuno and their formal qualities, let us go on to consider his thought. We plan to deal with it in three sections under the following titles: critical ideas, philosophical ideas, and mystic ideas.

Critical Ideas

1. Literary Judgments

In this section we will deal first with Unamuno's literary judgments, and secondly, with his sociological ones. In either case we will limit ourselves to his criticisms of the literature and sociology of the Hispano-American countries, presenting them as they appear in the diverse writings of the master but without committing ourselves to them.

In the opinion of Unamuno Hispano-American literature has not attained the highest level due to the noxious influence of the French. He confesses suffering from *misparisiensismo*, stating that what is Parisian has been fatal for the Spanish race. Unamuno is shocked by the positivist spirit of the French, which makes him lament the fascination that Paris and things French exert on the Hispano-Americans. He gives the French no credit for having produced any mystic of the first order. He is of the opinion that English and Italian literature, due to a higher moral robustness, as in their more idealistic tone, should exert much more beneficial effects over the young American republics than the French.

It is true that the French people have stood out more in the exact and natural sciences than in realist literature and positivist philosophy. But it is necessary to recognize that the French spirit has been undergoing modification for a long time. The most original thinker of modern philosophy is a Frenchman, Bergson, who is not only a spiritualist, but almost a mystic. We

---

86. The official organization that makes rules on proper Spanish language and usage. —Trans.

have also witnessed nowadays from the time when the guardian angels of France overran the German host at the river Marne the apparition of new susceptibilities in the French soul. It seems certain that, when years have passed and the Bergsonian spirit will stand up in triumph over the ashes of Auguste Comte, this judgment of Unamuno will have no basis. But at least the suggestion he makes about the cultivation of English literature seems to be very sound. In view of the growing spirit of fraternity between the Hispano-American nations and the Anglo-Saxon ones, and in view of the determination of the British and Americans to make any effort that will lead to due appreciation of their brothers that speak Spanish, by founding, for this purpose, chairs of Spanish language and literature in all their universities, the nations of this continent cannot delay in taking a reciprocal action, facilitating the study of English language and literature in their university lecture halls, because it is easy to understand that nations of such diverse language and customs will never understand each other until both of them substitute the superficial language of commerce for the classic language of their thinkers.

Almost the only books published currently in Spanish that Unamuno reads are by American[87] authors. So that when he talks about Spanish literature in the New World, he does it as a passionate friend, and he criticizes some tendencies that he believes he finds in them. He alleges that in many American authors there is a greater concern for the form than for the substance of their writings. These "literary cabinetmakers," as he calls them, busy themselves in the externals of literary art, producing an "oily" prose, florid and resounding, an "artistically loathsome" product. But they, because of their desire to be called stylists, end up not having any style. In the opinion of Unamuno the Hispano-American authors do not excel in the works of pure imagination. Those that deal with real matter over an objective background are better such as works on science and history, for example. He has found true humor and irony in only one American author, and that is in the patriarch of Peruvian letters, Don Ricardo Palma. The passage involved is so interesting that it deserves to be quoted completely. Explaining that the Castilian, Spanish literature lacks humor and fine irony because the Spanish temper is so passionate and fiery that, trying to be ironic or to mock, it insults, he adds:

> There, in America, Don Ricardo Palma is the most exquisite cultivator of irony that I know, and it may be due, as more than one critic, among them José de la Riva Agüero, has indicated, that

---

87. The author applies the term "American" to both North and South America. —Trans.

in Perú, with a moderate and even climate and soft living, sweet and easy, a soul has been formed that has some analogy with the French soul, and perhaps with the Hellenic soul.[88]

But perhaps the most accurate observation that Unamuno makes on literary matters has to do with international opinion of literary values. Such opinion is not, in the end, more than a judgment on "battleships, cannons, and material wealth." Among the cases to which he attributes this, we find the following:

> When I have heard more than one person talking of Chilean intellectual strength and science as superior to that of other South American countries, I suspect that those who issue such opinions based them less on any knowledge of Chilean literature or scientific works—knowledge which is here almost nil—than on the result of the war of the Pacific that earned for Chile the name of the "Prussia of America."[89]

This may be the reason why a French or North American author may consider himself, based only on the greater warlike spirit of their countries, as superior to a Spaniard . . . or to a Peruvian.

2. Sociological Judgments

Towards sociology, as the science that seeks the origin, traces the history, and solves the problems of social phenomena, Unamuno adopts the same attitude that his master Carlyle did attributing to it the loss of sight of the supreme importance of the individual, in its enthusiasm for institutions. We know already that Unamuno is interested mainly in individual human souls. It is very interesting to read his opinion of the science that so many acclaim as the savior of society.

> To this praised and well-trodden sociology I have a strong idiosyncrasy. For me there is scarcely anything more unbearable than books labeled as sociology, collections of platitudes and nonsense, mixed in general with fantastic syntheses. I imagine that within a half century a disrepute will fall upon this brand-new sociology as great as the one that today affects the philosophy of history of half a century ago.[90]

---

88. Unamuno, *Soliloquios y conversaciones*, 108.
89. Ibid., 189.
90. Unamuno, *Contra esto y aquello*, 72.

If this criticism is applied to Spencerian sociology, it has a sound basis, since the name of Spencer is rarely mentioned in European universities, and then, only to criticize his system. Otherwise Unamuno shows the most transcendental interest in the problems that tend to preoccupy sociology, which makes one think that he does not oppose this science as such, but only a pretentious school of it. In his many articles we find discussions on sociological issues, as, for example, "Games of Chance," "Pornography," "Feminism," etc., problems that interest modern society. But now we should look briefly at a problem that Unamuno presents that is at heart a sociological one and to which he gives an original and unexpected answer. But, as he has not devoted any complete article to the subject, we will rely on data from many different articles to reach our presentation of his point of view.

The problem in question can be presented in the following terms as "the lack of confidence in themselves shown by the South American peoples." Unamuno specifies several symptoms of this state of continental attitude. One of them is found in the book of a Chilean author who had the daring to state that "the so-called Latin nations are inferior to the Germanic and Anglo-Saxon ones, and are destined to be ruled by them." It is true that for Unamuno such a statement carries a fatal error, so that, after mercilessly assailing the book of such an outrageous author, he says, "It is necessary to end up with that boring sermon of inferiority and superiority of races, as if it existed in a generic and permanent way and it were not, so to speak, that whoever surpasses someone else in one respect, will surpass him in another, and whoever is on top today, was underneath yesterday, and he may be back there tomorrow, to go up, once again, on the next day. Perhaps what makes some less qualified for the type of civilization that dominates the world today, may be the reason why it will be better suited in a future type of civilization."[91] But given the incorrect nature of the judgment of the Chilean author, the fact that he brought it out reveals to the Spanish writer a grave disease in the spirit of this continent.

A second symptom of the same disease appears in a fact that was remarked by the outstanding Uruguayan thinker, Dr. Vaz Ferreira, in words that Unamuno quotes in his book *Monologues and Conversations*. It deals with young South Americans who return to their countries after having studied in Europe.

> In the European milieu our students are outstanding or at least have an honorable role, and I do not refer only to those with an extraordinary intellectual capacity, no! What is truly worthy of notice is that many that among us are mediocre are distinguished

---

91. Ibid., 14.

over there. But what happens afterwards? These students return with their courses finished. They are seen "sparkling," we may say, for a time, and then they "turn off." As professionals they may be most distinguished, good physicians, good lawyers, good chemists, but nothing else in their professions. They do not make any original discovery; they do not propel any science.[92]

According to Unamuno, the same happens with the Spanish fellows who return to their country from foreign universities. Vaz Ferreira and Unamuno are in agreement that the true cause of this phenomenon is not due to the lack of incentives for original research, nor in the lack of means to work, nor even lack of time on the part of the professionals, but it is due "to the condition of the spirit with which the South American researcher works. It is because he works in a state of passivity of the spirit, receptive, and does not believe he has got the capacity, or the duty, to make personal use of his observations; or, in other words, to a kind of collective humility, to a lack of confidence in themselves. It is as if the chemist, for example, Uruguayan, Argentinian, or Spaniard were to say, 'Me, oh my, an Uruguayan, Argentinian, Spaniard, what am I going to discover that has not already been discovered by a German, a Frenchman, or an Englishman?'"

The absence of interest in politics is the third symptom of the same psychological disease. "I am not a politician." "He is a politician." "The government does not give me anything."—These and other expressions repeated persistently are all equally humiliating, and they are the ones that were satirized years ago by the eminent Spanish author Mariano José de Larra in his article titled "In This Country." What are they but indications of lack of confidence of a people in its political life, and as a consequence, in themselves, who have to choose politicians, and also in the future of the nation? Because, as Unamuno says very well, "Where the people lose interest in politics, there is decay of science, art, and even industry."[93]

The last revealing trait of the same pathologic condition is what Unamuno called "the fear of ridicule." Due to the obsession of this fear there are few who try, who experiment, who make new tests, who get out of the routine. They would do it joyfully "if they were sure of success, but considering the perspective of failure, and after that, the jeer and banter, perhaps to be considered crazy, or duped, or half-witted, in view of that, they get frightened and do not try."[94] They forget that all the leaders and heroes of progress, whose faith in the success that was to crown their efforts, that led

---

92. Unamuno, *Soliloquios y conversaciones*, 178.
93. Ibid., 271.
94. See, Unamuno, *Vida de Don Quijote y Sancho*, 210.

them to face the momentary taunt, were considered great fools. They forget, also, that "when the fear of ridicule takes possession of an individual or of a people, they are lost for any heroic deed."[95] And "only by attempting the absurd can the impossible be conquered."[96]

In view of this subordinate spirit that, according to Unamuno, the men of letters, the professional, and plebeian South American classes suffer from, it is interesting to note the remedies that he prescribes. First, he suggests that the Spanish speaking nations get to know each other, so that they will be able to form an ethnic conscience. Second, a true nationality must be formed, be it Argentine, Bolivian, or Peruvian, by the conscious development in all the citizens of a country of the potential of the national soul. If this were to find its full expression, a nation could appreciate itself, discovering at the same time the role that it has to play among the nations of the world. The only cradle of this true nationality will be a national school. It will also be the concern of every citizen to become imbued with the eternal more than the modern, the universal more than the cosmopolitan. An individual could free himself from servile imitation with the new orientation that he would attain in this way. The last prescription that Unamuno proposes for the formation of this true nationalism is a religious base. We cannot do anything better than to listen to his own words.

> I do not understand a country that is true, a people that is true, a people that has some inkling of its mission and role in the world, if its collective conscience does not respond, even in a dark manner, to the great and eternal human problems of our ultimate purpose and our destiny.[97]

Philosophical Ideas

Unamuno's philosophy can be called the "philosophy of desperation." It is a spiritualistic philosophy, eclectic, and profoundly Spanish. It has deep roots in Spinoza, Kant, Carlyle, and William James, authors with whom Unamuno discovers many affinities, but the soul of the system is the revived spirit of Don Quixote de la Mancha. The most elaborate and complete expression of his ideas that Unamuno has given up to now is found in the book with the title *The Tragic Sense of Life*, a book published in 1912 and which, together

---

95. Unamuno, *Contra esto y aquello*, 124.
96. Unamuno, *Vida de Don Quijote y Sancho*, 211.
97. Unamuno, *Contra esto y aquello*, 78.

with his poems, the *Life of Don Quixote and Sancho*, and *About Authenticity*, contains all his fundamental ideas.[98]

With this preliminary orientation let us go back to consider the philosophical doctrines of Unamuno. And so that the discussion may be clear and concise, we will consider them under three sections, namely anti-rationalism, vitalism, and Hispanicism.

1. Anti-Rationalism

When Unamuno is called anti-rationalist, it is necessary to clear up the sense with which we use this word, because, from some points of view, he is a most radical rationalist. He demands absolute freedom of thought and assails any system, be it political, ecclesiastical, or philosophical that attempts to impose itself despotically over the conscience. Since the free exercise of reason is so sacred for him, even to the point of contradicting himself, he refuses flatly to refer to himself by the name of any school of thought. Man has to think, yes, but he must think in a "vital" not "logical" way. He must think with his body, his heart, and all the powers of his soul, not merely with his brain. To think that way is to be set free of the despotism of ideas, or, as Unamuno states, paradoxically, somewhere.—"To rethink the commonplace is the best way to get rid of its evil spell." In this way it should be clear that Unamuno does not impugn the legitimate use of reason, better yet, he promotes it. What he fights is the *pretensions* of reason. First, he denies that reason is a pure and simple faculty, assessing the concept of "pure reason" as purely fictitious. In the same way that a thinker is a man of flesh and bones, the exercise of reason is determined by the integral condition of his conscience. He finds the position that reason can attain the truth equally untenable. Hellenic reason will never be able to get to the core of things. When it does not lead to skepticism, it reaches only the "shadow of truth, cold and cloudy." Unamuno calls formal logic "a most hard tyrant of the spirit," and he loathes the syllogistic method. Neither does he consider acceptable the ideal proposed by rationalism, that is contemplation, which can never be an ideal for a man of flesh and bones, who longs to rejoice, not only to contemplate. He also denies reason the capacity to improve ethics. Contrary to all the great idealists, he states that "to reason on ethics is to slay it," and rejects the famous opinion of Socrates that "virtue is science." The

---

98. At the time of Mackay's writing Unamuno's works *Saint Emmanuel the Good, Martyr* (1930) and *The Agony of Christianity* (1925) had not yet been published. Along with *The Tragic Sense of Life* they were included on the *Index Librorum Prohibitorum*. —Trans.

only thing useful to lift the moral level in life is "passion." It is not reason but passion that can make heroes and saints.

2. Vitalism

The starting point of the philosophy of Unamuno is not rational, but vital; not reason, but sentiments and will. He adopts the pragmatic position of William James that it is the will that makes the world. And instead of saying with Descartes, "I think, therefore I am," he says, "I desire, therefore I am." For him all philosophy is nothing but an attempt to provide an objective and rational reality to the desires of the heart. Consequently, beliefs are just creations, that, for the same reason, have only a relative value. The martyr, according to Unamuno, is the one who makes the faith, not the faith the martyr.

The end of the universe is the individual soul, which does not consist of superior and inferior parts, unified and ruled by reason, as all idealists have thought since Plato. As to the soul, it is preached that it lives; but the life of the soul will never correspond to the Hellenic ideal of harmony, because the soul discovers from the very beginning an absolute dualism between the rational and the vital elements that will never live in peace and harmony. An internal struggle originates between them that will not be terminated by the idealistic or the hedonistic solution, but will end only in death. This interminable struggle is the distinctive element in the philosophy of Unamuno, and the whole system revolves around this. It will be important to trace its course from beginning to end. In this way we will be able to decipher the intimate biography of the author and be able to notice, at the same time, the practical application of his ideas.

The essence of the soul is expressed in the universal longing to be eternal. The instinct of perpetuation is the foundation of human society. Each individual who has not become sophisticated not only thinks himself unique but desires to stay like that for all eternity. The longing for personal immortality springs up, in one way or another, from the heart of all men. It was the presence of this longing in Kant, the man, which made Kant, the philosopher, justify rationally his belief in the immortality of the soul, taking that remarkable leap over the abyss separating "pure reason" and "practical reason." It was this longing that Spinoza wished to express with his idea of the "conatus," that is, the striving with which each thing tries to persevere in its being. Between the existence of this longing and the existence of God, Unamuno intersperses the following steps. Man desires to be immortal, soon he believes it to be so; but his personal immortality requires the guarantee of a God that guarantees it. Having created God in this way, in search of immortality, man then hopes and loves him. But in the meantime reason, following a different path, arrives at skepticism about all the beliefs of the heart. The conflict originates from this. Here we have the bottom of the abyss in which the heart and the head are sunken. In their strife the heart is broken, while from its wounds flow the tragic sense of life. From that point on man becomes a tragic and desperate contender with the mystery of life. The result is a "transcendental pessimism, which generates a temporal and earthly optimism." The desperation brought about by the struggle between reason and feelings may be the basis for "a vigorous life, of an effective action, of an ethic, of an esthetic, of a religion, and even of a logic."[99]

On the basis of this "transcendental pessimism" Unamuno builds a castle with three watchtowers to confront earthly life. One of them has its lookout open toward the region of thought, another toward popular opinion, and the third toward moral life. How do we have to think? How should we behave with reference to the judgment of others? How are we to live? With reference to our thinking, to struggle is worth more than victory. As struggle is the only true life, we should never demand peace or rest for the head, but only for the heart, no new light but "water from the abyss." As for popular opinion, one should never pay attention to it. Whoever lives under the light of eternity will have to face daily jeers and ridicule. As for life, Unamuno prescribes one ideal and one norm for it. The ethical ideal will be that each individual would treat his profession or job as a religious duty, that he would try to behave as if "our vocation be the position in which we find ourselves, or, in the last resort, to change it for something else."[100] So that for Unamuno the fundamental social problem is not the distribution of wealth, but of vocations. On the other hand, the norm with which to judge the morality of an individual, and in that way, his right to immortality, will be that, in the opinion of those who know him, he will be irreplaceable as father, as son, as professional, or as mechanic. Or, if we express the norm in different terms, adopting the words of Senancour, a man has to live in such a way that his annihilation, if it were to happen, would be an injustice.[101]

It is never pleasant to criticize a thinker with whose spirit and ideas one has deep sympathy. It is necessary, notwithstanding, that I finish this exposition of the philosophy of Unamuno with a critical judgment about it. First, the philosophy of Unamuno is indicative of a new and abundant tendency in modern philosophy. We are witnessing without a doubt the early dawn of a new, spiritualist age in the history of thought. All of a sudden the

99. Unamuno, *Del Sentimento Trájico*, 126.
100. Ibid., 265.
101. See ibid., 258.

last shadows that saddened the world, the positivism of Comte and the absolute idealism of Hegel, will have fled. The human soul receives the advent of its liberators. James and Bergson and a phalanx of illustrious thinkers that have followed them have brought to light once again a dialectical force which is invincible, and have established in a prestigious place the great doctrines of existence: liberty and immortality of the soul, and thereby also the existence and personality of a Supreme Being of the universe. As far as Unamuno advances under the banners of the new spiritualism, we are in complete accord with his ideas, and we recommend them passionately to all those who live under the Southern Cross, who recognize the iron crown of Auguste Comte. But there are some points in his system over which I would like to make several friendly reservations.

Among other points that we could mention, we list two of them that seem to me the weakest within Unamuno's system. One has to do with his epistemology, the other with his ethics. Although it is true that the direction that reason takes depends on the stimulus that it may receive from the sentiments, this has nothing to do with the capacity of reason to attain the truth. Because, if we believe, as we have to, that the universe is a rational whole, and if the function of philosophy is not to build an *a priori* system, but to interpret the whole experience,—provided that, we give reason a trustworthy original orientation, what prevents it from reaching the rational heart of things through a dialectic process of analysis and synthesis? Then there will be no reason why there has to be a persistent struggle between mind and heart, between science and religion, as one and the other form part of a rational and intelligible universe. But when Unamuno says, for example, that Christianity, even if he himself accepts it, is anti-rational, what he should say is that Christianity does not match the concepts of rationality that some authors have formed. It is not true, either, that "the struggle is worth more than victory." More human, and at the same time more philosophical, is Unamuno's other sentence, "How beautiful it is to get to port drenched in the water of the storm!"

The other objection to the philosophy of Unamuno is that it does not offer a practical and substantial basis for ethics. A desperate struggle in a limitless sea, where contrary winds of emotions and thoughts blow and where there is no certainty of ever arriving at the port, may certainly provide a basis for the morals of heroes and saints, but, as there are few of those, we cannot risk that all the other poor souls be drowned in the whirlpools of immortality. Man needs a solid basis for his faith and his life, a basis that will be rational for him, according to his concept of rationality. Besides this, nothing can be gained with the ethical norm that Unamuno suggests that is to become "irreplaceable." Is it not easy to imagine a man who lives in such a way to be irreplaceable, not only in his own judgment but also in the judgment of a group of his acquaintances, and who would be convinced that his annihilation would be unfair, and at the same time he would not have higher moral principles than those of a Moor who kills an infidel to gain heaven? This is due to Unamuno's use of the word "immortality" only in its traditional Spanish sense, that is, quantitative, without considering that the fundamental sense of such word is qualitative, corresponding to a state of the soul. May the man fight, advancing from faith to faith, and from concept to concept, but serene and strong!

> And whoever hates evil and vice finds
> a nuptial bed of roses in his death.

3. Hispanicism

This essay has become longer to such a degree that it has already exceeded the limits proposed at the beginning. We still have to deal with Hispanicism, the mystical ideas, and the influence of Unamuno. These topics I will have to treat with much less attention than they deserve. Following the example of our author when he finds himself in a similar situation, we will postpone the adequate discussion of those topics for some other occasion and limit ourselves for the time being to treat them briefly.

Unamuno makes constant claim that through his veins flows the most genuine Spanish blood. As a Basque, and a fellow countryman of Ignatius Loyola, he believes himself Spanish of Spaniards. Although he is one of the most cultured writers that Spain has produced, and even when he is fully aware of the great trends of European civilization, Unamuno is, perhaps, the one among contemporary Spanish writers who has crossed the borders of his country the least frequently and who has allowed himself to be influenced the least by the European spirit. For him it is unimportant that someone may say that Africa starts at the Pyrenees or that Spain extends to the Atlas Mountains. At the same time we find in Unamuno that one of his most absolute contradictions has to do with his prescription for the future of his country. He speaks sometimes as if the only hope for her were to renounce the ascetic ideal, opening wide all its windows to allow the entrance of European winds. At other times he seems to maintain that Spain must remain the same as she is, living quixotically with dreamed-of glory and charging against the windmills of a materialist civilization.

In his book *About Authenticity* that he wrote in his early years of literary life, Unamuno gives a most deep and valuable interpretation of the

Spanish spirit. After having analyzed the historical and authentic qualities of the Spaniards and having talked about the profound paralysis in which Spain is currently found, he adds the following text:

> Only opening the windows to European winds, soaking in the Continental environment, having faith that we will not lose our personality by doing so, becoming Europeanized to transform Spain, and involving ourselves with the people, will we regenerate this moral steppe.[102]

At that time Unamuno spoke as a social reformer for whom what is human was worth more than what is genuine. But since then he has written his *Don Quixote and Sancho* and *The Tragic Sense of Life*, books in which he seems to oppose the Europeanization of Spain. Now he is speaking more as a poet or a metaphysician than a reformer. He states that the only philosophical book that Spain has ever produced has been *Don Quixote* by Cervantes. This book, that in the last analysis is a book of jokes, is a brief summary of the history of Spain, and should be the "national and patriotic Bible" of Spain. Don Quixote, who lived in the flesh, without a doubt, before showing up in the pages of Cervantes, is the "Spanish Christ," "our lord Don Quixote." But between true and original observations, we seek in vain for a solution. How could El Quijote be the savior of Spain? Is it through his crazy life, or his sane death? We can hear the shout, "Long live Don Quixote!" or the opposite, "Death to Don Quixote!" We can conclude with this, that whatever is the value of the life of Don Quixote, and whatever the meaning of his death, a revived Don Quixote would be a pastor of souls, probably a writer, something that he himself suggested when after having been vanquished by the Bachelor[103] Carrasco, he took the shepherd's crook. Commenting on this incident in the life of the "Knight of the Sad Countenance," Unamuno says, "If Don Quixote were to return to the world, he would be the shepherd Quijotiz, no longer an errant knight with a sword. He would be a shepherd of souls, taking, instead of the crook, the pen or addressing his burning words to all the goatherds. And who knows if he may have revived! Who knows if he has revived . . . !"[104] These words taken in connection with others equally meaningful with which Unamuno ends his comments on the life of Don Quixote, cast new light on the renowned "quijotismo"[105] of the scholar of Salamanca. "And I say that Don Quixote

---

102. Unamuno, *En Torno al Casticismo*, 218.
103. A high school graduate.—Trans.
104. Unamuno, *Vida de Don Quijote y Sancho*, 423.
105. "with the quality of a Quijote." —Trans.

and Sancho were born so that Cervantes was able to tell us his life, and I was born so that I could comment on it . . . No one can tell your life, nor explain it or comment on it, my lord Don Quixote, except somebody who is afflicted of your same madness not to die."[106] From this we can conclude that Unamuno not only believes himself to be the only legitimate commentator on "el Quijote" of Cervantes, but that he believes himself to be a resuscitated Don Quixote, who has as a modern mission, to straighten with ink and pen the genuine wrongs of his beloved Spain.

Mystic Ideas

We will finish this study of the ideas of Unamuno with a glimpse at his mystic and naked spirit. As we know, he is interested in all the great problems that may concern a man and a Spaniard, that is why he deserves the name of critic, philosopher, and patriot; Unamuno is, in the depth of his soul, a mystic. His thinking is drenched in the mysticism of his homeland, and it is not the unworthy descendant of the line of Granada, León, and the Saint of Avila.[107] The intense individualism that distinguishes the mysticism of Unamuno from the pantheistic German mysticism is a feature that he has inherited from the mystical author of *The Dark Night of the Soul*.[108] Genuine son of his people, he would not be content with the perspective of losing himself in the soul of the universe, where he would forsake thinking and feeling as an individual. He seeks personal immortality, and he would prefer to be "an eternal atom than a fleeing moment of the whole universe."

Nonetheless, the mysticism of Unamuno is much more human and less ascetic than the genuine Castilian one. He does not make the same total separation between God and nature. The only Spanish mystic who really felt the charm of nature was Fray Luis de León, the predecessor of Unamuno in the University of Salamanca. For Unamuno, God is not only a transcendent being, but penetrates everything and lives and suffers in men. We find his eternal arms beneath all things. The belief that God is present, not only in the world but in the personal life of men, is one of the most deeply rooted ideas of Unamuno. Because of that belief we can understand a passage in his work that otherwise would seem meaningless and even cruel. Here is that passage:

---

106. Unamuno, *Vida de Don Quijote y Sancho*, 464.

107. The references are to Fray Luis de Granada, Fray Luis de León, and St. Teresa of Avila. —Trans.

108. St. John of the Cross. —Ed.

> Man floats in God without need of any board, and the only thing I want is to take away the board, leave him alone, give him encouragement so that he feels that he floats ... We have to throw men in the middle of the ocean, and take away all boards, so that they learn to be men, to float. Do you have so little trust in God that being in Him, in whom we live (Acts 17:28) you need a board to grasp? He will hold you without board. And if you sink in Him, what does it matter?[109]

The confidence of Unamuno in the presence of God in the universe flows from his personal experience. There is no passage in all his work, as deeply mystical as the following:

> I believe in God as I believe in my friends, because I feel the breath of His affection, feel His invisible and intangible hand, drawing me, leading me, grasping me; because I possess an inner consciousness of a particular providence and of a universal mind that marks out for me the course of my own destiny. And the concept of law—it is nothing but a concept after all!—tells me nothing and teaches me nothing.
>
> Once and again in my life I have seen myself suspended in a trance over the abyss; once and again I have found myself at the cross-roads, confronted by a choice of ways and aware that in choosing one I should be renouncing all the others—for there is no turning back upon these roads of life; and once and again in such unique moments as these I have felt the impulse of a mighty power, conscious, sovereign, and loving. And then, before the feet of the wayfarer, opens out the way of the Lord.[110]

The childlike simplicity with which Unamuno refers to God is truly admirable. The following words where we find him in the "inner castle" could have been written by Saint Teresa.

> This voice that tells me: shut up, buffoon! Is it the voice of an angel of God or the voice of the tempting demon? O my God, You know that I offer to You the plaudits and also the censures. You know that I do not know how or where You are taking me. You know that if there are some who judge me badly, I judge myself worse than they. You, Lord, know the whole truth, only You. Improve my luck and twist my judgment, so as to straighten

---

109. Unamuno, *Vida de Don Quijote y Sancho*, 426.

110. Unamuno, *Del Sentimiento Trágico*, 193–94. [Translation at Unamuno, *Tragic Sense*, 194–95. —Ed.]

out my steps to walk through a better road than the one I am following.[111]

But in spite of his evident faith in God, Unamuno wishes that his life here be an endless struggle. He wants his heart to rest confidently, but not his head, ever.

> As long as I live, Lord, give me doubt
> pure faith at my death
> give me life in life
> and at death, death.[112]

He does not desire full light.

> You, my heart, are not seeking light, but water
> from the chasms
> and thus you will find the forge
> of the visions of eternal love.[113]

He does not succeed in understanding what Jesus meant by his words, "My peace I leave you."

> It is hard, Jesus, the war you brought me
> and the peace you left us has been lost;
> your peace, gentle rabbi, what does it contain
> because you have closed for us the serene Olympus?[114]

As a child, when he was a member of the congregation of St. Aloysius Gonzaga, Unamuno had a dream of becoming a saint. From that moment until the present he has never stopped for one moment having yearnings of holiness and eternity.

"When will I rest, my God, which will be my last yearning? This one, as in the present? May it be the will of God."[115]

His Influence

The loving task that I set for myself at the beginning is finished. My awareness of its imperfections could not be any deeper. I have dealt lightly upon the personal and intellectual life of Don Miguel de Unamuno, that "Knight

---

111. Unamuno, *Vida de Don Quijote y Sancho*, 374.
112. Unamuno, "Salmo II," lines 26–29. —Ed.
113. Unamuno, "No Busques Luz, mi Corazón, si no Agua," lines 80–83. —Ed.
114. Unamuno, "La Siete Palabras y dos más," lines 9–12. —Ed.
115. Unamuno, *Recuerdos de Niñez*, 172.

of the Sorrowful Countenance" of current Spanish literature; and now, following the example of the likeable Moor, Cid Hamete Benengali, I hang up my pen, which has not stopped spotting the beautiful Spanish language. But, confident that after what I have written, someone else will take the pen to discuss the significance of the life and theories of the sage of Salamanca, with a few more words about his influence, I conclude.

"I know that in the worst case even if these sheets dry up and rot in the memory of the reader, they will form there a layer of compost that will fertilize his own understanding."[116] Unamuno wrote this at the beginning of his work *About Authenticity*. And in this way, even if there are relatively few of those who, up to now, have been able to communicate all his spirit and ideas, there is a great range of fine youngsters whose minds have been "fertilized" by his writings, and it is true that sometimes his influence has had a more dramatic dénouement than the slow action of a fertilizer. "I, at least, would be ungrateful if I did not recognize that I am in your debt for having climbed over the wall of my yard or of my kitchen garden."[117] Here we have the confession of the poet Antonio Machado that he stated in a letter to Unamuno. Among other enthusiastic supporters of the eminent thinker, we find José Ortega y Gasset, chair of philosophy at the University of Madrid and a writer of great talent; Federico Onís, professor at the Oviedo University and editor of *The Names of Christ* of Fray Luis de León, and Alberto Jiménez Fraud, director of the Student Residence in Madrid. All of them have felt the inspiration of Unamuno, and they live in close friendship with him. Imbued with his spirit they devote themselves to improve the intellectual and moral condition of their country. The Student Residence of Madrid, the institution that provided me with lodging during my stay in Spain and where I had the honor of being introduced to Unamuno, incarnates his spirit and ideals. There one can find together under the same roof the finest students of all Spain, and there one can appreciate the profound influence that Unamuno is exerting over the pleasant Spanish youth.

Don Alberto Jiménez told me once, "If Unamuno continues talking as he is doing, we will have a new civil war." And in this way it will have to be. One of these days, Spain will have its "new civil war," and the soul of the new Spain that will arise glorious from the present decay, will be that of Don Miguel de Unamuno, the sublime "crazy" of Salamanca.

The South American countries where Unamuno has a greater number of readers are Argentina and Chile. It seems that up to now, judging by the bookstores and libraries of Lima, his name is not well known in Peru. But

---

116. Unamuno, *En torno al Casticismo*, 24.
117. Unamuno, *Ensyos*, 5:30.

as soon as his fascinating words resound in Peruvian hearts, others, like Machado, "will climb over the wall of his yard." Numerous good causes need support, and from beyond the ocean, from a room in one of the narrow streets of old Salamanca, we receive the provocative words that the master told his disciples, "Somebody has to do it, why should I not be the one?"

10

The Christ of the Spanish Mystics

THE MEANING OF THE word *mystic* and the word *Christ* depends upon who uses them. In Argentina to say that a man is a disgrace, a human wreck, a poor devil, you say, "he is a poor Christ." The followers of Gandhi, seeking a term to describe their great leader, called him "like Christ." This is what happens with the term "mystic." For some a mystic is a dreamer, has lost touch with reality, and lives in the clouds; for others a mystic is dynamic and a creator who has found the highest values of the spirit. Philosophically speaking a mystic is one who is in immediate contact with the reality of the spiritual universe and, in religious understanding, has a love of God.

Contemporary thinking has made great strides in religious matters. It feels a very deep concern for the problems of the spirit, and some of the most eminent thinkers of our time are profoundly mystical. The religious order has become a field ready for the application of thought and analysis. William James says that the main factors of human progress have been the mystical. Keyserling in his book *Diabolical Figures* says that Jesus is the magician who has managed to infuse a new sense of life into the creative conception.

Spanish mysticism had its golden age, and it is estimated that between the sixteenth and seventeenth centuries about two thousand persons lived who could be called mystical. The Spanish mystics made up the school of religious passion the most powerful and influential that the history of Europe records. This influence was not only upon Catholics but also Protestants outside Spain. Let us call attention to those mystics who lived in the time of the conquistadors and scoundrels. The very motive for the conquest of America, it must be recognized, was of a religious character, but as the conquistadors were bursting forth and while Hernán Cortés and Francisco

Pizarro attacked fortresses in the Andes, the mystics opened up passes to cities on high. They were the "knights of the divine" who wanted to take by assault celestial cities. Unamuno believes that mystical philosophy is the only Spanish philosophy. Spain has had no technical philosophy, but certainly a human philosophy: mysticism and the *Romancero*. The most genuine Spanish reform was the wish to produce great mystics.

Spanish mysticism is individualistic and cannot cease to be so because the Spanish spirit is an individualistic one. It is said that each Catalan has a king within. They are aristocrats in the depths of their souls. The German mystic has no objection to being lost in the universe and plunged into Buddhist nirvana, but the Spanish mystic wishes to absorb the divinity itself and speaks like Saint Teresa:

> This divine passion of love
> with which I live
> has made God my captive
> and my heart free;
> and it arouses in me such passion
> to see God my prisoner
> that I die because I do not die.[118]

She has made the deity captive in her heart and has achieved spiritual freedom.

Spanish mysticism is also characterized by its activism. It is not intellectual or platonic or quietist. Its mystics do not formulate great philosophical systems; these great adventurers tell their own experiences of taking the cities of heaven by assault.

Spanish mysticism is also christocentric. The Spanish mystics established everything in Christ and made no distinction between him and God. For Teresa of Jesus, God is Christ the Redeemer, the powerful and the spiritual, who became flesh and still lives. The Christ of the Spanish is the Christ of experience not of dogma or history. What interested them was their innermost religious experience, the Christ that they felt in the depths of their souls. These great heretics, Friar Luis de Granada, Saint Teresa, Saint John of the Cross, Friar Luis de León, all were persecuted, ridiculed and some were imprisoned ... and much later canonized.

See how the Spanish mystical notion is presented to us in the following sonnet attributed to Saint Teresa:

---

118. Teresa of Avila, "Vivo sin vivir en mí," lines 11–17. The word in line 1 of the excerpt is "pasión" ("passion"). The word in that line in the critical edition of Teresa's *Works* is "prisión" (prison). See, Teresa, *Obras*, 6:77–78. The present translation follows the text of Mackay's article. —Ed.

I am not moved, my God, by desire
for heaven that I trust in as promised
nor am I moved by fear of dreaded hell
to avoid that I have offended.
You move me Lord, to see the Beloved
nailed to the cross and mocked.
I am moved seeing your body injured,
I am moved by your insults and your death.
Beloved your love moves me in such way
that, though there were no heaven, I would love you
and although I had no fear of hell.
I do not have to give because you want;
though as much as I hope, I would not hope,
that I love you just as you would desire.[119]

In this sonnet we encounter the most crystalline sentiment not only of Spanish mysticism, but also of Christian sensitivity of all the ages. "I do not have to give because you want." The writer of this verse was interested only in that which has worth in Christ; loved him only for that which he signifies and represents. This is what constitutes the quintessence of religion: the love of God for himself, and not because the love is a good business deal in this world or the next world. It is to care about love's qualitative value and not the quantitative value of any reward.

Raymond Lull, one of the most sympathetic figures and one to whom we cannot do justice here, is the knight errant of philosophy whose religious spirit is revealed in the title of his foremost book, *The Book of the Lover and the Friend*. To Raymond Lull the quintessence of religion is transcendental friendship, and he has a classic phrase that penetrates to the depths of Christianity: "He who does not love does not live, and living life cannot die." Life and love: two preeminent aspects of religion. When you love God, you yourself live, and when you live for him, you do not die, you are immortal.

Saint Teresa, the most extraordinary woman who has lived on earth, whom Machado called "Soul of Fire"; Saint Teresa is the mystic of passion, the passion for her husband, who seals it with an arrow in her heart,[120] comparable only to the stigmata of Saint Francis. The notion appears in Saint Teresa that Christ searches for the passionate soul; that God is trying to seize the self and transform it, an experience that many have felt, and that Thompson, the English poet, has described in an immortal ode in which

---

119. Attributed to Saint Teresa, "No me mueve, mi Dios, para quererte." —Ed.

120. See and compare, for example, the sculpture by Bernini, *The Ecstasy of Saint Teresa*, located in the Church of Santa Maria della Vittoria in Rome. —Ed.

he refers to some feet chasing him and a voice that spoke of love.[121] Saint Teresa told of a vision that once appeared to her in which she saw her soul transformed into a reflection that portrayed the figure of Christ; and that, as a symbol of the interpenetration of the ethical and the religious, every time she committed a fault, the image was tarnished. In this admirable image the Saint teaches that religion and ethics are two sides of the same thing. Another admirable figure of speech of Saint Teresa is contained in her saying, "Christ walks among the pots," that is to say that in both menial things and in those with more nobility one ought to feel the divine presence, and that a true man can lead a religious life in all spheres of his activity.

Saint John of the Cross, a flaming spirit who pierced the secret of the divine as no other person has done, admirably painted his religious experience in his most beautiful poem, "The Dark Night of the Soul," written in the inquisitorial prison.

> On a dark night
> inflamed, with longing, in love
> Oh, blessed fortune!
> I went out without being noticed
> my house being now quiet.
> On the blessed evening
> in secret, that no one saw me
> nor saw I anything,
> without light or guide
> except what burned in my heart.
> The light guided me
> truer than the light of noonday
> where He whom I knew well
> expected me.
> Oh night that guided me
> Oh night lovelier than the dawn.
> Oh night that united
> Beloved with the loved one,
> loved one transformed into the Beloved.[122]

Thus is the religious search with the extraordinary light that burns in the heart, a passion for Christ, for him supreme; an adventure in which one wholeheartedly risks everything to encounter a new being that energizes and transforms into his very image.

---

121. The reference is to Francis Thompson's poem "The Hound of Heaven." —Ed.

122. John of the Cross, "En una noche obscura," lines 1–5, 11–15, 16–19, 21–25. Mackay's excerpted text does not include line 20 ("En parte donde nadie parecía.") of the poem. See John of the Cross, *Obras*, 2:1–2. —Ed.

Friar Luis de León, one of the greatest singers of nature, brought religion outdoors to the sound of the sparrows, and in his poetic corner exclaimed, "Christ lives in the fields." There is nowhere better to feel the divine than in the fields. Christ is the interpretive character of the cosmos, and we must meet him, and merge with him, and recover him for life and thought. Religion is not something that is only part of life, but rather all of life. Christ is health, perfect balance, the pure air that one breathes in order to live.

Don Francisco Giner de los Ríos and Don Miguel Unamuno are two modern mystics who can be considered fathers of the new Spain. The first, "my Don Francisco," as they all say, hardly talks of religion, but at heart he was a secular saint whose life was purely translucent. He introduced the religious spirit into everyday life because he considered it not a formula but a vital function. He was a friendly spirit; his ideal was friendship without borders. He lived with his disciples in the Guadarrama mountains, and even though the religion of his nation did not wish to bury him, he became a piece of the national soul. He possessed the religious sense of life.

The second, Don Miguel de Unamuno, the leading European moralist, in the presence of whose roar the voices of Bernard Shaw and Wells are very faint, presents us with the Christ of Judea, the Christ of the barren, bleak plateaus, and in him sees the tragic, sees the Christ of Calvary. In his youth he dreamed of being a saint and has come to be one. For Unamuno life is a struggle between the reason and the heart. The reason does not solve the awesome human problem. The ethical must be eternal. If the ethical does not survive, the universe is unjust; but it will be just. "I believe in God," Unamuno said, "as I believe in my friends, because I feel the breath of His affection, feel His invisible and intangible hand, drawing me, leading me, grasping me; because I possess an inner consciousness of a particular providence and of a universal mind that marks out for me the course of my own destiny."[123] His religion is to wrestle with God, side by side with God in order to solve human problems. For him, the Spanish Christ crucified is the everlasting symbol and a symbol of the race. In Unamuno two Christs are brought to light: *The Recumbent Christ* of Palencia, Christ black, dead, and inert that is the Christ of everlasting death that says nothing to life; Christ who is "earth, earth, earth." "Christ of the heavens, redeem us from the Christ of earth!"[124] . . . That Christ is not the Spanish Christ . . . The other

---

123. Unamuno, *Tragic Sense of Life*, 194. —Ed.

124. The preceding two quotations are from the closing lines of Unamuno's poem "The Recumbent Christ of Santa Clara." Unamuno, *Velázquez*, Appendix B, 377. The subject of that poem, the statue of the dead Christ of Palencia, is contrasted with *Christ Crucified*, Velázquez's painting. See Unamuno's book poem (and masterpiece) *The Velázquez Christ*. William Thomas Little noted that much of *The Velázquez Christ*

Christ is that of Velázquez, the one that struggles . . . Like Pascal, Unamuno affirms that "Christ has not stopped his agony," agony in the Greek sense of the word, that is, struggle. This agony for Unamuno is the quintessence of religion. Life is struggle, action, war; in it we must hit and fight, not with men but with false values. Unamuno wishes for peace but peace in the war, not peace of the pond, but the peace of the river that flows into the sea in constant and serene activity.

We must wrestle with God who made us, not that we would be corpses or have canes for the blind. We must wrestle and have peace like the peace of Christ, sleeping when the storm blows and his disciples shout; a peace in the soul that nothing can snatch from us, a peace that comes from our union with Christ, with God. There are great problems to be solved, but their solution is not found in the library, or in the cell, or in the jungle. We must wrestle in the solitude of the road, that is to say, always walking, always acting, beside the sublime wayfarer who leads through the countryside and villages for the sake of God on earth, the road to Emmaus.

---

was written while Unamuno was on a spiritual retreat at the Benedictine monastery of Santo Domingo de Silos. —Ed.

11

The Cultural Value
of Studying English Literature

I AM DEEPLY THANKFUL to the members of the Faculty of Letters, and especially to the illustrious Professors, Doctors Deustua and Wiesse, for the high honor they have bestowed by calling upon me to offer this course on English literature. I present myself this afternoon with a heart full of pleasure and pride—of pleasure for the opportunity to speak on the literature of my motherland—of pride for the privilege of working together in the teaching at this the oldest and most renowned university in Latin America.

I warn you, however, that you have me here without pretensions of any kind and with severe nervous tension. I have to let you know, also, from the beginning, that when one tries, at the present time, to prepare a course on English writers, one finds more than a few difficulties. To me, the first problem is one of language: I have acquired a very simple, ordinary command of the beautiful language of Cervantes, but there are other difficulties that anyone would experience who was called upon suddenly, like me, to give a series of lectures like these. The scarcity of the original texts of classic English literature in the city of Lima; the relative scarcity of the translations of them into Spanish; and the shortage of great books of literary criticism are some of the circumstances that make difficult, for the time being, the proper performance of the task that I have hastily engaged. But in spite of all these obstacles I have resolved not to spare any effort to make this course as useful as possible. And, if your interest and good will encourage me to offer a similar but more extensive course at the beginning of next university year, I promise to make a more worthy task of English letters in keeping with the high traditions of San Marcos University.

Now, without any further preliminaries, I will take up the announced topic for this evening, "The Cultural Value of the Study of English Literature."

The Pragmatic Spirit

The word "value" opens up a fertile field for thought. We live in an age permeated with the pragmatic spirit. The new philosophy of practical values has provoked tremors in many traditional systems. We do not ask so much, "What is?" or "What does this mean in relation to absolute and immeasurable reality?" but "What is this for in the limited and definite present?" In other words, a person's main concern with regard to this or that is not to know its truth but its usefulness.

In the high regions of abstract thought the influence of this movement has been eminently liberating. But in other spheres of life it has had consequences that, in the opinion of many, have been unfortunate and hurtful. Under the thrust of this spirit the old Latin and Greek classics have not only been demoted from the prestigious pedestal they used to occupy in scholarship, but the voices of Homer, Plato, Virgil, and Horace are barely recognizable in many university lecture halls. In many cases, also, the tough intellectual discipline required to study the great classics of philosophy has been replaced, for academic purposes, by the light pastime of reading the output of the latest philosophaster[125] who has given birth to poorly digested thoughts. But the most unfortunate consequence of the mistaken interpretation of pragmatism can be found in the concept, prevalent in some social groups, that no study deserves the effort if it does not lead directly to the acquisition of material riches. It turns out that any new study that may be proposed must submit inescapably to the dominant criterion, that is, its value as an instrument to improve the social condition of the student.

---

125. *Philosophaster* is a Latin satirical comedy by Robert Burton (1577–1640). Since the play is about someone who pretends to be a philosopher, the term itself is used to refer to a pretender to philosophy. —Ed.

The Pragmatic-Commercial Criterion and the Study of the English Language

If the English language is the subject of this utilitarian or commercial criterion, it receives the highest grade, so to speak. This language, born among savage tribes in the thick forests of Saxony and in the cloudy shores of Friesland and removed afterwards to ancient Albion,[126] that had to fight, at successive moments in history with Latin, Dutch, and French, now promises to become the commercial language of the world. For this reason knowledge of English is considered indispensable for a commercial career. People who would consider the most minimal study of English literature as a waste of time discover a remarkable enthusiasm for the language.

Dangers Involved in the Exclusive Study of the English Language

Incidentally, I would like to refer to certain serious dangers that are involved for a country like Peru in the exclusive study of the English language. First, this study can lead to some *misconceptions*, such as, for example, that North Americans lack spiritual ideals. Such a mistaken concept has been able to spread because of the almost exclusive contact of the South American public with the merchants of the republic of the North, and they constitute, in general, a money-mad class, heartless and not representative of their country. A war has been necessary to overcome that idea. In the second place, such study, practiced as it is at present, tends to *denaturalization*. Here is the psychological process. First step: many persons learn and utilize a foreign language to which they owe their job in industry. Second step: they reach the point of imitating what is superficial and frothy from an exotic civilization. Third step: they begin making confused contrasts between their country and the foreign one. Fourth step: following the line of least resistance, they end up losing their faith in their country and lose interest in serving it; and they become disgusting in the eyes of the foreigners themselves, because of the nauseating excuses they make about the misfortune of their nationality, "I am Peruvian, but I think as a foreigner," etc., etc., *ad nauseam*.

But a complementary study of English literature would give those people a different orientation and would form another spirit in them. Through studying English literature they would reach a true understanding of the Anglo-Saxon spirit and a knowledge of the social and industrial problems that England has lived through in its long history. It would

---

126. "Albion" is the oldest known name of the island of Great Britain. Here, it is used poetically to refer to the island. —Ed.

protect the Peruvian student from servile imitation, on the one hand, and also from the chronic discouragement from which he suffers on the other; and it would infuse him with ideas that he could use to solve the problems of his own country.

The Idea of Culture

The real value of the study of English literature will stand out if we consider it as a cultural discipline. But then the question arises, what is culture? And with what concept of culture does such a study best fit? I propose to set up an ideal of culture, and then to show that the study of English literature can contribute to the realization of such an ideal. Consider, therefore, negatively and positively, the concept of culture.

Culture is not mere *linguistic ability*. Those who have as their ideal in life to be able to speak many languages, as they are great enthusiasts of cosmopolitan thinking and behavior, are often individuals without a definite point of view, intellectual hermaphrodites, who have the features of many countries, but do not have the power or the individuality of any one.

Culture is not *encyclopedic knowledge* either. It is true that scholarship does not exclude culture, but it does not imply it, either. It often happens, on the contrary, that the ones called scholarly who are fond of boasting of their knowledge are nothing but devout members of a cult of notions, shallow charlatans, intellectual skeletons without flesh, blood, or spirit, submissive slaves of mediocrity. *Humanism*, with its study of the past, especially of the old classics, its involvement with an ideal world of beauty, may offer a more attractive ideal. Humanists are, by and large, men of refinement, but with a cold and narrow mind: beautiful, frigid statues, brittle and unyielding. They live devoid of sympathy for the social convulsions of the present age, which they cannot interpret. Their criticism tends to be cynical.

We have, at last, *modernism*, that is the cult of the modern without reference to the past. The devotees of this cult in its literary expression are professional swallowers of everything new and newly published. All their interest is for the most recent novelty, after which they let themselves be dragged. They are literary chameleons who, devoid of their own color, take the shade of the place where they find themselves at the moment.

Culture in the proper sense of the word implies: (1) An *attitude*. This attitude consists in having the soul turned toward the light of truth, an open and tolerant mind, and enthusiasm for learning. (2) A *perspective*. With the above-mentioned attitude one will reach, in the end, a high point of view where one will be able to contemplate all ideas and human institutions with serenity, being able to award each one of them their due importance. All things will be seen as they are. (3) A *passion for perfection*. This passion will be expressed in seeking the ideal in personal, intellectual, and moral life, and in its communication to the whole society.

According to this conception, culture becomes something eminently moral and social. It has nothing of asceticism or selfishness. It discovers an enthusiasm for the good in all its forms. It is serene and does not care for popularity, which is for puppets, not for men. It initiates and is practical. One of the most suggestive sayings of Plato, in the seventh book of his *Republic*, was that, "The philosophers must be the kings." The great academic was right: because culture, and nothing else, is what gives the right to rule and administer, and to point the direction to a country or a movement. Let us remember that Aristotle was the tutor of Alexander the Great, and that the men who direct the current war and lead the future civilization are not irresponsible romantics but old thinkers, such as Wilson, Clemenceau, Poincaré, Orlando, Lloyd George, and Balfour. And if modern democracies are going to escape the risk of mediocrity that threatens them, they will have to revise their ideas about culture.

Having already explained the meaning of cultural value, the path is open to consider what English literature can contribute to our realization of our cultural ideal.

English Literature

Literature can be defined as the artistic expression of the best thoughts about universal life. Restricting in this way the meaning of the word to artistic productions, we exclude from consideration the works of science and philosophy, since they are not pure literature because they do not need to employ artistic forms. English literature is one of the three complete literatures that the world has had, the other two being the Greek and the French. Every complete literature must express four artistic attitudes towards life, namely *describe it, feel it, idealize it,* and *live it*. Using this logical analysis of the idea of literature, I would like to show to what extent English literature can provide a perspective and a passion to whoever brings the required attitude to its study. But because of lack of space, I can only mention, without speaking at length about the individual merits, some typical works whose study may help to develop the desired orientation.

1. Life Described

(1) Plain description. (a) Description of landscapes and natural life: *The Seasons* by James Thomson, and the works of George Crabbe,[127] and William Morris. (b) Narrative descriptions: *The Canterbury Tales* by Geoffrey Chaucer; *The Traveler* and *The Deserted Village* by Oliver Goldsmith; *Childe Harold's Pilgrimage* by Byron; and a number of essays and travel books that include narrative and description, such as *The Travels of David Livingstone*; *Essays of Travel* by R. L. Stevenson, etc., etc. (c) History: more complicated descriptions of the life of nations and institutions, and of the course and causes of great movements, *The History of England* by Macaulay; *The History of the Decline and Fall of the Roman Empire* by Gibbon.

(2) Imaginative description. (a) Epic and romantic poems: personifications of the forces of nature or descriptions of the life of mythical or historical characters, the old epic of *Beowulf*; *Paradise Lost* by Milton; *Ossian* by MacPherson; *Morte d'Arthur* by Tennyson. (b) Allegory: personification of ideas, *Pilgrim's Progress* by Bunyan, one of the most remarkable books of the English language; *Gulliver's Travels* by Swift. (c) Drama: descriptions of situations and persons who are representative or typical, either tragic or comic; the dramas of Marlowe, Shakespeare, Jonson, Ford, Oscar Wilde, Bernard Shaw. (d) Novels: a later genre with descriptions of situations and persons of common, daily life. The development of the novel has been toward the concrete, provincial, and conversational. Typical novelists are Fielding, Scott, Thackeray, Dickens, Eliot, Conan Doyle, Chesterton, Wells, Ralph Conner,[128] Gilbert Parker.[129]

2. Life Felt

In the English lyric we can find three cardinal feelings, those of freedom, love, and mystery.

(1) Freedom: This feeling appears in Byron in the form of an exaggerated license and rebellion; in Shelley as metaphysical freedom; in Campbell[130] and Kipling as national freedom.

---

127. George Crabbe (1754–1832) was an English poet, clergyman, and surgeon. His career was aided by the statesman Edmund Burke. —Ed.

128. Ralph Conner is the pen name of the Rev. Dr. Charles William Gordon (1860–1937), a Canadian novelist and church leader whose father was a Free Church of Scotland missionary in Upper Canada. —Ed.

129. Sir Gilbert Parker (1862–1932) was a Canadian novelist and British politician who served in the British House of Commons as a Conservative member of Parliament. —Ed.

130. John Campbell (1708–1775) was a Scottish writer and historian. —Ed.

(2) Love: Wordsworth and Thomson express love of nature; Blake and Hood,[131] love for humanity; Burns and Byron, sentimental love; Tennyson and Browning, spiritual love.

(3) Mystery: A sense of the mystery of life and a spirit of reverence toward it has been a characteristic of English literature from its origins. Classical expressions of this feeling are found in *Sartor Resartus* of Carlyle; *In Memoriam* of Tennyson; and *Hound of Heaven*, by Francis Thompson.

3. Life Idealized

Among the authors who have looked at life philosophically with a point of view, we find More, Bacon, Burke, Carlyle, Arnold, Ruskin, and Wells. They have attempted to analyze, criticize, and build a better life than the one lived by society at the moment. Carlyle and Arnold will be remembered as apostolic critics; Burke, Ruskin, and Wells, as visionary architects.

4. Life Lived

English literature has a remarkable wealth of great biographies, that is, literary monuments about how the lives of some of the children of the nation have been lived. Biographic masterpieces that deserve to be read for the literary qualities and the greatness of the characters represented are the *Life of Johnson* by Boswell, that of Nelson by Southey, the one of Scott by Lockhart, and the one of Gladstone by Morley. A study of biographical English literature brings out the interesting fact that many of the great men whose public and intimate lives have been reported, combined in their being Hebraism and Hellenism, tendencies that are so frequently opposed, that is, character and intellect, morality and esthetics.

Whoever sincerely starts the study of English literature and walks restlessly through the paths that I have just pointed out, will find in the end a wider vision, a strengthened heart, and a fortified character. That person will be able to understand the spirit of a people, to enjoy exquisite sensations of art, will feel the inspiration of eager and fulfilled spirits, and will learn a great deal that he will be able to apply in his own intellectual and moral life, and also in the social and political life of his country.

---

131. Thomas Hood (1799–1845), a British humorist and poet, was the father of Tom Hood (1835–1874), a satirist and playwright. —Ed.

Part Four

The Message and Political Life

12

The Regeneration of Peru

IN 1919, THE NINETY-EIGHTH year of the independent life of the Peruvian Republic, a book appeared in Lima titled: *The First Century: Moral and Material Progress of Peru in its First Century of Independent Life*. The author of the work is the well-known Peruvian sociologist, Don Pedro Dávalos y Lissón. It seems to disclose that a disinterested study of Peruvian history during the past hundred years reveals not the progress of the country but the lack of progress. From which it may be gathered that the dawn of the second century, which is just beginning to light up the horizon, must break over a land that has known more shadow than light through the long period since the July 28, 1821, when San Martín constituted Peru a free and independent nation.

The motto with which the present government began its work is "*Patria Nueva*" (New Country). Special stamps of large size record the great event of promulgating a new constitution. But these same stamps, which flaunt the banner of the new regime, while symbolizing aspirations for the future, contain a judgment of the past—and the present.

"If he speaks ill of Spain, he is a Spaniard," said José Mariano de Larra, in his famous satire, *Things in This Country*. So we may say, "If he speaks ill of Peru, he is a Peruvian." Spain's national weakness for defaming the homeland has become endemic in Peru, to such an extent that one often hears the remark, hardly flattering to the proud Peruvian, "I am a Peruvian, but I have the ideas of a foreigner." But, disregarding this horde of slanderers who dishonor their own nation, having no regard for the country except bitter judgments, the fact is that Peru today is not realizing all the hopes that her founders of a century ago marked for the future of the nation. Much as he might wish to do so, no good patriot, nor foreign lover of this country can close his eyes to the sad fact that, after a hundred years of experimenting with republican life, in spite of many material advances, this country is still groping and stumbling about in the dark as regards spiritual matters. There are moments when from the lips of all Peru's friends issue the words of Fray Luis de León, written in prison:

> Here all night long we wake; and wretched day
> Brings no relief but tears; each morning's woe
> Swallows up yesterday's.

What is going on in the ancient mansion of the Incas? Many are those who devote themselves to diagnose the ills of which the country makes complaint. Every nook of the national mind has been pried into in a corresponding number of articles and pamphlets. The characteristic habit of thinking subjectively concerning matters of national importance is little less than morbid. "What is being done?" or "What else could be expected?" are the refrains that sound eternally. Now it is the Spanish blood, now the native, now the heterogeneous mixture of other bloods that is to blame. Now the dominant church is impugned, or scarcity of money, or lack of means of transportation. But whatever might be the ulterior cause of the trouble, those who have studied the problem most seriously agree that the immediate cause is the lack of character and that this lack of character comes from the lack of an ideal. Peru needs an ideal that might mould the nation into a strong and upright people, one with its own true individuality.

Where will Peru find an ideal to serve her through the second century, an ideal which will outline a future destiny for her and inspire her with enthusiasm to attain it? This is the problem laid down by José de la Riva Agüero[132] toward the end of his remarkable book, *The Literature of Independent Peru*. Does he solve it? He says, "To be able to produce a fruitful collective ideal, we Hispanic Americans need ethnic homogeneity, confidence in our own power, intense and concentrated intellectual life, as well as social and economic development." Commenting upon this statement of Riva Agüero, Unamuno exclaims, "And they need something more, the same thing we Spaniards need in order to have again an ideal which may give us originality; namely, the religious sentiment of life."

This learned gentleman is right. Nothing can take the place of "the religious sentiment of life" in establishing and developing a people. Nothing

---

132. José de la Riva Agüero (1783–1858) was an historian, politician, soldier, and president of Peru. —Ed.

but religion can serve as a guide to men who have lost their way; only religion can supply that dynamic force by which a feeble people may grow strong. Neither commerce nor industry can do this. They may fill the land with machines and profits, make fabrics and smelt metals, yet they are unable to plant in the national mind a single altruistic sentiment, or to forge a noble character for a single citizen. The greatness of a country is the greatness of her men, and that is produced by other factors than economic ones.

Nor can culture accomplish the desired end. Culture gives light but not force, provides implements for work, but not the will to labor, ornaments life without changing its substance. Intellectual culture has but a negative value where the spirit is concerned. If, by it, a virtuous man can gain a more pleasing manner for social life and greater mental shrewdness in business matters, likewise by it the thief may steal in a more dexterous way. Even moral culture cannot replace religion in the life of a people. A country is not made more moral nor does its civilization change by the simple enforcement of rules of morality. For however good these rules might be, they are unable to arouse enthusiasm to comply with duty, or bring it about that virtue shall be the natural and spontaneous expression of the mind. No permanent moral state can be produced thus.

In one of his poems Schiller tells the story of a young man who tried to gain virtue by obedience to moral law, that is to say, by fulfilling his duty. What was the result? His spirit was kept in restraint. The requirements of the law became more and more repugnant to him. He reached the point where he tolerated religion without enjoying it. His conscience, instead of renovating his will, did nothing more than spur it. Finally, realizing that his nature had not changed, he exclaims in disgust, "O virtue, take back your crown, and let me sin."

Thus it happens in the life of a people, and with greater reason, for great masses of human beings are concerned. Certain privileged spirits may perhaps reach civic virtue without a religious basis for their morality, but for the great majority of men this is impossible, and even in those cases where apparently a blameless moral life is combined with religious sanction, religion is there, nevertheless. It has been observed by Balfour, a well-known statesman and thinker of England, that, when a study is made of the life of those men who are the perfection of honor, but who acknowledge no religious faith, it will be found that their characters have been formed in surroundings made and penetrated by the very faith that they later disavow.

Few will deny that religion is the greatest dynamic and renovating force known. William James, the eminent North American philosopher, has established in an incontrovertible way the fact that a religious life has also a great pragmatic value for the individual as well as for the society in which he lives. In his famous treatise, *The Varieties of Religious Experience*, in the chapter called "The Value of Saintliness," he says, "In a general way then, and 'on the whole,' our abandonment of theological criteria and our testing of religion by practical common sense and the empirical method, leave it in possession of its towering place in history. Economically, the saintly group of qualities is indispensible to the world's welfare. The great saints are immediate successes; the smaller ones are at least heralds and harbingers and they must be leavens also, of a better mundane order. Let us be saints then, if we can, . . ."[133] There were saints in England when the United States was founded. And even more saintly were those Pilgrims who founded this great Saxon republic.

The problem of Peru, as of other countries, is much more than a political, sociological, economic, or educational problem; it is after all the problem of the production of saints. "Lima has no saints," says Dávalos y Lissón in the book previously mentioned, not even any of those epileptic saints that appear from time to time in the provinces. I share in the opinion of Unamuno, Francisco García Calderon, and others, that the religious problem is the principal problem of the country, and hold that the solution of it will give the keep to the solution of all others. Regeneration must begin in the mind, and must express itself first in the new, or if you will, old, type of "the Saint."

---

133. James, *Varieties*, 364—Ed.

13

The APRA Movement

THE TERMS APRA AND Aprismo are becoming as familiar in Latin America as the terms fascism and communism have been for some time in the rest of the world. Whether as an international political philosophy or a national political party, the APRA movement is a genuinely Latin American product. It is, one might say, the first truly indigenous and, at the same time, completely formulated system of political thought that has emerged in the history of Latin America. Thus far, it is true, neither the principles nor the spirit of this movement, nor the practical statesmanship of its promoters have been tested in the seat of power; yet the ideas that lie at the heart of it, the influence that they have already had in a number of Latin American lands, the personality of its founder and chief exponent, and the brief political history of the APRA Party in Peru, are so significant as to entitle the movement to close and serious attention by all who are interested in future political developments in Latin America. The topic falls naturally into three main sections: 1) The origin and history of the APRA movement; 2) The APRA as an international political philosophy; and 3) The APRA as a national political party.

I. The Origin and History of the APRA Movement

The APRA movement is the child, and indeed the only living child, of a widespread cultural revolt carried on by university students in Latin America against the traditional university system in vogue throughout the continent. The reform movement began in 1918 in the Argentine university of Córdoba and spread rapidly to other university centers in Argentina, Uruguay, Chile, and Peru. In 1919 the students of the University of Lima, Peru, declared a strike after the University Senate refused their demands for reform. Under the leadership of a young man, Victor Raúl Haya de la Torre, a student in the Faculty of Law and president of the Students' Federation of Peru, the strikers succeeded in securing many of the reforms for which they had been agitating. These included the removal of incompetent professors, the modernization of courses, and student representation on the governing board of the university.

The following year a conference of Peruvian students held at Cuzco, the seat of the old Incan empire, passed a series of resolutions bearing upon the social issues before the country. With a view to contributing to the uplift of the masses, the students organized a scheme of university extension. The name of *Universidades Populares González Prada* (González Prada Popular Universities) was given to the new organization. González Prada was an outstanding Peruvian writer who, until his death in 1918, had mercilessly and fearlessly analyzed the problems of Peru in a series of brilliant essays. A saying of his, "Age to the grave, youth to the task,"[134] had already sounded as a slogan of the new student generation in Latin America. His young Peruvian countrymen called their new "Peoples Universities" by his name and applied themselves with enthusiasm, insight, and abnegation to face needs that he had taught them to see and feel. Thus, a new interest in social reform was added to the original interest in university reform.

The González Prada Popular Universities, themselves the creation of a new attitude on the part of youth towards education and social problems, became the mother of the APRA movement and transmitted to this movement a number of its essential features. A number of new notes were struck in Latin American social history in the sacrificial and disinterested labors of a choice group of Peruvian students on behalf of working men and women in Peru. To begin with, the traditional gulf between students and workmen in South America had been bridged. Here was a new type of student, one who–repudiating the cultural ideals of previous student generations according to which a man of culture should not be a *sectario*, that is, identify his life with any one idea or cause–relinquished all claim to special privilege. The new student regarded culture as a crusading instrument for human betterment and social needs as a challenge to the socially privileged. The working man's traditional distrust of the student class and the traditional disdain of the student class for the work and the manual worker were soon replaced by a united front of intellectual and manual workers. Proletariat

134. "Los viejos a la tumba, los jóvenes a la obra."

pupils received from their student mentors not only an elementary education in the ordinary sense but also instruction in hygiene, in sociology, and in social science. Notions of personal purity and of group discipline and loyalty were strongly inculcated. Politics in the party sense were banned, and all politicians were suspect. At this stage it was considered that the ideals of the new united front would be betrayed if any of the members were to take part in political activity under the existing order.

In May 1923 an event occurred that brought the Peoples Universities to an end and the APRA movement in its international aspect into being. A colossal demonstration of students and workmen organized and led by Haya de la Torre prevented the consecration of Peru to an effigy of the Sacred Heart of Jesus, which the dictator Augusto Leguía had planned as the expression of the deference of its government to the traditional religious forces in the country. This action was taken on the ground that the projected religious act was unconstitutional and that it signified the surrender of the administration to a system that in the opinion of the "allies" was one of the chief sources of the social evils of Peru. In the month of October, Haya de la Torre and a number of other student and workmen leaders of the Peoples Universities were banished from the country to different points of the Americas.

Haya de la Torre found asylum in Mexico, the holy land of South American radicals. This young man, a native of Trujillo in northern Peru, and twenty-eight years of age at the time of his expulsion from the country, had been the soul of the *Universidades Populares*. For several years before his exile he had been a teacher in the Anglo-Peruvian College, Lima, a high school conducted by the Free Church of Scotland Mission in the country. He was destined to spend eight years away from his native land, which time he devoted to travel, study, writing, and the organization of the APRA movement.

The APRA idea was launched by Haya de la Torre in 1924, while he was still in Mexico, and consisted of five points. These points set a new direction for political thought and action in Latin America and today constitute the maximum program of the APRA movement. They are as follows: 1) action against American imperialism; 2) for the political unity of Latin America; 3) for the internationalization of the Panama Canal; 4) for the nationalization of land and industry; 5) for the solidarity of all oppressed peoples and classes.

Thereafter Haya de la Torre went to Russia to study communism. He became convinced that the Soviet system was not what Latin America needed. He later became a student at the London School of Economics and Ruskin College, Oxford. Contact with British economists and labor leaders greatly matured his thinking and character. At the same time it gave him unbounded love and admiration for the British spirit and brought home to him very forcibly a fact, traditionally denied in social revolutionary circles in Latin America, that personal religion and social radicalism are perfectly compatible. Banished a second time from Latin American territory in 1928 when on his way back to Peru, he spent nearly three years in Germany, until his return to Peru in 1931 as leader of the newly organized APRA Party, and as candidate of this party for the presidency of the republic. What happened thereafter belongs to the story of the APRA as a political party. Haya de la Torre is once again a fugitive, but he and his ideas have so caught the popular imagination in Peru and other countries of Latin America as to make him today the most significant political thinker and leader in the whole Latin American world. This fact gives importance to the conceptions that underlie and inspire the APRA movement.

II. The APRA Movement as an International Political Philosophy

The word APRA is a combination formed from the initials of the official title of the movement, *Alianza Popular Revolucionaria American* (The Popular Revolutionary Party of America). This title connotes what the APRA aspires to be: a united front of all groups having an inherent place in the social structure of Latin America, with a view to achieving a complete transformation of life in the political sphere, the social sphere, and the sphere of personal character throughout the continent. The title of a book by Haya de la Torre, *Por La Emancipación de la America Latina* (*For the Emancipation of Latin America*), is a concrete expression of this ideal. Continental life, it is suggested, has needed a "New Ayacucho," a decisive battle for economic and spiritual freedom to carry forward the reality of the political freedom that was achieved in 1824 at the Battle of Ayacucho, in the Peruvian Andes, when the might of Spain was finally broken in South America.

The chief sources for a study of APRA ideology are the books of Haya de la Torre, most of which consist of articles and addresses, and those of such other Aprista leaders as Manuel Seoane, Carlos Manuel Cox, Luis Alberto Sánchez, and Luis Heysen. The life of Haya has recently been written by Sánchez under the title of *Una Vida sin Tregua* (*A Life without Truce*).

A brief interpretative comment on each of the five points previously listed will form the simplest introduction to APRA thought.

> (1) Action against so-called "yanqui" imperialism indicates no antipathy towards the North American people or government.

It stresses rather the imperative need of collective defense, on the part of Latin American countries, against those sinister and hitherto uncurbed economic interests in the United States that have in recent years, in the case of more than one country and at more than one time, subjugated national life and prejudiced national development.

(2) The APRA considers that only a federation, at least economic in character, of all Latin American states, will make it possible for those states to defend themselves against foreign economic imperialism. The Federation dream of Bolivar is a central element in the philosophy of the movement, which dreams of the United States of Latin America.

(3) The APRA advocates the nationalization of land and basic industries to avoid exploitation and to make sure that the vital means of subsistence and progress are in the hands of each state.

(4) The proposal is made that the Panama Canal be internationalized as is the Suez Canal, so that no single nation should be in a position to use it for carrying out its own policies, to the detriment, it might be, of other countries.

(5) The full international sweep and human passion of the movement comes out in its plea that all oppressed peoples and classes stand solidly together. One of the precepts in the code of APRA youth, the FAJ (*Federación Aprista Juvenil*) runs thus, "The oppressed peoples of Peru, of America, and the world are your brothers: love them. For them thousands of APRA martyrs died. Follow their example."

The thought structure of the APRA is Marxist but not communistic. The Marxian dialectic and the economic interpretation of history are accepted, but the dialectic principle is accepted so thoroughly by APRA leaders as to lead them to criticize official Marxism in the name of it. Quoting the words of Marx that the dialectical stages are not suppressed by decree, and those of Huxley that "Reality is not invented," Haya de la Torre shows how different the social structure of Latin American countries is from that prevailing in highly industrialized countries and in Russia. Capitalism, for example, is only incipient in Latin America. Here it has not yet fulfilled its necessary historic role. The middle class has not yet come into its own. "The middle class," said the APRA leader in December, 1924, in explanation of the significance of Alianza Popular in the official title of the movement, "has not fulfilled its French Revolution, nor its Reformation, nor its Cromwellian stage. It has not yet been the dominating class. It is impelled by its destiny to join its fortunes with the incipient proletariat and the feudalized farm laborer of the continent. For that reason a Popular Alliance was necessary, to which a revolutionary spirit and a continental sense had to be imparted."[135] Thus, in Latin America the three historic stages of the Marxian dialectic coexist. For that reason the APRA refuses to allow Russian communism to be superimposed on Latin American reality, and by this refusal it has earned the overt hostility of the Third International.

Another point to be noted is that the APRA leaders believe in democracy and think in terms of it. It is natural that they should do so in a continent which has known democracy only in name and not in reality and where each succeeding dictatorship has left a legacy of social and political evils. But Haya de la Torre and his friends are aware of two things that mark them off from previous political leaders in Latin America. They realize, first, that economic rights and freedom are as essential as political rights and freedom for the expression of a true democracy; and, second, that a high degree of moral character is necessary for the worthy exercise of the democratic function. The former insight has led to the conception of functional democracy, the latter to the preoccupation of APRA leaders with the private as well as the public morals of those who profess the APRA philosophy or belong to an APRA group.

Functional democracy as expounded by Haya de la Torre is a significant conception. To begin with he insists that the organization of the APRA party is democratic. There is no hierarchy or *führer* involved. The program comes out of the best thought of the party and is not an imposition from above. The desire of the chief *commander* is that what the APRA stands for shall be in the soul of each member and that the rank and file shall not blindly follow this or that leader. He is eager to depersonalize politics and to be himself neither a *caudillo* in the old Latin American sense nor a *duce* or *führer* in the new European sense. In this respect Haya de la Torre has not ceased to be a schoolmaster at heart. The proof of this is that he has resolutely opposed old fashioned revolutionary methods to reach the seat of power. And yet he does not believe that the pedagogic office of educating men and women for democracy is sufficient in Latin America, because conditions in these lands are such that civic ideals can only be fulfilled if the idealist has the power to put them into practice, otherwise he will find that the government is always against him. Therefore the APRA, which is essentially a movement of thought and life, aspires to political power of a democratic order.

135. *Vida de Haya*, p. 109.

The APRA democracy, however, would be of a *functional* character. That is to say, it aims at securing, on the one hand, that citizens enjoying political status shall enjoy an economic status corresponding to their needs and aptitudes, and on the other, that all recognized interests in the life of the state shall be directly represented in the national parliament. Such interests would center on the incipient city proletariat, farm workers, and the middle class, which, as already stated, has never fulfilled its destiny in Latin America. The intellectual worker, it is presupposed, belongs to this third group. It would be the function of the state to create and maintain an equilibrium between the activities of these three classes and at the same time to guarantee an equal equilibrium between national and foreign interests in the country. For in the APRA scheme of things there would be a secure and necessary place for foreign capital in the national economy. The state would see to it, however, that it was carried on to the advantage and not the disadvantage of the nation.[136]

III. The APRA as a National Political Party

Since 1925 APRA cells had functioned in Paris and Buenos Aires and in some other Latin American capitals where groups of young Peruvian radicals had taken refuge, exiled from their country by the dictator, Leguía. The members of these cells, most of them Peruvians, had met regularly to study some aspect of political science and prepare themselves for future political action. Bound together by a rigid discipline, they gave special prominence to general economic and international questions. Their influence was considerable in radical circles in the countries where they lived. Their opponents in these countries accused them of trying to Peruvianize (*peruanizar*) Latin America; their Peruvian opponents accused them of trying to internationalize Peru. A new law had been actually approved in the Peruvian congress to make it impossible for any party with international affiliations to present candidates for the national elections.

The fall of President Leguía in August, 1930, made possible the return of Haya de la Torre and other Aprista leaders from the different countries where they had lived in exile. In November of that year the Partido Aprista Peruano (Peruvian Aprista Party) was organized in Lima, with a view to taking part in the forthcoming national election. The party sponsored the candidacy of Haya de la Torre for the presidency of the republic. Haya arrived in Peru in July 1931. The elections took place on October 1st. The Apristas won a considerable number of seats in the National Congress, but

136. See Haya de la Torre, "Mensaje."

the presidency was won by Sanchez Cerro, the army colonel who had deposed Leguía the previous year.

Following the installation of the new president in November, the APRA Party, which in the meantime had challenged the fairness of the elections, was ruthlessly persecuted by the government in power, and thousands of its members became martyrs to their cause. APRA members in the National Congress were unseated and exiled, and Haya de la Torre was imprisoned. The latter suffered untold horrors during a fifteen months' imprisonment in Lima. He was released only after the assassination of Sanchez Cerro and when the provisional president Benavides felt himself to be so securely seated in power as to be able to express his natural sense of justice, despite the continued opposition of the leaders of the Sanchez Cerro party. An amnesty was declared. With Haya de la Torre again at its head, the APRA Party was reconstituted and prepared for the elections. Six hundred thousand members were enrolled, each of whom paid a small weekly contribution to party funds. But on successive occasions the date for the elections was postponed. Restiveness in the APRA ranks gave occasion to the government to suppress the party. Representing as it does the traditional political forces in Peruvian life, that is to say, the old Civilista Party, the government greatly feared the consequences should the new party come into power. The ranks of the Apristas were again broken through the imprisonment of many of their members and the exile of their leaders. After months in hiding in Peru as a fugitive, Haya de la Torre finally escaped to Chile in July 1935. The APRA Party has thus again been shattered momentarily as a political force, but its organization continues, and its influence grows. If the Peruvian government schedules a national election to be held in 1936, the constitutional date, and grants a political amnesty in view of that event, the APRA Party will go to the polls with the probability of success.

Existing in Peru as a national political movement, the Peruvian APRA Party stands in particular for the minimum program of the international movement. The minimum program applies to the conduct of affairs in each individual state. Such a program involves a realistic scientific study of the country to ascertain its resources in things and people. It contemplates concentration upon the indigenous population which, as in Mexico, represents the stable element in the nation's life. It advocates a policy of regionalism and the decentralization of power. A conference of experts would determine how the national wealth should be most adequately exploited in the interests of the inhabitants of the country and how the welfare of the latter should be most adequately promoted. The ideal political regime would be, of course, that of a functional democracy. Church and state would be separated, but the state should not interfere with the practice of religion. In Peru, the majority of the members of the APRA Party profess, nominally at least, the Roman Catholic faith.

One of the striking features of the leaders of the APRA Party in Peru is their appreciation of religious values and their insistence upon the supremacy of the ethical. This is strikingly revealed in the code for the FAJ, the Federation of APRA Youth. Here are a few articles of the code. The code begins, "APRA youth, prepare thyself for action and not for pleasure. This is thy law," and goes on:

> Rule 4: Be sincere. Never be afraid to tell the truth.
>
> Rule 5: When you give your word, fulfill it.
>
> Rule 7: Distinguish between strong language and foul language. Use the former, reject the latter.
>
> Rule 11: The oppressed peoples of Peru, America, and the world are your brothers. Love them. For them thousands of Apristas died. Follow their example.
>
> Rule 22: Teach him who knows less and learn of him who knows more. The knowledge you acquire is not for you alone; put it at the service of your organization.
>
> Rule 33: Wherever you are, indoors or out of doors, conduct yourself in an exemplary fashion, showing that Aprismo is, even in its outer manifestations, a complete renovation of personality.
>
> Rule 37: Select the shows you attend. Elect those that offer you healthful teaching and high artistic values, and that teach you lessons of morality and energy. Set yourself against the frivolous and pornographic cinema.
>
> Rule 39: Do not waste your vitality. Put a rein on sensualism. Reserve your sexual energy. On your continence and health today depends the health of your children tomorrow. Condemn Don Juanism ... Do not forget that our country is sunk in corruption owing to the lack of true virility and authentic moral discipline.

The interesting thing about these rules is that they represent a brake with many of the traditional vices and prejudices of Latin American life.

Devotion to the APRA Party and its principles by the membership in general puts the movement among the great mystic political movements of our times. Cases could be instanced of individuals who have passed through radical transformation of character as a result of their affiliation with the party and its activities. Notable is the case of Luis Alberto Sánchez, one of the most brilliant among the younger figures in the world of Latin American letters. At the close of a pamphlet written in exile in Ecuador in 1933 and titled *Aprism and Religion*, he writes:

> One of the things I am most proud of is to have comprehended in time the emptiness of professional intellectualism, to have allowed my heart to beat in unison with that of manual workers and students, to have felt their inspiration and to be guided by their infallible sense of justice and life. My gratitude is due to my party, and never more than now when I settle my scale of values and revise hierarchies. Never have I felt more satisfied at having as my home an ambulatory fatherland—this exile in which I live, and as my university a school of sacrifice—the ideals of the APRA.

With these things in mind, we are in a position to appreciate the force of that almost religious passion with which APRA members repeat the words of the rubric on all official documents of the party, "Only the APRA will save Peru."

14

The Truth That Makes Men Free

LIBERTY WAS ONE OF the many things in modern life that we had accustomed ourselves to take for granted and to regard as an imperishable part of our heritage from the past. Until quite recently, no one believed that the great liberties, fruits of long centuries of struggle—liberty of thought and of speech, liberty to dispose of one's goods and one's person, liberty of public assembly and of religious worship—would ever be challenged again. How rudely we have been aroused from our romantic slumber! Not only have those liberties been challenged in places where they had been taken for granted, they have been destroyed in places where they had been regarded as sacred and inviolable.

The chief symbol of the eclipse of liberty in our time is the coming of the new state. The founders of the great totalitarian systems have sounded freedom's death knell over wide areas of the world. "Liberty is precious," said Lenin, "so precious that we must ration it." "Liberty is dead," said Mussolini, "and its corpse is already putrescent." The rationing and death of freedom in many lands is the most disturbing feature in the human situation today.

The unexpected eclipse of freedom in some parts of the world and the probability that its torch will grow increasingly dim in others forces Christians everywhere to rethink what freedom means and how the freedom they enjoy has been achieved. The new situation has developed so suddenly that we have all been taken unawares. Not long ago a group of Christian philosophers and jurists were called together to give their counsel upon problems arising from the loss of religious liberty by missionaries and national Christians in certain countries. In the course of discussion, the observation was made that no fundamental treatise had been written on the subject of religious toleration since the days of John Locke in the seventeenth century. The need had not arisen for such a treatise. But now the problem of freedom has become the most crucial in the life of the world and the most worthy of earnest thought.

In this paper we shall limit ourselves to one phase of the subject—the relation of the Bible to human freedom. We shall consider first, the part being played by the Bible where freedom is being eclipsed; secondly, the contribution made by the Bible in securing the principal liberties that we enjoy; thirdly, the particular quality of freedom with which the Bible is supremely concerned.

I

One of the striking and significant things in the present-day crisis of liberty is that the last stand for freedom in many lands is being inspired by the Bible. When we survey the world of today, we discover that the groups which, despite persecution and the loss of all outward liberty, are offering the most resolute resistance to the new despotisms, are groups which have found their inspiration in the Christian scriptures. The book whose pages relate the most significant crisis in human history, whose influence has revolutionized the life of individuals and of societies, never comes to its own so much as at times of crisis and revolution.

Take, for example, the situation of Germany. When Dr. Albert Einstein came to America some years ago, an exile from his native country, he made a very significant statement. He said that, when National Socialism came to power in Germany and began to challenge the traditional liberties of the country, he felt certain that the standard of revolt would be unfurled within the German universities and learned societies. What was his surprise to discover that the challenge to freedom was met with resolution only within the Christian church—a community which until that time he had despised! But who were the men within the German church who proved to be the most unflinching in their opposition to the new pagan order? They were invariably churchmen who took the Bible seriously. Listen to the voices from a German prison—to the words of comrades of that noble Christian, Martin Niemoeller. One imprisoned pastor says, "It is most wonderful to read the Bible at such a time! How alive it suddenly becomes and how real! It really gives you the impression of having been written specially for prisoners and for prison."[137] And another, referring to the famous Barmen declaration of the Confessional Church, says, "If anyone can prove that one sentence of our Declaration is not in accord with the Holy Scriptures and the Word of God, I am absolutely ready to sign a statement that I will keep silence as regards that sentence."[138] Men like that are invincible.

II

The book that today inspires men who stand in the last redoubt of freedom has been itself the great pioneer of human liberty. Let us look at the process of freedom in the outward lot of mankind through the influence of the Bible and of biblical religion.

The Bible has made a supreme contribution to popular education. More than any book or force in history, it has been the great liberator of the human mind. It has burst open the prison doors of superstition. Its translation into each new language has been a classic event in the educational advance of the people speaking that language. The reign of illiteracy begins to come to an end in the life of a people from the time the Bible comes among them, and they are free to listen to its message.

Educationally speaking, no country owes more to the influence of the Bible than the United States. For a hundred years the *New England Primer*, which was essentially a Bible primer designed by the early colonists to teach children to read and to know the Bible, was the schoolbook of the overwhelming mass of Americans in colonial days. Known as the "Little Bible of New England," it was popular in all the colonies until after the Revolution. It is estimated that, in the course of a hundred and fifty years, three million copies of the epoch-making little textbook were sold and used.[139] Later, when the movement began to people the great spaces to the west, the little schoolhouse was ever the companion of the little church on the advancing frontiers of civilization.

As with elementary, so with higher education. The foundation of Christian colleges by the different denominations and their rapid growth in influence and numbers from the Atlantic to the Pacific, is perhaps the greatest educational epic of all time. These colleges, from the founding of Harvard onward, were primarily designed to give a thorough grounding in the classics and in general secular learning to the men who looked forward

---

137. Macfarland, *"I Was in Prison"*, 40.
138. Ibid., 42.
139. See Simms, *The Bible in America*, 42–44.

to be preachers of the Word. They became the precursors and patterns of the great state universities of a latter day.

How different has been the course of popular education in areas where the Bible has been traditionally banned! The official church in Spain and Latin America refused to give the Bible to the people. Christianity in these countries gave birth to no great popular movement in education. So far as religion was concerned, the masses were left in ignorance and superstition through the lack of schools. Mexico before the revolution was a typical case. To this day the percentage of illiterates is appalling in the lands that make up the Hispanic group. And yet, how many cases are known of men and women in those lands, beyond the age of three score and ten, who, on becoming gripped by Bible truth, learned to read in order to enjoy the book that set their spirits free. The literacy among members of the evangelical community in Latin American countries is overwhelmingly greater than it is in the community in general.

The link between the Bible and civil liberties is equally striking. William Wilberforce, a lover of the Bible, a man who owed his soul to its liberating truth, led the great crusade to emancipate Negro slaves in the British Empire. Wilberforce's contemporary, Anthony Ashley Cooper, Lord Shaftesbury, a man of one book from boyhood to old age, championed the cause of factory workers in industrial England and succeeded in securing the passage of one act after another through the British parliament to alleviate their lot.

The same relationship exists between the Book and rights and privileges of citizens in a democratic order. Those Christian churches that were zealous to order the lives of their members in accordance with the principles of Holy Scripture, became nurseries of liberty and training places for civic and political responsibility. Their insistence, to the point of sacrifice, upon the rights according to the Word of God obliged the state to which they belonged to cultivate tolerance and to make provision for the coexistence of varying viewpoints within the national family. Church membership schooled men and women in the discharge of responsible duties. It prepared them to claim and to exercise the rights of citizens in the affairs of state. It made them sensitive to community needs which it was their responsibility to meet.

The extent to which the Christian church has been the great school of democracy, with the Bible as the principal textbook of democratic freedom and responsibility, is best appreciated when we compare the history of democracy in the United States with that of democratic institutions in the sister republics of Latin America. A distinguished Argentine thinker was discussing the long series of revolutions that have marred the political history of Latin-American countries, and the reasons why it has been difficult for democratic principles to become fully indigenous in the Hispanic world. He made in substance this luminous statement.

> Only those countries have ever made a success of democracy in which the people, or at least a strong minority of the people, have cultivated personal religion and taken up an attitude of personal loyalty to God. The experience of God and the appeal to God, gives people a sense of dignity; it instills into them settled principles of right living, and inspires them with a deep sense of responsible action. . . . In our countries religious inwardness has been lacking throughout our history, with the result that we have not found it possible to be consistently loyal to the democratic system.

Spiritual inwardness is inseparable from the Bible. As more than one great South American writer has pointed out, this inwardness which is the necessary prerequisite of democracy has been lacking in Latin America because the people have not known the Bible at first hand. A reasoned and dispassionate study of Hispanic history makes it plain that the unhappy political annals of Spain and her ancient colonies derive from the fact that official Christianity of those lands placed a decisive ban upon a knowledge of the Bible by the people.

The case is not different when we come to the high realms of cultural and religious freedom. Freedom of thought and freedom of conscience—the twin liberties that are most precious to civilized man—without which no civilization is worthy of the name, are children of the Bible. While it is true that the demand for intellectual freedom originated in Greece rather than in Judea, and that the right to think freely has been as much insisted upon by secular as by Christian thinkers, this should be remembered. Greece and her thinkers would have lain buried in their graves and remained lost to history but for a renaissance of the Bible and of interest in the Bible. For "Greece," as has been beautifully stated, "arose from the grave with the New Testament in her hand." All this is true despite the fact that Christians have sometimes interpreted the Bible and its teaching in such a way as to show intolerance and bigotry with respect to the ideas and religious practices of other people. Alas many a scandal has been perpetrated down the ages in the name of the Bible and professed loyalty to biblical truth. But Christianity and the Bible have not been to blame for the misguided zeal of many of their devotees.

Not only so; it was the Bible's insistence that truth is one because God is one that made the scientific spirit and the freedom of scientific research possible. Evangelical Christians have been among the most unswerving champions of freedom of research, even when research was carried out on the Bible itself and views of the Bible were expressed that conflicted with those traditionally held. Cultural freedom, moreover, will follow the fate of the Bible. Let the Bible be repudiated as the supreme guidebook of mankind, and intellectual freedom will die. The proof of this is the death of intellectual freedom in Russia and Germany where Christianity and its records have been rejected.

As for freedom of conscience, that is to say, religious freedom, nowhere has it been more effective than in countries where the principles of biblical Christianity have swayed the popular mind. The United States, which more than any other country was founded by men mastered by the Bible, has been the most hospitable country in history to divergent religious ideas and of sects. The battle for religious liberty was won in America by men whose faith was grounded in the scriptures. Who can forget that that great Christian, Roger Williams, was "the first person in modern Christendom to assert in its plenitude the doctrine of the liberty of conscience, the equality of opinions before the law?"[140] How can civilization in America ever forget its debt to the Baptists, "the first body of Christians to formulate and enforce a doctrine of religious liberty?" The Presbyterians, whose historical love of freedom made them the first in the political realm to advocate American independence, have enshrined in their standards the foundation principle of religious liberty that "God alone is Lord of the conscience." Because this principle has been recognized, Protestant and Roman Catholic, Jew and Buddhist, are able to live in this free land in peace and liberty.

It is natural that this unbreakable link should have been forged across the centuries between the Bible and human freedom—and that the "book of a thousand tongues" should have taken part in a thousand battles for liberty. Increasing insight down the centuries into the Bible view of man and his destiny led to the removal of obstacles to the development of free personality. For, in the Bible, man is set forth as a being who has infinite value for God, his creator and redeemer. Inasmuch as God has called him to the high destiny of sonship, certain important consequences follow. No human authority has the right to degrade or enslave man or deprive him of his right to self-development. He should be free to assume responsibilities for which he is fitted. None should demand of him a love or loyalty that are due to God alone. It is the duty of society and the state to do what lies in

---

140. Bancroft.

their power to free men from such conditions as make it difficult for them to fulfill their destiny as children of God.

III

Freedom, however, means a great deal more than freedom to obtain an education, freedom from inhuman treatment, freedom to assume responsibility according to one's capacity, freedom from the necessity of believing or worshipping in opposition to one's conscience. These liberties are all precious. They were the birthright of successive generations of people in the Anglo-Saxon world. The Bible played a major part in securing them. But one might enjoy all these liberties to the full without being free. A man might be free from all external authority and yet be a slave—a slave to his own self-will. True freedom is positive in character. It is much more than freedom from evil conditions that prevent the full development of personality. It is the freedom that is born when personality in its wholeness dedicates itself to the pursuit of the good. It is freedom in the truth; freedom born of a full commitment to God in whose love and service man becomes fully free and truly man.

> Make me a captive, Lord,
> and then I shall be free.

Perfect human freedom is captivity to the divine. It is "to become to the Eternal goodness what his own hand is to a man." Only in rendering loving service to the Almighty Father does the creature achieve the freedom of sonship in the universe and become a constructive member in God's kingdom.

The Bible opens up in concrete personal terms, the meaning of the highest human freedom and of the truth that leads men to it. Light is flashed upon the basic problem of human nature. The chief state of servitude in which man finds himself is not bondage to external ills but bondage to his own evil will. He is a sinner in servitude to the law of sin within him. He loves himself more than God and his neighbor; he determines his actions by self-interest; he hates the thought of full submission to the will of God; and, in consequence, he hates God who requires such submission from men. At the heart of the Bible is the great truth of reconciliation whereby God-haters become friends of God; whereby a slave-consciousness is transformed into a consciousness of sonship. The quest of reconciliation to God, oneness with the Almighty, is the great quest of the ages. A cattle drover once said to a Scottish minister, "ise gie ye twa coos if ye 'gree me and God."[141] The rough

---

141. "I'll give you two cows if you bring God and me to an understanding."

man had become concerned about his relationship to God and was eager to know how to come to an understanding with his Maker.

The pathway to reconciliation with God and to the freedom of sonship is declared by the Bible to be Jesus Christ. Truth and freedom are associated with him. "I am the Truth,"[142] he is represented as saying. He is "the Word become flesh,"[143] the incarnate personal Truth. "You shall know the truth," Jesus said, "and the truth shall make you free."[144] St. Paul, who himself had been delivered from bondage to sin through faith in the Crucified, and had become one of the spiritually free, said, "Stand fast in the liberty wherewith Christ has made you free."[145] So absolute was this liberty to be, that Christians should owe no man anything but love.[146] It was a freedom perfected in love. For to love is to fulfill the law.[147] To love is to be free; to hate is to be a slave.

Therefore, loyalty to Jesus Christ as the true Lord of Life produces that spiritual freedom which manifests and fulfills itself in love. Here are two germinal truths which are supremely important. The first is that Jesus Christ is ultimate. He is the absolute truth, the theme of the Bible, and the beginning and end of life. Truly to know him is to achieve freedom. He is life's greatest liberator. He is the only figure in history who is utterly worthy of being followed, the only master whose discipleship will not lead to eventual bondage. "The liberator of one generation," it has been said, "becomes the gaoler of the next." Christ is the only one who ever lived of whom this is not true. He is everlastingly our contemporary who sets men free today as he did yesterday. Therefore,

> "I bind my heart this tide
> To the Galilean's side."

The other truth is this. If spiritual freedom manifests and fulfills itself in love, no one who is free can be an individualist or live merely for himself. Love has no meaning except where others are concerned. It involves a giving of oneself to God and to other people. It means friendship and community. Only in fellowship with kindred spirits, bound together in the same great loyalty to God and to his scheme of world fellowship in Christ, can one be fully free. The Christian church is designed by God to be the great home of

---

142. John 14:6. —Ed.
143. John 1:14—Ed.
144. John 8:32. —Ed.
145. See Gal 5:1. —Ed.
146. See Rom 13:8. —Ed.
147. See Rom 13:10. —Ed.

freedom as it is of truth. It is the church's supreme task now as ever to be the great mother whose sons and daughters around the world shall be friends of God and of one another and of all men.

IV

We return to the place where we began. What has been said provides a mirror in which to study the new challenge to freedom by the totalitarian powers. The new order which these powers have created has important lessons to teach us.

Who will deny that, if that freedom which manifests itself in the love of God and man had prevailed in human relations during the last few decades, the revolt against freedom in many parts of the world would never have taken place? If, instead of diplomatic maneuvering and sentimental good will there had been actual friendship between the world's rulers, together with a willingness to pay the dues of friendship, the present crisis of freedom would not have developed. As it is, in the vast modern cemetery made up of those lands in which today "freedom lies putrescent," there are significant epitaphs well worthy of our study.

The epitaph of self-expressionism is there. This corpse while in life had regarded the license it claimed as perfect freedom. The freedom of self-expressionism consists in the unbridled manifestation of instincts however low, and the untrammeled pursuit of interests however selfish and antisocial. In demanding that every expression of the self shall serve the community, the totalitarian rulers have secured by force a virtue which ought to have been cultivated by free choice. They have reminded us of something which hosts of people had, alas, forgotten; namely, that personality grows when men respond to the claims of something greater than themselves. For young Communists and Nazis who give themselves with joyful abandon to the cause of class or blood the question of freedom becomes a purely academic issue and does not concern them. Only devotion to their cause interests them.

The epitaph of relativism is also there. The relativist contends that a free man should adopt an attitude of complete detachment from all human absolutes. True freedom, he believes, can only be maintained by a refusal to identify oneself completely with any single idea or cause. It lies in preserving oneself unattached—a perpetual bachelor. A free man, according to this view, appreciates the values inherent in all ideas and causes, but he never marries himself to any. And so he lives and dies spiritually childless. To a generation which believed that the essence of free personality consisted in the endless discussion of viewpoints and the maintenance of poise and measure, the totalitarian systems have taught that true personality, and with it true freedom, can be obtained only by commitment to some master—a great idea, a great cause, a great person.

But who shall the master be? That is the ultimate question. The truth and error of totalitarianism become clear at this point. To live in any worthy sense means to commit oneself utterly to something greater than oneself. That is the everlasting truth proclaimed by the totalitarians. Their error is equally plain. Commitment in their scheme is produced by force that destroys the elemental birthright of personality, the right of free choice. Not only so; the commitment they demand is made to an unworthy master. No man or state, no class or race or imperial tradition, is worthy of the unreserved devotion of a human soul. Where this demand is made, God is supplanted, and a human idol is enthroned in his place. Where human spirits submit to be mastered by some man-god, grave consequences follow. Their humanity dies. They are reduced to the status of cogs in the machinery of state. Their horizons are narrowed. They cannot look with sympathy and longing beyond the bounds of the territory claimed by their master. Parochialism prevails. Universal friendship is rejected. The dream of world brotherhood dies.

In such a situation what shall we do? What shall the future be? The famous words of old John Erskine, spoken in the Scottish General Assembly, in the eighteenth century, after he had listened to a discourse in which the world mission of Christianity was disputed, are a worthy slogan for our time. "Rax me that Bible, Moderator"[148] said the old man. At a time when the Christian view of life is being disputed in its individual and corporate aspects, and men are asked to bow the knee before new Baals, let the slogan resound, "Rax me that Bible." When the old Book is placed in our hands, we open it afresh where John Erskine did, and read, "Go ye into all the world, and make disciples of all nations."[149] Let Christianity become missionary again. Trembling for the future of freedom in the world, we listen to the words, "If the Son shall make you free, ye shall be free indeed."[150] How widespread shall that freedom be? "He shall have dominion from sea to sea, and from the river unto the ends of the earth."[151]

But, "Oh God," I hear some say, "what if the whole earth be soaked in blood by men who are a blot upon thy world?" Listen and read again: "Even the creation waits with eager longing for the sons of God to be revealed."[152]

---

148. "Reach me that Bible, Moderator."
149. See Mark 16:15; Matt 28:19. —Ed.
150. John 8:36. —Ed.
151. Zech 9:10. —Ed.
152. Rom 8:19. —Ed.

And yet, again, "The creation itself shall be delivered from the bondage of corruption into the liberty of the glory of the children of God."[153] Redeemed nature and redeemed men shall yet rejoice together in the freedom of the Truth that makes all things free.

---

153. Rom 8:21. —Ed.

Bibliography

Adams, Jasper. "The Relation of Christianity to Civil Government in the United States, (1833)." In *The Sacred Rights of Conscience*, edited by Daniel L. Dreisbach and Mark David Hall, 597–610. Indianapolis: Liberty Fund, 2009.
Alexander, Robert J. "Victor Raúl Haya de la Torre and 'Indo-America.'" In *Prophets of the Revolution: Profiles of Latin American Leaders*, 75–108. New York: Macmillan, 1962.
Anderson, Allan. *Spreading Fires: The Missionary Nature of Early Pentecostalism*. London: SCM, 2007.
Arbaiza, Genaro. "Benavides of Peru." *CuH* 48 (May 1938) 15–17.
———. "Latin-American Notes." *CuH* 48 (June 1938) 12–13.
———. "South America's No. 1 Tyranny." *CuH* 49 (October 1938) 26–29.
Arciniegas, Germán. "The Military vs. Aprismo in Peru." In *The State of Latin America*, 79–94. New York: Knopf, 1952.
Arias, Oscar. "Culture Matters: The Real Obstacles to Latin American Development." *FA* 90 (January/February 2011) 2–6.
Baez-Camargo, G. "The Earliest Protestant Missionary Venture in Latin America." *CH* 21 (1952) 135–45.
———. "Evangelical Faith and Latin American Culture." In *The Ecumenical Era in Church and Society*, edited by Edward J. Jurji, 126–47. New York: Macmillan, 1959.
Ballor, Jordan J. *Ecumenical Babel: Confusing Economic Ideology and the Church's Social Witness*. Grand Rapids: Christian's Library Press, 2010.
Barnes, M. Craig. "John R. Mott: A Conversionist in a Pluralist World." PhD diss., University of Chicago, 1992.
Beals, Carleton. "Black Shirts in Latin America." *CuH* 49 (November 1938) 32–34.
Belaúnde, Víctor Andrés. "The Alienation of the Latin-American Mind from Christianity." *BR* 8 (1923) 578–86.
Beyerhaus, Peter P. J. *God's Kingdom and the Utopian Error: Discerning the Biblical Kingdom of God from Its Political Counterfeits*. Wheaton, IL: Crossway, 1992.
———. *Missions: Which Way? Humanization or Redemption*. Grand Rapids: Zondervan, 1971.
Beyerhaus, Peter, and Henry Lefever. *The Responsible Church and the Foreign Mission*. Grand Rapids: Eerdmans, 1964.
"Blake Charges Deliberate U.S. Bombing of Dikes." *NYT*, July 21, 1972, 2.

Braaten, Carl E., and Robert W. Jenson. *In One Body Through the Cross*. Grand Rapids: Eerdmans, 2003.

Branch, Taylor. *Parting the Waters: America in the King Years 1954–63*. New York: Simon & Schuster, 1988.

Brown, Stewart J. *Thomas Chalmers and the Godly Commonwealth in Scotland*. New York: Oxford University Press, 1982.

Burton, Wilbur. "Dictators for Neighbors." *CH* 47 (October 1937) 63–68.

Butterfield, Herbert. *Christianity in European History*. London: Collins, 1952.

Caird, G. B. *Our Dialogue with Rome; the Second Vatican Council and After*. London: Oxford University Press, 1967.

Carter, Stephen L. *New England White*. New York: Knopf, 2007.

Castro, Emilio. "Pentecostalism and Ecumenism in Latin America." *CC* 89 (September 27, 1972) 955–57.

Chadwick, Owen. "Chalmers and the State." In *The Practical and the Pious: Essays on Thomas Chalmers (1780–1847)*, edited by A. C. Cheyne, 56–83. Edinburgh: Saint Andrew, 1985.

Chanamé, Raúl. *La Amistad de dos Amautas: Mariátegui y John A. Mackay* [*The Friendship of Two Wise Men: Mariátegui and John A. Mackay*]. Lima, Peru: Editora Magisterial, 1995.

Charter and Plan of the Theological Seminary of the Presbyterian Church in the United States of America, Princeton, New Jersey. Princeton, NJ: Princeton Theological Seminary, 1953.

Chesnut, R. Andrew. *Born Again in Brazil: The Pentecostal Boom and the Pathogens of Poverty*. New Brunswick, NJ: Rutgers University Press, 1997.

———. *Competitive Spirits: Latin America's New Religious Economy*. Oxford: Oxford University Press, 2003.

Cheyne, A. C. *The Practical and the Pious: Essays on Thomas Chalmers (1780–1847)*. Edinburgh: Saint Andrew, 1985.

Cox, Harvey G. "The 'New Breed' in American Churches: Sources of Social Activism in American Religion." *D* 96 (1967) 135–50.

Dias, Elizabeth. "The *Evangélicos!*" *T* 181/14 (April 15, 2013) 20–26, 28.

Didache. In *Early Christian Writings*, translated by Maxwell Staniforth, 227–37. New York: Dorset, 1968.

Douthat, Ross. *Bad Religion: How We Became a Nation of Heretics*. New York: Free Press, 2012.

Editorial, "Ominous Peru." *CC* 61 (April 5, 1944) 422–23.

Escobar, Samuel. "La Huella de Juan A. Mackay en la Historia Peruana." [The Imprint of John Mackay on Peruvian History]. In *El Sentido de la Vida y Otros Ensayos* [*The Meaning of Life and Other Essays*], por Juan A. Mackay, 5–15. Lima, Peru: Ed. Presencia, 1988.

———. "The Promise and Precariousness of Latin American Protestantism." In *Coming of Age: Protestantism in Contemporary Latin America*, edited by Daniel R. Miller, 3–35. Lanham, MD: University Press of America, 1994.

Fairbank, John K. "Assignment for the '70's." *AHR* 74 (1969) 861–79.

Farr, Thomas F. *World of Faith and Freedom: Why International Religious Liberty Is Vital to American National Security*. New York: Oxford University Press, 2008.

Finke, Roger, and Rodney Stark. *The Churching of America, 1776–2005: Winners and Losers in Our Religious Economy.* 2nd ed. New Brunswick, NJ: Rutgers University Press, 2005.

Fonseca Ariza, Juan. "Unamuno y la Intelectualidad Protestante en el Perú: El Caso de John A. Mackay (1916–1925)" [Unamuno and the Protestant Intelligentsia in Peru: The Case of John A. Mackay (1916–1925)]. *E de D* (Fraternidad Teológica Latinoamericana) 1 (September–December 2004). Online: http://www.cenpromex.org.mx/revista_ftl/num_1/textos/juan_fonseca.htm.

Gill, Anthony James. *Rendering unto Caesar: The Catholic Church and the State in Latin America.* Chicago: University of Chicago Press, 1998.

Gill, Jill K. *Embattled Ecumenism: The National Council of Churches, the Vietnam War, and the Trials of the Protestant Left.* DeKalb: NIU Press, 2011.

Goldbrunner, Josef. *Holiness Is Wholeness.* Translated by Stanley Godman. London: Burns & Oates, 1955.

González Prada, Manuel. *Free Pages and Other Essays.* Translated by Frederick H. Fornoff, edited with an Introduction and Chronology by David Sobrevilla. New York: Oxford University Press, 2003.

Goslin, Thomas S., II. "Protestantism in Peru." *JPHS* 26 (September 1948) 149–64.

Harbison, E. Harris. "The 'Meaning of History' and the Writing of History." *CH* 21 (1952) 97–107.

Harrison, Lawrence E. *The Central Liberal Truth: How Politics Can Change a Culture and Save It from Itself.* New York: Oxford University Press, 2006.

Harrison, Lawrence E., and Samuel P. Huntington. *Culture Matters: How Values Shape Human Progress.* New York: Basic Books, 2000.

Haya de la Torre, Victor Raul. "Mensaje a la Nacion Peruana" [Message to the Nation of Peru]. February 1932. In *Construyendo el Aprismo [Building the APRA].* Buenos Aires: Coleccion Claudia, 1933.

Hefling, Charles. "Who Is Communion For?" *CC* 129 (November 28, 2012) 22–27.

Hoover, W. C. "Pentecost in Chile." *WD* 10 (April 1932) 155–61.

Huntington, Samuel P. *The Clash of Civilizations and the Remaking of World Order.* New York: Simon & Schuster, 1996.

———. "Religion and the Third Wave." *NI* 24 (Summer 1991) 29–42.

———. *The Third Wave: Democratization in the Late Twentieth Century.* Norman: University of Oklahoma Press, 1991.

Hurtado, Osvaldo. "Know Thyself: Latin America in the Mirror of Culture." *AI* 5 (January–February 2010) 92–102.

James, Earle K. "Apra's Appeal to Latin America." *CuH* 41 (October 1934) 39–44.

James, William. *The Varieties of Religious Experience.* London: Collins, 1971.

Jeal, Tim. *Livingstone.* New Haven: Yale University Press, 2001.

Jenkins, Philip. *New Faces of Christianity: Believing the Bible in the Global South.* Oxford/New York: Oxford University Press, 2006.

Jenson, Robert W. "Christian Civilization." In *God, Truth, and Witness: Engaging Stanley Hauerwas,* edited by L. Gregory Jones et al., 153–63. Grand Rapids: Brazos, 2005.

John of the Cross. *Obras del Místico Doctor San Juan de la Cruz.* Ed. crítica y la más correcta y completa de las publicadas hasta hoy, con introduciones y notas del Padre Gerardo de San Juan de la Cruz, C.D., y un Epílogo del Excmo. Sr. D. Juan Vázquez de Mella. Vol. 2. Toledo: Impr. Librería y Encuadernación de Viuda é Hijos de J. Peláez, 1912.

Johnson, Byron R. *More God, Less Crime: Why Faith Matters and How It Could Matter More*. West Conshohocken, PA: Templeton, 2011.

Kantor, Harry. *The Ideology and Program of the Peruvian Aprista Movement*. 1953. Reprint, New York: Octagon, 1966.

Kelley, Dean M. *Why Conservative Churches Are Growing: A Study in Sociology of Religion*. New York: Harper, 1972.

Keyes, Ralph. *The Post-Truth Era: Dishonesty and Deception in Contemporary Life*. New York: St. Martin's, 2004.

Keyserling, Hermann. *The World in the Making* [*Die Neuentstehende Welt*]. Translated by Maurice Samuel. New York: Harcourt, Brace, 1927.

Kimball, Roger. *The Long March: How the Cultural Revolution of the 1960s Changed America*. San Francisco: Encounter Books, 2000.

Krauze, Enrique. *Redeemers: Ideas and Power in Latin America*. New York: Harper, 2011.

Landsman, Ned S. "Revivalism and Nativism in the Middle Colonies: The Great Awakening and the Scots Community in East New Jersey." *AQ* 34 (Summer 1982) 149–64.

Latourette, Kenneth Scott. *A History of Christianity*, vol. 2: *A.D. 1500 – A.D. 1975*. New York: HarperSanFrancisco, 1975.

———. *The Unquenchable Light*. New York: Harper, 1941.

Liebert, Robert. *Radical and Militant Youth, A Psychoanalytic Inquiry*. New York: Praeger, 1971.

Lindbeck, George. "Ecumenisms in Conflict." In *God, Truth, and Witness: Engaging Stanley Hauerwas*, edited by L. Gregory Jones et al., 212–28. Grand Rapids: Brazos, 2005.

Macfarland, Charles S. *"I Was in Prison": The Suppressed Letters of Imprisoned German Pastors*. New York: Revell, 1939.

Mackay, John A. *Christian Reality and Appearance*. Richmond: John Knox, 1969.

———. *Christianity on the Frontier*. New York: Macmillan, 1950.

———. "Dos Apóstoles de la Democracia: Woodrow Wilson y Lloyd George." [Two Apostles of Democracy: Woodrow Wilson and Lloyd George] *MP* 1 (November 1918) 255–60. Online: http://www.filosofia.org/hem/dep/mer/n005p255.htm.

———. *Ecumenics: The Science of the Church Universal*. Englewood Cliffs, N.J.: Prentice-Hall, 1964.

———. *Heritage and Destiny*. New York: Macmillan, 1943.

———. "Life's Chief Discoveries." *CT* 14 (January 2, 1970) 3–5.

———. *The Other Spanish Christ*. New York: Macmillan, 1932.

———. *Preface to Christian Theology*. London: Nisbet, 1942.

———. "Protestantism." In *The Great Religions of the Modern World*, edited by Edward J. Jurji, 337–70. Princeton, NJ: Princeton University Press, 1946.

———. *Realidad e Idolatría en el Cristianismo Contemporáneo*. Buenos Aires: La Aurora, 1970.

———. "A Representative American of the Sixties: James Joseph Reeb." *PSB* 60 (October 1966) 33–39.

———. "The Rôle of Princeton Seminary." *PSB* 31 (November, 1937) 1–2.

———. "Student Life in a South American University." *SW* 13 (July 1920) 89–97.

———. "Student Renaissance in South America." *SW* 17 (April, 1924) 62–66.

———. *That Other America*. New York: Friendship Press, 1935.

---. "A Theological Meditation on Latin America." In *Christianity on the Frontier*, 153–68. New York: Macmillan, 1950.

---. "Two American Civilizations and their Implications for Reformed Theology." *PR* 18 (March 1943) 90–96.

---. "The Unfulfilled Dream of Columbus." In *Biennial Book*, 84–93. New York: Board of National Missions, Board of Foreign Missions of the Presbyterian Church USA, 1935.

---. "Valor Cultural del Studio de la Literature Inglesa" [Cultural Value of the Study of English Literature]. *MP* 2 (May 1919) 354–60. Online: http://www.filosofia.org/hem/dep/mer/no11p354.htm.

---. "Who and What Are We?: The Fundamental Ideals and Purposes of the Association Movement Need to Be Given New Vitality." *AF* 10 (October 1929) 1, 2, 17, 18.

Mackay, W. M. *Thomas Chalmers: A Short Appreciation*. Edinburgh: Knox, 1980.

MacPherson, John M. *At the Roots of a Nation: The Story of San Andrés School in Lima, Peru*. Edinburgh: Knox, 1993.

Martin, David. *Tongues of Fire: The Explosion of Protestantism in Latin America*. Oxford: Basil Blackwell, 1990.

McCoy, John. "Robbing Peter to Pay Paul." *LAP*, June 29, 1989, 2.

Metzger, Bruce M. "Implications of Inclusive Language in Biblical Translation." Lecture, Princeton Theological Seminary, May 29, 1984.

---. *Introduction to the Apocrypha*. New York: Oxford University Press, 1957.

Metzger, John Mackay. *The Hand and the Road: The Life and Times of John A. Mackay*. Louisville: Westminster John Knox, 2010.

Míguez Bonino, José. *Faces of Latin American Protestantism*. Grand Rapids: Eerdmans, 1997.

---. *Rostros del Protestantismo Latinoamericano*. Buenos Aires: Nueva Creación, 1995.

Miller, Francis P. "The Relation of the Christian Faith to Democracy." *C & C* 2 (February 23, 1942) 3–6.

Moorhead, James H. *Princeton Seminary in American Religion and Culture*. Grand Rapids: Eerdmans, 2012.

Mott, John R. *Liberating the Lay Forces of Christianity*. New York: Macmillan, 1932.

Mudge, Lewis Seymour. *In His Service: The Servant Lord and His Servant People*. Philadelphia: Westminster Press, 1959.

Navarro Monzó, Julio. "Conceptions of Christ Found in Latin America." *CQ* 9 (1931) 19–31.

---. "Need for the Social Gospel in South America." *SW* 17 (April 1924) 57–62.

---. "The New Reformation." *SW* 21 (July 1928) 269–81.

---. *The Religious Problem in Latin American Culture*. Translated by Webster E. Browning. Montevideo, 1925.

---. "What I Learned at High Leigh." *SW* 17 (October 1924) 177–79.

Newbigin, Leslie. "Reply to Konrad Raiser." *IBMR* 18 (1994) 51–52.

Newbigin, Leslie, Review of *Ecumenism in Transition: A Paradigm Shift in the Ecumenical Movement?* by Konrad Raiser. *IBMR* 18 (1994) 2–5.

Obama, Barack. "Wesleyan University Commencement Address." Middletown, CT, May 25, 2008, as prepared for delivery. Online: http://www.politico.com/pdf/PPM42_remarks_of_obama.pdf.

Oldham, J. H. "A Responsible Society." In *The Church and the Disorder of Society*, 120-54. Man's Disorder and God's Design 3. New York: Harper, 1948.

Olivera, Mario. "Juan A. Mackay y El Movimiento Ecumenico en America Latina" [John A. Mackay and the Ecumenical Movement in Latin America]. Licenciatura en Teologia tesis, Seminario Biblico Latinoamericano, San José, Costa Rica, 1990.

Oppenheimer, Mark. "For Episcopal Church's Leader, a Sermon Leads to More Dissent." *NYT*, June 22, 2013, A16.

Putnam, Robert D., and David E. Campbell. *American Grace: How Religion Divides and Unites Us*. New York: Simon & Schuster, 2010.

Ramsey, Paul. *Who Speaks for the Church?* Nashville: Abingdon, 1967.

Reisner, John H. "The Church and the Community." In *The Church Faces the World*, edited by Samuel McCrea Cavert, 58-62. New York: Round Table Press, 1939.

Reisner, Sherwood. "Protestant Mission in Latin America Today." *SW* 53 (1st and 2nd quarter 1960) 187-94.

Rembao, Alberto. "The Presence of Protestantism in Latin America." *IRM* 37 (1948) 57-70.

Richardson, Herbert. "Civil Religion in Theological Perspective." In *American Civil Religion*, edited by Russell E. Richey and Donald G. Jones, 161-84. New York: Harper & Row, 1974.

Rieff, Philip. *Triumph of the Therapeutic: Uses of Faith after Freud*. New York: Harper, 1966.

Rostow, W. W. *The Stages of Economic Growth, a Non-communist Manifesto*. Cambridge: Cambridge University Press, 1960.

Rudd, Mark. *Underground: My Life with SDS and the Weathermen*. New York: W. Morrow, 2009.

Rycroft, W. Stanley. *Indians of the High Andes*. Report of the Commission appointed by the Committee on Cooperation in Latin America. New York: Committee on Cooperation in Latin America, 1946.

———. *Memoirs of Life in Three Worlds*. Cranbury, New Jersey: 1976.

———. *On This Foundation*. Foreword by John R. Mott. New York: Friendship Press, 1942.

———. *Religion and Faith in Latin America*. Foreword by Alberto Rembao. Philadelphia: Westminster, 1958.

———. Review of *The Ideology and Program of the Peruvian Aprista Movement* by Harry Kantor. *IRM* 43 (1954) 220-23.

Sánchez, Luis Alberto. *Haya de la Torre o el Político; Crónica de una Vida sin Tregua* [Haya de la Torre or Politician: Chronicle of a Life without Truce]. Santiago: Ediciones Ercilla, 1936.

———. "John A. Mackay y el Anglo-Peruano" [John A. Mackay and the Anglo-Peruvian School]. *L* 47 (1972) 49-53.

———. "John Mackay y la Educación Peruana" [John Mackay and Peruvian Education]. *L* 48 (1973) 63-70.

Schulz, Klaus Detlev. *Mission from the Cross: The Lutheran Theology of Mission*. St. Louis: Concordia, 2009.

Schweitzer, Albert. *The Quest of the Historical Jesus*. Translated by W. Montgomery. 2nd Eng. ed. London: A & C Black, 1926.

Sigmund, Paul E. *Liberation Theology at the Crossroads: Democracy or Revolution?* New York: Oxford University Press, 1990.

———. *Models of Political Change in Latin America*. New York: Praeger, 1970.
———. *Religious Freedom and Evangelization in Latin America: The Challenge of Religious Pluralism*. Maryknoll, NY: Orbis, 1999.
Simms, P. Marion. *The Bible in America: Versions that Have Played Their Part in the Making of the Republic*. New York: Wilson-Erickson, 1936.
Sinclair, John H. "W. Stanley Rycroft, Latin American Missiologist." *JPH* 65 (Summer 1987) 117–33.
Smith, Adam. "Of the Expence of the Institutions for the Instruction of People of all Ages." In *An Inquiry into the Nature and Causes of The Wealth of Nations*, 309–38. Chicago: University of Chicago Press, 1976.
Smith, George. *The Life of Alexander Duff*. 2 vols. New York: A. C. Armstrong, [1880].
Soto, Hernando de. *The Mystery of Capital: Why Capitalism Triumphs in the West and Fails Everywhere Else*. New York: Basic Books, 2000.
———. *The Other Path: The Economic Answer to Terrorism*. New York: Basic Books, 1989.
"The South American Mission. Farewell Meeting in Edinburgh." *MRFCS* (November 1916) 157–60.
Starn, Orin, et al. *The Peru Reader: History, Culture, Politics*. Durham: Duke University Press, 1995.
Steigenga, Timothy J., and Edward L. Cleary. *Conversion of a Continent: Contemporary Religious Change in Latin America*. New Brunswick, NJ: Rutgers University Press, 2007.
Stoll, David. *Is Latin America Turning Protestant?: The Politics of Evangelical Growth*. Berkeley: University of California Press, 1990.
Taylor, Martin C. *Gabriela Mistral's Religious Sensibility*. Berkeley: University of California Press, 1968.
Temple, William. *Personal Religion and the Life of Fellowship*. London: Longmans, Green, 1926.
Tennent, Gilbert. "The Danger of an Unconverted Ministry Considered in a Sermon on Mark VI. 34." In *The Great Awakening*, edited by Alan Heimert and Perry Miller, 72–99. Indianapolis: Bobbs-Merrill, 1967.
Teresa of Avila. *Obras de Santa Teresa de Jesus*. Editadas y Anotadas por el P. Silverio de Santa Teresa, C.D., 6. Burgos: El Monte Carmelo, 1919.
Thomas, Hugh. *Rivers of Gold: The Rise of the Spanish Empire*. London: Phoenix, 2004.
Thrall, Margaret Eleanor. *The Ordination of Women to the Priesthood: A Study of the Biblical Evidence*. London: SCM, 1958.
Unamuno, Miguel de. *Contra esto y aquello*. Madrid: Renacimiento, 1912.
———. *Del Sentimiento Trájico de La Vida*. Madrid: Renacimiento, n.d.
———. *Ensayos V* . Madrid: [Est. tip. de Fortanet], 1917.
———. *En Torno al Casticismo*. Madrid: F. Fé, 1902.
———. *Essays and Soliloquies*. Translated by J. E. Crawford Flitch. New York: Knopf, 1925.
———. *Poesías*. Bilbao. Imp. de José Rojas, n.d.
———. *Recuerdos de Niñez y de Mocedad*. Madrid: V. Suárez, 1908.
———. *Soliloquios y Conversaciones* [*Monologues and Conversations*]. Madrid: Biblioteca Renacimiento, 1911.
———. *Tragic Sense of Life*. Translated by J. E. Crawford Flitch. New York: Dover, 1954.

———. *The Velázquez Christ: Poem*. Translation, notes, and introduction by William Thomas Little. Lanham, MD: University Press of America, 2002.

———. *Vida de Don Quijote y Sancho: Según Miguel de Cervantes Saavedra Explicada y Comentada*. Madrid: Renacimiento, 1914.

Van Dusen, Henry P. *One Great Ground of Hope: Christian Missions and Christian Unity*. Philadelphia: Westminster, 1961.

Vargas Llosa, Mario. *A Fish in the Water: A Memoir*. Translated by Helen Lane. New York: Penguin, 1995.

———. "Literature and the Search for Liberty." *WSJ*, November 8, 2011, A19.

Varon, Jeremy. *Bringing the War Home, The Weather Underground, the Red Army Faction, and Revolutionary Violence in the Sixties and Seventies*. Berkeley: University of California Press, 2004.

Véliz, Claudio. *The New World of the Gothic Fox: Culture and Economy in English and Spanish America*. Berkeley: University of California Press, 1994.

Washington, George. "Farewell Address." In *The Sacred Rights of Conscience*, edited by Daniel L. Dreisbach and Mark David Hall, 468–70. Indianapolis: Liberty Fund, 2009.

Watt, Hugh. *Thomas Chalmers and the Disruption, Incorporating the Chalmers Lectures for 1940–44*. Edinburgh: T. Nelson, 1943.

Weber, Max. *The Protestant Ethic and the Spirit of Capitalism*. Translated by Talcott Parsons. New York: Scribner, 1958.

Wright, Richard. "The Underground Christ." In *Pagan Spain*, 161–74. 1957. Reprint, New York: Harper Perennial, 2008.

www.ingramcontent.com/pod-product-compliance
Lightning Source LLC
Chambersburg PA
CBHW062018220426
43662CB00010B/1380